Commentary

New Heavens, New Earth

24- mystery of Providence

26- soul = person sometimes

48- study God

BOOKS BY GORDON H. CLARK

Readings in Ethics (1940)
Selections from Hellenistic Philosophy (1940)
A History of Philosophy (coauthor, 1941)
A Christian Philosophy of Education (1946, 1988)
A Christian View of Men and Things (1952, 1991)
What Presbyterians Believe (1956)
Thales to Dewey (1957, 1989)
Dewey (1960)
Religion, Reason, and Revelation (1961, 1986)
William James (1963)
Karl Barth's Theological Method (1963)
The Philosophy of Science and Belief in God (1964, 1987)
What Do Presbyterians Believe? (1965, 1985)
Peter Speaks Today (1967)*
The Philosophy of Gordon H. Clark (1968)
Biblical Predestination (1969)†
Historiography: Secular and Religious (1971)
II Peter (1972)*
The Johannine Logos (1972, 1989)
Three Types of Religious Philosophy (1973, 1989)
First Corinthians (1975, 1991)
Colossians (1979, 1989)
Predestination in the Old Testament (1979)†
First and Second Peter (1980)*
Language and Theology (1980, 1993)
First John (1980, 1992)
God's Hammer: The Bible and Its Critics (1982, 1987)
Behaviorism and Christianity (1982)
Faith and Saving Faith (1983, 1990)
In Defense of Theology (1984)
The Pastoral Epistles (1984)
The Biblical Doctrine of Man (1984, 1992)
The Trinity (1985, 1990)
Logic (1985, 1988)
Ephesians (1985)
Clark Speaks From the Grave (1986)
Logical Criticism of Textual Criticism (1986, 1990)
First and Second Thessalonians (1986)
Predestination (1987)
The Atonement (1987)
The Incarnation (1988)
Today's Evangelism: Counterfeit or Genuine? (1990)
Essays on Ethics and Politics (1992)
Sanctification (1992)
New Heavens, New Earth (1993)

---

*Combined as *First and Second Peter* (1980) and revised as *New Heavens, New Earth* (1993).
†Combined as *Predestination* (1987)

New Heavens, New Earth

First and Second Peter

Gordon H. Clark

The Trinity Foundation
Jefferson, Maryland

Cover: *Saints Peter and John Healing the Lame Man*. Nicolas Poussin (1594–1665). Oil on canvas. The Metropolitan Museum of Art, Marquand Fund, 1924.

The Trinity Foundation
Post Office Box 700
Jefferson Maryland 21755
ISBN: 0-94931-36-2

Contents

Foreword

Although the Roman Catholic church calls Peter the first pope, he nowhere gave himself that title, nor did anyone else in the early church. There is no evidence that an institution such as the papacy even existed until long after Peter's death. It is entirely foreign to the apostolic church, which knew only one head, and only one mediator between God and man, the man Jesus Christ. Peter refers to himself as an apostle, one of several appointed by Christ; it was the highest office in the New Testament church. The church on earth is not a monarchy; it is a republic, and Peter, in writing these letters, wrote part of its constitution.

Peter wrote to Christians scattered across the face of the earth to encourage them in a time of persecution. It is instructive to note how he encouraged them. Peter did not encourage the persecuted Christians by speaking of the political ascendancy of the church or of Christians; he did not encourage them by speaking of a triumphant institution or movement. He failed to mention Constantine; he ignored the millennium. To encourage the poor Christians Peter spoke only of their irrevocable election to salvation, of the "inheritance incorruptible and undefiled, that does not fade away, reserved in heaven for you who are kept by the power of God through faith for salvation ready to be revealed in the last time."

Scoffers—those openly anti-Christian and those professing to be Christians—ridicule this hope as "pie in the sky." It is typical of the worldly mentality of the scoffers that they can think only in physical terms, only in terms of pie. Apparently their god is their stomach. Had they but an inkling of what salvation means, they might see the foolishness of their efforts to build heaven on earth. Peter promised something far better: new heavens and a new earth. The Gospel promises eternal salvation, a salvation achieved by the power of the God: eternal life that can never be lost, eternal joy that can never end. It is an *incorruptible* inheritance from God. It is this hope—a certain hope, for Christ has already risen and ascended into heaven—with which Peter encourages the persecuted exiles.

The twentieth century is the bloodiest century in the Christian era, and most of that blood has been shed by institutions—churches and governments—that have sought to immanentize the eschaton. Ridiculing eternal salvation as "pie in the sky," they have not hesitated to make blood flow on Earth. But they have not and cannot deliver either pie in the sky or pie on Earth. They can deliver only death, both now and in the world to come.

The twenty-first century may be another time of harsh persecution of Christians. If so, they can be encouraged by reading Peter's letters and by being reminded that life eternal is theirs, that it can never be lost, and that no man, institution, or creature can take it away.

John W. Robbins
February 1993

First Peter

PREFACE

The first epistle of Peter is a message for the twentieth century, even though the fisherman and apostle died many centuries ago. The reason for the timeliness of the epistle lies in the fact that Peter wrote by the inspiration of the Holy Spirit; and when God revealed himself to Moses, to Daniel, or to Peter, his message was not limited in its application to the local conditions that Moses, Daniel, or Peter had to face; rather, when God spoke, he gave a message that he intended to guide Christians of all ages.

The following exposition of First Peter takes the form of a commentary; but it is a devotional and practical rather than a technical and critical commentary. A good critical commentary would list and discuss nearly all the different interpretations of each phrase. Such a study is very valuable, but the negative results of critical procedure are largely omitted from this book, and the space is occupied with a positive explanation of the text as the author understands it. I have also ordinarily omitted the technical appeal to the Greek wording. Although a study of the original underlies the whole, infrequent reference is made to it, and no reader need turn back because he did not take Greek in high school. As a substitute, phrases are retranslated or paraphrased in the body of the exposition where clarification of the King James version seemed desirable.

But more especially this study differs from the usual pattern of commentaries by leisurely detours into the wider scriptural background and by the inclusion of considerable illustrative material. It is hoped that the wider Scriptural background will serve, not only to show the unity of the Biblical message, but also to stimulate private meditation and habits of Bible study. With this it is also hoped that the illustrative material will not only make the reading enjoyable, but that it will provide teachers of Bible classes with sufficient material in available form.

The King James version is quoted at the beginning of each section. Some consider this version outmoded both by its errors and by its antiquated English. Translations in modern speech are attempting to displace it. But there are reasons for still using the familiar version. The familiarity itself is a reason, as well as the beauty of the language. This may not seem like a very scholarly reason; but will anyone assert that the less rhythmic language of the modern translations is a positive asset and that beauty is a defect? And unless the atomic age is to explode man's aesthetic endowment, I venture to predict that no modern version will displace the King James and gather to itself the affection of the Christian people without achieving pleasing English. And if the proponents of modern speech disdain considerations of beauty, may we not ask why it is unreasonable to demand pleasing English of scholarly translators?

Let us admit that the King James version suffers both because the best manuscripts had not been discovered, and because various grammatical mistakes were made. The American Revised Version is in most places more accurate, and a student should not be without it. Nonetheless, in what seems to have been an effort to be different for the sake of being different, it has ruined the rhythm of the familiar words.

Then too it is not always true that the modern versions are more accurate. While the new Revised Standard Version has a very excellent translation of First Peter, the New Testament is not uniformly good. For example, the first chapter of Ephesians is notably bad. And there is the mistranslation of the word for propitiation. To propitiate means to appease the wrath of an angry Deity, and this is exactly what the New Testament means where the word occurs. To expiate, and this is the word the contemporary translators have substituted, means to extinguish guilt, or to atone for, by suffering, by paying a penalty, or in some way or other. It could seem that the translators find the idea of propitiation distasteful, and accordingly replaced it with a less definite and therefore less obnoxious idea. But true scholarship requires the translation to reproduce the ideas of the original author and not to reflect the preferences of the translator.

But there is also another reason for using the King James version. Perhaps it is just personal prejudice, though I should prefer to call it taste and delicacy. The modern versions are copyrighted. Now, it costs a good deal of money to translate and publish the Bible. The translators should be well paid and the publishers deserve their profit. But legitimate though this financial consideration is, one wonders whether it is good taste to copyright and claim ownership of God's Word?

But what is worse, the copyright is not defended on the legitimate basis of paying expenses. The claim is made that a copyright was obtained to ensure the purity of the text. This is a most difficult statement to understand. The King James version has been printed by numerous publishers for over three hundred years, and there is no evidence that its text has been corrupted. The claim that the modern versions were copyrighted to ensure their purity is a claim that I find myself unable to accept.

Therefore, for a purpose such as this, I prefer to use the King James version. And for the rest I must content myself with the hope that someday a better translation will be made. To be better, it must be grammatically more accurate; and it must be produced, not by a hostile scholarship, but by a devout scholarship that gives the sense of the authors without altering or obscuring it by Unitarian footnotes or mistranslations of important terms; and last, perhaps least, though still indispensable, it must achieve a pleasing degree of euphony.

Introduction

The first epistle of Peter is very simple in outline and very practical in content. But its simplicity does not rob it of a divine profundity, nor does its practicality disparage doctrinal truth. On the contrary, Peter no less than Paul bases practical advice and exhortation on doctrine, or, if it may so be called, on theory. Practical people should not disparage theory. They cannot get along without it. Practical applications must always be applications of some theory; and it makes a world of difference what theory is applied. Consider the difference in application between Hapsburg, Bourbon, or Nazi political theory and that of English constitutional monarchy. Theory is indispensable, and Peter has it. Yet Peter is practical, not theoretical. Peter has doctrine; but compared with Paul's epistle to the Romans, this short letter is not doctrinal; there is neither the careful exposition, nor the refutation of objections that is found in Romans; and in particular there are not the logical divisions and subdivisions of an articulated argument. The outline of First Peter is simple, but it is also unbalanced, for the epistle is divided into two very unequal parts.

After the address and salutation in the first two verses, there is a doctrinal section dealing with the greatness of God's mercy in salvation. This first main division, verses three to twelve in chapter one, becomes the basis of the series of exhortations composing the remainder of the epistle. Since this second main division is subdivided into particular topics, a formal scheme will prove an aid to the eye.

A. The Doctrinal Basis
   - 1:1–2 Address and salutation
   - 1:3–12 God's great mercy in salvation, the basis of the following exhortations

B. The Practical Applications
   - 1:13–2:10 General exhortation to hope and holiness
   - 2:11–4:7 Particular exhortations relative to specific situations
   - 4:7–5:11 Personal Relations
     - (a) Relations among Christians
     - (b) Relations between Christians and unbelievers (this involves the matter of persecution and may have been the compelling motive in writing the epistle).
     - (c) Further relations among Christians
   - 5:12–14 Concluding paragraph

I have already explained in what sense the epistle is not doctrinal. It is not doctrinal in comparison with Romans; it is not doctrinal in that it lacks any extended explanation of justification or the atonement or providence. Nonetheless the epistle, both in its first division where it is to be expected and in the series of exhortations as well, refers to and sheds light on many doctrinal issues. In fact in the New Testament as a whole it is not the most fundamental doctrines that receive the most careful exposition. In Romans and Galatians Paul argues for justification by faith in chapter after chapter; but nowhere can there be found any such argument for the deity of Christ. And yet would not one say that the deity of Christ is more fundamental than justification by faith? But while no exposition of Christ's deity is found, there are many references to it. The deity of Christ is fundamental in that it underlies all New Testament teaching; the particular discussions of the various chapters presuppose rather than explain it. To assume that Christ is not very God of very God would turn half if not all the verses of the New Testament into nonsense. Similarly in First Peter doctrines are assumed without explanation, and bits of information are added which are not found elsewhere. What Peter says enriches our understanding of passages in other books, and conversely the hints and references in other books enable us to discover and appreciate Peter's meaning.

Now all of this may sound trite, and certainly no genius is needed to grasp it. Yet the extent to which this is true may be tremendously underestimated. If any section of an epistle is devoid of doctrinal content, surely it would be the address and salutation. What great truths can be contained in the writer's signature, the address on the envelope (so to speak), and the "Dear Sir"? To those who, very naturally, think on this wise, there comes a surprise. And not to delay it, let us turn immediately to the first two verses.

Dear Sir . . . Yours Truly

1 Peter 1:1–2

Peter, an apostle of Jesus Christ, to the strangers scattered throughout Pontus, Galatia, Cappadocia, Asia, and Bithynia,

Elect according to the foreknowledge of God the Father, through sanctification of the Spirit, unto obedience and sprinkling of the blood of Jesus Christ: Grace unto you, and peace, be multiplied.

When we receive a letter today, we sometimes read the first page before guessing who has written to us. Or else we look at the end of the letter before reading the first sentence.

Contrary to this modern style of letter writing, it was the custom in antiquity to sign one's own name first. Then the writer would put the name of the person or persons addressed, and third, he would add an appropriate greeting. Thus the main import of these opening verses is that Peter wrote the letter to elect sojourners of the dispersion, wishing them grace and peace. A glance at the map of Asia Minor will quickly show the location of the several provinces or districts mentioned. In some of these places the apostle Paul had preached; into others, such as Bithynia (Acts 16:6, 7), Pontus, and possibly Cappadocia, the Holy Spirit had not permitted him to enter. But Peter was not writing particularly to the converts Paul had made. It is mainly the Jews that Peter has in mind, for to them applies the word *dispersion*.

There may have been local congregations almost or entirely composed of Jewish Christians; undoubtedly there were individual Jewish Christians surrounded by Gentiles and unbelieving Jews; but whatever the racial complexion of these churches and localities may have been, and regardless of a verse or two that seem to refer to the Gentiles, Peter addresses the Jews.

That he addresses the Jews in his epistle no more detracts from its value for Gentiles than the fact of its first century date makes it useless today. In discussing the situations the Jews faced at that time and in those places, Peter by the inspiration of the Holy Ghost makes use of principles that are valid for all times and all places. Matthew too addressed his Gospel to the Jews; he quoted Old Testament prophecies with which they were quite familiar; but Christ's acts of redemption and the contents of his teaching are not restricted to any one audience. Accordingly, if Peter gave advice to Jewish Christians about to face Nero's persecution, that advice applies to the Reformation martyrs, to the Korean Christians who faced Japanese persecution in World War II, and should be taken to heart by those who now suffer under the Communists.

Not only do the first two verses give the signature, the address, and the greeting; they also briefly anticipate the message of the epistle. It is not an entirely unreasonable simplification to say that the theme of the epistle is found in the words, "Elect . . . unto obedience." The notions of election and of obedience occur and recur throughout the five short chapters.

The doctrine of election is one of the most important doctrines in Holy Scripture, but because those who fear to acknowledge God's sovereignty have attached invalid inferences to it, the easier of these two notions, namely that of obedience, will be discussed first, and election will be deferred until we come to verse nine of chapter two. For the moment let us merely remember that Christ said, "Ye have not chosen me, but I have chosen you" (John 15:16).

These opening verses were not intended as an explanation of all that they refer to. This is so little to be expected that the wonder is rather that Peter was able to refer to so much in his address. When the epistle as a whole is considered, the emphasis seems to lie on one of the important purposes of God in election: obedience. Obedience by itself does not exhaust the purpose of election; it is not the ultimate purpose God has in mind; but it is the phase of God's purpose that the recipients of this epistle needed to read about. And all in all, obedience may be more comprehensive than at first appears.

At the mention of obedience one naturally thinks of an act performed. In the army an officer orders, "Forward March," and the soldiers step forward. Or one may think of it negatively as a not-doing. The Scriptures say, "Thou shalt not steal," and he who obeys refrains from certain overt actions. Peter has all this in mind when he uses the term obedience, but he has more than this in mind. Obedience, while it may always involve some sort of activity, is not exhausted by ordinary overt action. "Search the Scriptures" is a command; and while obedience to it may require a sort of action, it is the action of sitting still, reading a book, and, presumably, thinking about it. Moreover, after searching the Scriptures and learning what they say, we are commanded to believe them. Believing is even less overt than turning the pages of a book, but it is obedience nonetheless. Mental and physical obedience both come within the scope of Peter's statement. Further emphasis on obedience will be postponed for discussion under 1:14, 22; 2:7, 8; 3:1, and 4:17 below. Here let us only note that God has a purpose in electing some to everlasting life, and that purpose is to make them obedient to his precepts.

Conjoined with obedience is the sprinkling of the blood of Jesus Christ. It would not be sufficient for God's purpose (even were it a fact, which it is not) that a man obey perfectly from the moment of his conversion onward. He should have obeyed before. God demands perfect obedience at all times, and tomorrow's obedience does not excuse yesterday's disobedience. Therefore, as guilty before God, and as deserving of God's wrath and curse, a man must be cleansed of all guilt and pollution. This also is the purpose of God's election, and the method of cleansing is the sprinkling of the blood of Jesus Christ.

Let it be borne in mind that Peter is writing primarily to Jews. They were familiar with the Old Testament. To them the mention of sprinkling called up fond memories and definite ideas.

In the Old Testament sprinkling formed a most important part of the ritual of sacrifice. There were sprinklings of blood, of water, and of oil. In Exodus 24:6–8 we read that after the oxen had been burned on the altar, "Moses took half of the blood, and put it in basins; and half of the blood he sprinkled on the altar. And he took the book of the covenant, and read in the audience of the people: and they said, 'All that the Lord hath said will we do, and be obedient.' And Moses took the blood, and sprinkled it on the people, and said, 'Behold the blood of the covenant, which the Lord hath made with you concerning all these words.'" This procedure was designed to teach the people the nature of expiation. The oxen had been offered as a sacrifice to appease God and their blood was sprinkled on the altar. This indicates, as even the heathen tribes know, that a sacrifice first of all is designed not to cause a change of heart in man, for which change God then accepts the worshipper, but a sacrifice is primarily intended to cause a change of disposition in God. A sacrifice is supposed to act on God, not on man. God sets aside his wrath and becomes gracious. Then in the Mosaic ritual, after the blood had been sprinkled on the altar, the law was read and the people voluntarily accepted the covenant God had proposed; and finally the blood was sprinkled on the people to show that they had been forgiven, accepted, and included in the covenant. For other instances of sprinkling with blood see Exodus 29:16, 20, 21; Numbers 18:17; II Kings 16:15, and many other references.

The New Testament naturally throws some light on Old Testament sprinkling. Hebrews 9:13, 19, 21 with the context teach that the sprinklings of blood sanctified the patterns of heavenly things, but in reality true sanctification is accomplished by the blood of Jesus Christ. In the following chapter (Hebrews 10:22) there is a reference to purification from evil by sprinkling and washing (compare Hebrews 12:24).

In view of this background, the Jews to whom Peter was writing would instantly understand that the blood of Jesus Christ cleanses from all sin, that the sacrifice on the cross satisfied the just demands of the righteous God; and that cleansing and obedience were purposes of election.

Before the exposition passes to the main argument of the epistle, one more fact should be emphasized. This short address, by declaring that Father, Son, and Holy Spirit act unitedly in the salvation of men, substantiates the doctrine of the Trinity and rules out all forms of unitarianism. From a crabbedly literal viewpoint, the Trinity and the Nicene phrase, "of the same essence" are, as the Arians insisted in their struggle against Athanasius, not mentioned in the Bible. And for that matter neither is the Holy Ghost called a person. But the important point is not the presence or absence of certain words; the important point is the presence or absence of certain ideas. Wolves in sheep's clothing sometimes disguise themselves in a surface loyalty to Scriptural wording in order to deny Scriptural teaching. There is no mention of vicarious or substitutionary atonement—atonement, yes; substitution, no. Therefore they argue, let us not insist that Christ took our place and suffered in our stead. These words do not occur in Scripture. Correct; but Peter soon emphasizes the ideas and doctrines. And in these first two verses the Trinity is taught. Unless the three Persons are substantially equal in power and glory, how could we account for their conjunction, cooperation, and relationship as taken for granted throughout the New Testament? A mere man and God Almighty could not be so linked. And so it may be said, as others have said before, that God the Father plans salvation, God the Son merits salvation, and God the Spirit applies salvation. Grace unto you and peace be multiplied.

Kept by God's Power

1 Peter 1:3–5

Blessed be the God and Father of our Lord Jesus Christ, who according to his abundant mercy hath begotten us again unto a lively hope by the resurrection of Jesus Christ from the dead,

To an inheritance incorruptible, and undefiled, and that fadeth not away, reserved in heaven for you,

Who are kept by the power of God through faith unto salvation ready to be revealed in the last time.

The main body of the epistle is a series of exhortations to people who were facing temptation, opposition, and persecution for the name of Christ. To prepare these people and us for a proper attitude toward the wealth and fame of this world, so alluring to the underprivileged and perhaps even more alluring to power-sated dictators, Peter directs attention to God and his marvelous grace.

So great is the grace about to be described that the apostle can begin only with an exclamation of praise: Blessed be God!

The form of the exclamation of praise, however, may cause one a little wonder. That God is the Father of our Lord Jesus Christ is not surprising. The Trinity is constituted of Father, Son, and Spirit. In the Gospels Jesus is represented as the only begotten Son of the Father. With all this everyone is perfectly familiar. But in what sense is the Father the God of our Lord Jesus Christ? If the Trinity is one God, not three gods, how can one of the Persons be the God of another? Are they not all equal in power and glory? Is not the Son himself very God? Quite so; and Peter teaches no different doctrine, though the words at first seem to.

The first solution of this problem that comes to mind is the suggestion that the verse should be translated, Blessed be God, the Father of our Lord. The Revised Version actually makes such a suggestion in its footnotes. And it is true that in a half dozen instances in the New Testament the King James version has it so. Romans 15:6, 2 Corinthians 1:3, and 11:31 are cases in point. By so translating the phrase, one seems to avoid any inconsistency with the doctrine of the Deity of Christ. But there are two objections to this easy solution. The first is that it is a poor translation: the Greek wording does not favor it. Peter says, the God of our Lord. The second objection to this too easy solution is that even if it removes a difficulty in this epistle, the difficulty cannot possibly be dislodged from Ephesians 1:17. In this verse the word *Father* does not come between *God* and the phrase *Our Lord Jesus Christ* to complicate the matter. Paul distinctly says that God is the God of Christ. Hence, rather than seek some facile escape, it is better to try to discover the meaning of the text as it stands.

It ought also to be noted that Jesus himself in Mark 15:34 addressed the first Person of the Trinity as "My God."

The reason for this expression in Mark is perhaps clearer than the reason for it in First Peter. In the Gospels the human nature of Christ is extensively described. The boy Jesus grew in wisdom and stature and in favor with God and man. But none of this could be true of the divine nature. God is a Spirit; he does not grow. The man Jesus became weary and fell asleep. But he that keepeth Israel neither slumbers nor sleeps. The Trinity is one God. No three human persons can possibly be so united as the Father, Son, and Spirit. Within the Godhead no Person could possibly forsake another. Obviously, then, when the man Jesus on the cross cries, "My God, my God, why hast thou forsaken me?" it is the voice of his human nature, by which he was like us in all things except sin. And as with us, so with him too, God was his God.

Now, while all this is clear enough in Mark, it is far from clear in Ephesians 1:17 or in 1 Peter 1:3. Is there then any other possible sense in which God is the God of Jesus Christ? There is such a meaning, and it is a very important one. Many are the religions of the world;

many are the preachers and philosophers who speak of God. The Mohammedans have their god and the ancient religions of the East had theirs. The modernist today talks of a god and so does the theosophist, the Christian Scientist, and the Mormon. But do all these preach the same God? Are all these religions equally effective in bringing man and God into a blessed relationship? The New Testament answer to these questions is a resounding "No!" There is but one God, the living and true God, and no man can come to God but by Jesus Christ. The one true God, the Creator and preserver of the world, is the God of our Lord Jesus Christ. God is the God whom Jesus Christ made known. There is none other. Blessed be the God of our Lord Jesus Christ.

The reason that blessing is an appropriate expression on the lips of Peter or of any man is that God is great in mercy. The Psalmist in 130:3 asks, "If thou, Lord, shouldst mark iniquities, O Lord, who shall stand?" Men fail to recognize the great mercy of God because they fail to recognize their sinful condition. The unsaved man in his pride thinks that he is as good as any other man, and that he deserves the approval of God, not as a matter of mercy, but as a matter of right. What a fool! The beginning of wisdom is the fear of the Lord. A man who has long trusted Christ for salvation and has grown mature in grace is better able to evaluate the miry pit from which he was digged and to appreciate the greatness of God's mercy.

The fact that the new life which Peter is about to mention is the result of the grace of God shows once more that God did not choose us because he foresaw our faith or good works. If God had looked ahead in time and had seen that we were going to choose righteousness, and if he had elected us for that reason, then our salvation would not so much have been according to his mercy as it would have been because of our spiritual discernment and development. Grace rules out all merit, foreseen faith included, as the basis of our election and salvation.

God is gracious in many ways, but Peter here calls attention to a most eminent display of mercy. Blessed be God who begat us again to a living hope. Christ had told Nicodemus that except a man be born again, he cannot see the kingdom of God. The natural man is, as it were, not yet born—he is not alive. Before he can enjoy life and its pleasant functions, he must be born. This new birth, or regeneration, is the work of the Holy Spirit. A baby cannot choose to be born, nor does the baby do the bearing. Similarly the natural man cannot receive the things of the Spirit; they are foolishness unto him. In sin was he conceived, and "every imagination of the thoughts of his heart is only evil continually" (Genesis 6:5). Such a one needs a new life. As he is, he cannot call upon God because "no man can say that Jesus is the Lord but by the Holy Ghost" ( ). He needs to be born again.

Apart from regeneration, he has no hope of life, but God according to his great mercy has begotten us to a living hope. The hope is living, not so much because it lives in us, as because it is a hope of life. Heretofore we were without hope, troubled by a semi-conscious fear of the judgment. We had no confidence in the future, and beyond the grave lay the dark unknown. With the non-Christian the subject of death and beyond is not a welcome subject. By dint of much carelessness and preoccupation with other matters, he may be able to forget it for a while. Then a gruesome automobile accident takes one of his family, or war breaks out to remind whole nations of the stark realities they have tried to forget. The modern mind has tried hard not to be serious. It has labored at superficiality and, with the help of nervous amusements, has succeeded to a degree.

No doubt in other ages also there have been desperate attempts at light-heartedness. One of the most desperate provides involuntary evidence to the power of a fearful expectation of judgment, for it is a fearful thing to fall into the hands of the living God. This most desperate attempt to banish the fear of death was made by the old Epicureans. Lucretius, reporting the philosophy of his master, Epicurus, asserts that the fear of death, exploited by religion, causes more misery than war, disease, or anything else. It is for this reason that he denies the doctrine of creation, elaborates an atomistic science, and concludes that consciousness ceases at death. It was members of this school, among others, who laughed when Paul on the Areopagus spoke of judgment and the resurrection. They laughed; they had steeled themselves, and chromium-plated themselves, against the fear of death. But can we perhaps detect in their strenuous philosophic effort, and underneath their laughter, the power of that fear working in themselves?

Death does not dismay the Christian, because God has begotten him to a hope of life. He may sing, he does sing, and sings truly

When I tread the verge of Jordan,
Bid my anxious fears subside;
Death of death and hell's destruction,
Land me safe on Canaan's side:
Songs of praises, Songs of praises,
I will ever give to Thee.

There is an excellent reason for this praise in the face of death; there is a sure foundation for this hope of life. Peter does not offer some subtle and tenuous argument in favor of immortality as Socrates did the day of his death. Peter points to death conquered in an historical setting. We have this living hope by the resurrection of Jesus Christ from the dead. By him and in him death has been vanquished. He is the firstfruits of them that sleep, and we shall be raised in our order.

It is a distinctive feature of the Christian religion that it is historically grounded. Not only has God given man a written revelation in the Bible, but he has accomplished objective works of redemption in history. Setting aside the preparatory works in the Old Testament, we may center our attention on the work of Christ. During his earthly ministry, he taught the people many things. Parables, maxims, warnings, and encouragements came from his lips. But true and precious as all this is, his main work was not teaching. He came to give his life a ransom for many; he came to accomplish redemption on the cross. To the apostles could well be entrusted the writing of revelation. The Holy Ghost would so inspire them as to preserve them from error. But to no one else could God entrust the work of redemption. And regardless of all else that Christ said or did, his dominating purpose in coming to earth was to die. There was no other good enough to pay the price of sin; he only could unlock the gate of heaven and let us in.

Christ came to die, but he came also to rise again; and by his resurrection we have the hope of life eternal.

This life for which we wait is an inheritance incorruptible, undefiled, that fadeth not away. In these words Peter contrasts for his Jewish readers the future inheritance with the inheritance that had been their national hope. Their forefathers had told them that the land of Palestine was their inheritance. But that land was not incorruptible. Its wells could dry up; its fields could lose their fertility; the national independence could be lost; and it could seem as though God had cast Israel away forever. Furthermore the land of Canaan was not undefiled. Its plains had been the place of battle; its hills had held the altars of strange gods; its kings had caused Israel to sin; they had shed innocent blood and had oppressed the poor. The country had been conquered by the heathen; the temple had been defiled and destroyed; and at the time Peter was writing, all this was about to happen over again. Certainly the inheritance of the land was a fading inheritance.

But the heavenly inheritance was of quite a different sort. That fair, future land is the land of fadeless day. Its enjoyments are abiding. In it neither moth nor rust can corrupt, nor do thieves break through and steal.

How lovely! But is it attainable? Are we sure to inherit it? The answer is yes, and for two reasons. The first reason is that God has reserved the inheritance in heaven; his omnipotence defends it. But more than that—God reserves it for *us*. Of what use is it to talk of a home over there, if we are not to enjoy it? Why should those mansions excite our imagination, if they are intended for someone else? The emphasis that Peter gives to his words does not fall so much on the treasure that is reserved, as it does on the fact that *we* are guarded by that same omnipotent power to ensure our getting the promised possession: "Kept by the power of God, through faith, unto salvation ready to be revealed in the last time."

On one occasion there was gathered a large group of Christian young people to hear the words of an elderly gentleman. He had been a missionary for many years, he had traveled widely, and his venerable appearance of distinction equaled his reputation. The young people had every reason to expect words of wisdom out of a rich experience. But what a disappointment! The elderly gentleman chuckled about Calvinists and Arminians. The former teach "once saved, always saved," while the latter may be saved at breakfast and lost at lunch. Then he asserted that there was so much to be said on both sides of the question that he had no view to offer. And with an emphatic thump on the desk he concluded, "Let us leave the matter just where God left it and add no more." What a disappointment!

To be sure, a Christian ought not to add to what God has revealed; neither should he subtract from that revelation. The venerable gentleman implied that God had said nothing about security in Christ, and he dismissed the conflict between Calvinists and Arminians with a superficial chuckle. One wonders about the heathen to whom he was sent as a missionary. Did he tell them that Christ's death might possibly save them? Of course the results could not be guaranteed, but it was the best remedy for sin he had. They might as well become Christians, since heathenism certainly was not any better. Is this what he told his natives? It is not what Peter told the people to whom he wrote. Peter says not only that the inheritance is safe, but also that *we* are kept by God's great power.

The security of the believer, to be sure, can be misunderstood. If anyone thinks the Christian is preserved in a state of grace by his own efforts, he is terribly mistaken. "Prone to wander, Lord, I feel it; prone to leave the God I love." We are not kept by our own feeble power. "Let thy goodness, like a fetter, bind my wandering heart to thee."

Then too, the security of the believer can be misinterpreted to mean that one may, after regeneration, sin with impunity. To lay naked the absurdity of such a misinterpretation, someone has parodied a hymn to read:

Free from the law, O blessed condition,
I can sin as I please, and still have remission.

On the contrary, Paul in Romans 6, 7, and 8, teaches that we are justified in order to become sanctified. One who comes to Christ for salvation from sin does not intend to continue in sin. If he knows what salvation is, he has turned with grief and hatred from his sin and endeavors from then on to please God. Because of these misunderstandings, it might be wise to avoid the phrase "eternal security," and to use the phrase "the perseverance of the saints." Nothing is gained by quarreling about phrases if their meaning is the same, but yet the latter phrase can be made to emphasize the fact that the truly regenerate man perseveres in grace. His progress may be fast or slow; he may seem to backslide; but if he is truly born again, he will neither totally nor finally fall from the state of grace, but will certainly persevere therein.

The doctrine of perseverance, or security, is the doctrine of Peter, of Paul, and of Jesus Christ himself. In Philippians 1:6 Paul says he is certain that "he that began a good work in you shall perfect it until the day of Jesus Christ." Jesus himself said (John 10:27–29), "My sheep hear my voice and I know them, and they follow me: And I give them eternal life; and they shall never perish, neither shall any man pluck them out of my hand. My Father, which gave them me, is greater than all; and no man is able to pluck them out of my Father's hand."

There was a minister who, though he seemed to believe that he was secure in Christ, never preached on the subject because, as he said, it is a controversial subject. He was a kindly gentleman and did not care to disagree with anyone. But after all, what is not controversial? The deity of Christ, the infallibility of the Bible, and the very existence of God are all controversial subjects. Is a Christian minister, to whom God has entrusted his Gospel, to keep silence whenever someone disagrees? If this policy of silence were followed, the contents of sermons would soon become so dilute that the people would starve for lack of nourishment. In fact, this is about what has happened in America. Ministers have been so intent upon keeping the peace of the church that they have sacrificed its purity. Or they have tried to defend the fundamentals to the neglect of all the rest of God's revelation. Thus they have sought the fewest things to believe. They seem to ask themselves, not how much of the Bible can I give my congregation, but how little and still maintain a reputation for faithfulness. Is it not reasonable for the people to expect their ministers to tell them what sort of salvation Christ offers? Does he offer a precarious hope, or does he offer a sure and permanent salvation? Having begun the good work in us, is God going to forsake and forget us? Let us have done with weak-kneed ministers who shun important doctrines through fear of controversy; and let us sing lustily

E'en down to old age all My people shall prove
My sovereign, eternal, unchangeable love.
The soul, that on Jesus hath leaned for repose,
I will not, I will not desert to his foes.
That soul, though all hell should endeavor to shake,
I'll never, no never, no never forsake!

A doctrine so important as that of the perseverance of the saints deserves emphasis, and yet such is the wealth and variety of God's revelation that emphasis on even a main point should not be allowed to obscure the wonderful details. That God will preserve us in grace is a source of comforting assurance, but he has not left us ignorant of the method by which he accomplishes his purpose. Presumably if we knew only God's purpose, it would be sufficient for confident Christian living, and yet God has in addition described his way of working. We are kept, to be sure, by God's almighty power, and that guarantees the result; but it is the faith that God works in us that is the means and method.

The question of means and method is often important. Someone who little understands God's dealing with men might ask, If I am sure of my heavenly home, why should I keep on believing in Christ? Or, If God before the foundation of the world has elected some to eternal life, why should we preach the Gospel to the heathen?—if they are elect, they will be saved anyway. But this is not true. Of course, if God's power be abstractly considered, one might say that God could have saved the heathen without the preaching of the Gospel, or that he could have guaranteed us a home on high without an abiding faith. If God had not done what he has done, there is no telling what he might have done. But the chief question is not what God could have done but did not; the chief question is what has God actually done? He has actually decreed that the preaching of the Gospel is a necessary means for the conversion of the elect, and that perseverance in grace is accomplished through faith. It is not true that these things will come to pass in just any way. They will come to pass in just the one way that God has decided to bring them to pass. While it is not the prerogative of any man to sit in judgment on another, if a hypothetical case were presented of a man allegedly regenerated on one occasion but at present having no faith, the most plausible diagnosis of the case would be that the man had not been regenerated in the first place. For God has definitely revealed that he will preserve every child of his through faith. Experience—or, more accurately, man's fallible analysis of experience—can never supersede God's word.

As a concluding corroboration of the necessity of faith, one may refer to Hebrews 3:12, 19 and 2 Thessalonians 2:13. In the former passage hardness of heart and God's punishment are connected with unbelief; and in the latter Paul almost duplicates the words of Peter. He writes, "God hath from the beginning chosen you to salvation through sanctification of the Spirit and belief of the truth." Therefore let us daily exhort one another and beseech God to increase our faith.

Two more ideas need a minimum of explanation before the exposition of verse five is complete. The first of these represents salvation as something future. Often salvation is spoken of as complete: We have been saved, it happened once for all, and that is the end of it. Now while we have been saved once for all, it is not true that that is the end of it. If Christians would be more particular in their use of words, they would escape many unnecessary misunderstandings. Salvation is a very broad term, and its phases are so diverse that what is true of one phase is not true of another. No doubt it is necessary on occasion to speak of salvation taken in its entirety, but it is more frequently necessary to focus attention on some part. For this reason the Christian should know—should have learned in Sunday School—the correct definitions of *regeneration, justification, repentance, sanctification,* and *glorification.* These are all parts of salvation, but not all have happened once for all. Regeneration is an instantaneous, subjective, moral change; justification is an instantaneous, objective, forensic change. Repentance and sanctification are subjective but not instantaneous. The notion that one has been born again rather implies that it is not all over with, but that a new life should follow. And the completion is still in the future, ready, as Peter says, to be revealed at the last time. It simply awaits God's word, and though we may weary at the seeming delay, God will speak in due season.

The final point of verse five is the notion of the last time. What the phrase means must be determined by the sense of the argument. Not everywhere in Scripture does it have exactly the same significance. In 2 Timothy 3:1 the last days are prior to the return of Christ, as also in Jude 18. In 1 John 2:18 it was the last time when John was writing the epistle nineteen centuries ago. And Hebrews 9:26 calls the crucifixion of Christ the end of the world. Obviously Peter has in mind the return of Christ, the glorification of the body, and our everlasting blessedness in heaven.

Necessary Hardships

1 Peter 1:6–9

Wherein ye greatly rejoice, though now for a season, if need be, ye are in heaviness through manifold temptations:

That the trial of your faith, being much more precious than of gold that perisheth, though it be tried with fire, might be found unto praise and honor and glory at the appearing of Jesus Christ:

Whom having not seen, ye love; in whom, though now ye see him not, yet believing, ye rejoice with joy unspeakable and full of glory:

Receiving the end of your faith, even the salvation of your souls.

The first phrase of verse 6 is a little ambiguous in its wording. *Wherein* may mean *in the last time,* or it may better refer to the whole idea of assured salvation. And the word for *greatly rejoice* may be either indicative or imperative, for there are not two distinct forms for these moods in Greek. Therefore there are four interpretations of this phrase logically possible: (1) In the last time, rejoice greatly. (2) In the last time, you are greatly rejoicing. (3) With respect to salvation, rejoice greatly. (4) With respect to salvation, you are rejoicing greatly.

Although from a strictly grammatical standpoint *wherein* is most easily taken as designating time, it seems a little premature to command

Christians now to rejoice in the last time; and, of course, they cannot now be rejoicing in the future. Therefore, probably, Peter meant to command them to rejoice now because of their salvation, or, as the English versions take it, he is not commanding but describing the actual joy his readers have.

In either case there is a contrast between the joy of salvation and the vexations of manifold trials. However severe these trials may be, and for those to whom Peter wrote they were indeed severe, there are still considerations of comfort. In the first place the trials are temporary. The magnificent eleventh chapter of Hebrews tells of some of God's servants who were stoned, sawn asunder, or slain with the sword. Although no one should minimize their martyrdom, yet their sufferings did not last long. Christians have been burned at the stake for their faith in Christ, and no one can deny the pain and horror of such a death. There are others, not martyrs, who have labored among heathen tribes through plagues, in filth, and with vermin for bedfellows. They have suffered, not torture, but the pain of fever, of the burning sun, of the steaming jungle. Of these too the world is not worthy. And though their tribulations are longer in duration than those of the martyrs, yet, when compared with everlasting glory, they too are short.

Then in the second place a consideration of comfort is to be found in the fact that these trials are not useless. God sends them only if need be. He who believes in Christ should know that God does all things well. Does not the infallible Word say that all things work together for good to those who love God? Not that the "things" control their working together as if our lives were but the baubles of coincidence; but rather that God, who sees the end from the beginning, works all things after the counsel of his sovereign will. When a man has faith in God, he may be vexed or suffer pain by manifold temptations, but he should know better than to complain against what God does. For the persecutor could have no power at all against God's elect unless it were given him from above. And yet God, ever merciful, has not asked us to trust him altogether blindly. He has not confined his revelation to the bare statement that he rules in the army of heaven and among the inhabitants of the earth. Although that would have been sufficient, he has also disclosed some of his purpose. In one place we are told that whom the Lord loves, he chastens, for what son is he whom a father does not chasten? The absence of chastening casts doubt on one's sonship. Of course no child enjoys a spanking; nevertheless, by not "sparing the rod and spoiling the child," a peaceable fruit of righteousness results. Peter's passage also repeats and expands the same idea. He goes back to the rich imagery of the Old Testament with which his mind had been improved as a Jewish lad in the synagogue and at home. How many times since he had become a Christian apostle must he have thought of the verse (Job 23:10), "He knoweth the way that I take; when he hath tried me, I shall come forth as gold." And he had often read Psalm 66:10, "Thou, O God, hast proved us: Thou hast tried us, as silver is tried." Gold and silver are tried in the fire because they are so valuable. Taking the trouble to refine them is worth the effort so that the metal may come out pure and free from dross. But Christian faith is far more precious, and no impurities may be left to mar it. And thus God in the Old Testament set forth in his illustration a principle of spiritual life that should apply not only to the Old Testament saints, but to all his servants in all ages.

This is all easily understood—when our lives are free from anxiety and suffering. But when affliction comes, it is human nature to forget fine principles about chastisement. The present tribulation obscures our vision and we bemoan our fate. This is true even when we merely think of the hardships of others without being injured ourselves. Why was it that the Japanese imprisoned a Korean Christian woman and released her only when the rigors of an unheated prison had given her pneumonia and she was about to die? Was it necessary for God to try her faith so severely? Why was it that some seventy-five thousand Calvinists had to be massacred on St. Bartholomew's Day? Only evil came of it, for France was lost to Protestantism and was gained first by Romanism and later by infidelity. Did it need to be?

The Scriptures say yes, it needed to be. We do not see how God was working out his plan in such ordeals. The intricacies of providence, more complicated than the most masterful game of chess, are too complex for us now. But someday he will make it plain to us; someday we shall understand. We understand the principles now; they are not hard to grasp. When we see all the details, we shall understand them too. We shall understand not only the great events of history—how the St. Bartholomew's Day massacre and Bloody Mary fit into the divine scheme—we shall see also how our more insignificant troubles have purified us and glorified God. Perhaps we shall be a bit crestfallen over the great complaining we made about our minor inconveniences, when others fought to win the prize and sailed through bloody seas. We shall understand then; but now let us remember that there is no sorrow like his sorrow, no suffering worse than Christ's suffering.

The praise and the honor and the glory resulting from our manifold vexations may be the glory of God displayed in working all things together for our good. His power and might and wisdom will be revealed to the dullest eye. But instead of the intrinsic glory of God, perhaps Peter had more in mind the glory that God will confer on us. It is our dross that shall have been purged away, and we shall be spotless and pure. Paul also refers to this glory when he says (1 Corinthians 15:42–49), "So also is the resurrection of the dead. It is sown in corruption, it is raised in incorruption . . . it is raised in glory. . . . And as we have borne the image of the earthly, we shall also bear the image of the heavenly." To the same intent is Philippians 3:21, "The Lord Jesus Christ, who shall change our vile body, that it may be fashioned like unto his glorious body." And besides the notion of the glory that shall be ours, it is to be noted that both Peter and Paul connect our receiving this glory with the revelation or appearing of Jesus. In that we love the Lord who has redeemed us, though we have not seen him, in that we look for him to return to judge the quick and the dead, in that we have God's assurance that our salvation is sure, and in that we rejoice in the blessings that Christ has given, we rejoice in that promised but delayed end of our faith, the salvation of our souls.

There is small probability that any of Peter's readers had seen Christ in the flesh. Yet they loved him. This suggests that love to Christ may exist, even in a highly developed degree, apart from physical sight. Faith receives the written record and grasps all that Christ said or did. Could eyesight do more? And what was true for the first recipients of this epistle is true also for us who read it today.

"Christians are in perpetual danger of overestimating the value of the personal vision of Christ in this world of flesh and sense; while on the other hand they are prone to underestimate the value of that simple faith which rests on his recorded words and deeds."*

**The Shorter Epistles*, by Henry Cowles. The thought of the preceding paragraph is from the same author.

This prepares the way for an answer to an objection to Christianity made by pagan-minded educators. They have sometimes ridiculed Christianity, in particular the conversion of children, on the ground that it is psychologically impossible for a child to love someone whom he has not seen. Now it may be impossible for a child or even an adult to love Athanasius or Martin Luther. But to judge the love of Christ on the basis implied is to misjudge the whole situation. Those who make this objection are thinking of love in purely naturalistic terms. They tacitly deny the supernatural. But if our minds are not circumscribed by the limitations of naturalism, we shall discover one factor—in addition to Christ's deity—that does not exist in any other human relationship. That factor is saving faith. There are other attitudes, to be sure, that are called faith. One may have faith in one's business, bank, or country. But saving faith is a gift of God that attaches us to Christ. It has neither a duplicate nor a substitute object. As a gift of God through which our justification is secured, faith ought not to be underestimated. And yet it seems to be a human tendency to place faith on a lower level than the eye of flesh. No doubt Jesus anticipated all this when he said: "Because thou hast seen me, thou hast believed; blessed are they that have not seen, and yet have believed" (John 20:29).

The end of our faith is the salvation of our souls. The word *soul* has several connotations in the Bible, and its later usage in the English language has increased rather than diminished the range of its meanings. At this point it need only be noted that the salvation of our souls is not meant to exclude the salvation of our bodies, but rather, as in  Genesis 2:7 and Acts 27:37, the word *soul* means *person*. A stupid literalism often produces strange doctrines. A kindly old gentleman—he was personally a lovely character—used to argue that man was composed of three things, body, soul, and spirit. (Genesis 2:7 shows that there were just two, not three, components.) Then on the basis of Ecclesiastes 12:7 he hinted that there was no salvation for the body. The body decayed into dust. The soul that sinned was to die, and other souls were to be saved. But the spirit returns to God who gave it; and so no spirit is ever lost. It requires no technical knowledge of Hebrew or Greek to avoid such peculiar conclusions. A good training in the Shorter Catechism in Sunday School will lay the foundation. Some acquaintance with Charles Hodge or Benjamin Warfield will provide logical analyses of Scripture. And for the rest, a little searching with a concordance will fill in the details.

Puzzled Prophets

1 Peter 1:10–12

Of which salvation the prophets have inquired and searched diligently, who prophesied of the grace that should come unto you:

Searching what, or what manner of time the Spirit of Christ which was in them did signify, when testified it beforehand the sufferings of Christ, and the glory that should follow.

Unto whom it was revealed, that not unto themselves, but unto us they did minister the things, which are now reported unto you by them that have preached the Gospel unto you with the Holy Ghost sent down from heaven; which things the angels desire to look into.

Peter continues to indicate the value of salvation so that his readers may despise the pain and ignominy of their coming persecution. This salvation is nothing to be lightly dismissed from consideration. The prophets, whom all the Jewish Christians acknowledged as God's servants, were studiously curious about it. They had prophesied of a great display of grace; they had foretold the sufferings of Christ and the subsequent glories; but the exact meaning of their own prophecies was not clear to them. Consequently, after writing down the message they had received from God, they examined its words with great care. Previous prophets had foretold the advent of Messiah; the ritual of the temple and several events of Hebrew history were types and shadows of greater deeds of redemption to come; but when were they to come? How long, O Lord, how long? And so the prophets searched their own writings to see whether the date could be discovered, or if the exact date were not to be found, perhaps there was a clue to the sort of time or characteristics of the age in which Messiah should appear. Their search was disappointing. No doubt they hoped that Messiah would come in their lifetime, but God revealed to them that they were writing not so much for themselves, their people, or their age, but that their ministrations were particularly to benefit a later time. It was to be four hundred years after the last prophet had laid down his pen before the fulfilment should begin, and how many thousands before the subsequent glories should be revealed? The prophets must have wished it were otherwise. But have not the Christians of later ages benefited by their ministry? Persecution may be imminent, but a salvation, not merely long foretold, but long prepared, outweighs present tribulation.

That this salvation was long prepared, and that it was to a limited extent revealed to the Old Testament saints, deserves consideration. The unity of the Bible is a testimony to its divine origin. Since it was written by a number of authors over a period not less than 1500 years, the unity of its message is evidence of supernatural guidance. These verses emphasize the unity. Does the Old Testament teach salvation by the Mosaic law while the New ushers in a day of grace? Not at all! The Old Testament preaches the sufferings of Christ. Moses, David, and Isaiah did not grasp the complete significance of the message, but it was the Holy Spirit of Christ who gave them the message, and the message was salvation through Christ's blood. Great as the prophets were, the message was greater and should not be reduced to the limits of their understanding. The grace of God in Christ has been preached in all ages. What the Jewish prophets preached was none other than the message "announced to you by those who preached the Gospel to you by the Holy Spirit sent from heaven."

The old prophets discerned the meaning dimly; many of the Jews of Christ's day were totally blind to it; and strange to say, nineteen centuries later there are self-styled Bible teachers who, while having a glimpse of grace in the New Testament, think they see other ways of salvation in the Old.

Once upon a time there was a man who preached a sermon on the significance of the Old Testament. It was a relatively long sermon and probably took over an hour to deliver. There were only two persons in the congregation, and while the sermon was never written down, it was undoubtedly the greatest sermon ever preached on the significance of the Old Testament. For it was Christ himself who said, "'O fools, and slow of heart to believe all that the prophets have spoken: Ought not Christ to have suffered these things, and to enter into his glory?' And beginning at Moses and all the prophets, he expounded unto them in all the Scriptures the things concerning himself" (Luke 24:25–27).

Need we wonder then that the angels desire to peer into such glorious matters?

HOLINESS

1 Peter 1:13–16

Wherefore gird up the loins of your mind, be sober, and hope to the end for the grace that is to be brought unto you at the revelation of Jesus Christ;

As obedient children, not fashioning yourselves according to the former lusts in your ignorance:

But as he which hath called you is holy, so be ye holy in all manner of conversation;

Because it is written, Be ye holy; for I am holy.

Here begins the second section of the epistle. So far Peter's main purpose has been to fix attention on the wonders and glories of salvation in Christ. In the remainder of the epistle he also exhibits the preciousness of our inheritance in Christ, but his main purpose will be to draw some practical conclusions from the doctrine. This is immediately emphasized by the first word of the section: *Wherefore*.

A threefold exhortation is contained in the first of these verses. The main admonition is to hope. Two subsidiary injunctions, which may be taken as conducive to a firm hope, are to gird up the mind and to be sober. The flowing robes of antiquity may have lent an air of dignity to Greek philosophers and Roman senators, but they did not expedite vigorous activity. Peter pictures the minds of some people as encumbered with the flowing robes of irrelevant thought. Perhaps a Christian was trying to understand the significance of Christ's death and was confused, if a Jew, by pharisaical interpretations of the Old Testament, or, if a Gentile, by Gnostic cosmological speculation. Or more probably and more simply he was confused as to what extent he should make known his Christian faith in the face of rising opposition. He began to weigh the probable consequences of different lines of action; he turned from the plain commandments of Christ to calculations of expediency. It is likely that I can do more good, so he might think to himself, if I compromise a little with the modernism around me, than if I bluntly resist it. If I should resist, I would be ejected from this large congregation where the numbers of people multiply my opportunity. I would at best have a very limited ministry. Or if I should be thrown to the lions, I could not preach Christ at all. It is plain then that it is better to deny Christ a little than to be silenced completely. How easy it is to put on the flowing robes of respectability and stumble into sin. Remember Christ's precious redemption, and gird up the loins of your mind.

Be sober. This command refers to eating and drinking, but not only, nor even primarily. The Romans, to be sure, among their many vices, were notorious gluttons; but there is no clear indication that gluttony was a besetting sin of Peter's audience. It is more likely that sobriety of mind is intended. Overt acts of transgression spring from evil thoughts. We must think correctly before we can act with firm, conscious virtue. If a man thinks that God's commands can be neglected under local conditions, it shows in his life; if he thinks that God allows no exceptions, people will judge him to be a stubborn and conceited fanatic, but God will judge according to truth. It is man's obligation therefore to think of all problems in their relation to God. Whether we eat or drink, whether we are capitalists or Communists, Greek Orthodox or Plymouth Brethren, we ought to solve every problem by thinking of God and his revealed will. Of course, we may then have to change our affiliations.

If then we follow these two subsidiary injunctions, the main command will be easier. To a person who thinks soberly and sees all things in their relation to God, it is not difficult to hope and to have courage in time of trial.

The translation both of the King James Version and of the American Revision reads, "hope for the grace that is to be brought." But the Greek text says, "hope for the grace that is being brought." The translations put it in the future because the time indicated is the revelation or appearing of Jesus Christ. But it is not impossible to suppose that though Christ's return is still future, Peter thinks of the grace and of Christ himself as being on the way. At any rate such a supposition may well encourage us to hope perfectly. The content of the grace on which we set our hope no doubt includes the redemption of our bodies in glorification, as in the previous allusion.

Peter now enters upon the theme of obedience; he had indicated it in the second verse and will return to the thought again. Here the Christian is asked to act as an obedient child. God is his Father, and to him the child owes filial devotion. We have not always been the children of God. Formerly we acted in lust and ignorance, and were by nature the children of wrath. But God adopted us and made us his children. This he did by free grace in and for his only Son. God has received us into his family and has given us his name. John Satanson has become John Godson. The Spirit of Jesus has been given to these adopted children, and they have been made heirs of all the promises and fellow-heirs with Christ in glory.

But if sonship involves such privileges, ought it not involve some obligations also? There is a story told of a king who found a bum in the street and invited him to come to the palace and to be his son. The bum, either because of experience or because of Scottish ancestry, asked what it would cost.

"Nothing," said the king, "it is all free." The king led him into the palace; the tramp was amazed at the display of wealth. "It is all yours," said the king.

"And I don't have to pay anything?" asked the tramp.

"Nothing at all," replied the king.

"And may I have all I want to eat?" asked the new heir.

"Yes," said his father, "you may eat all you want to." So the king called a servant and told him to see that the new prince would be ready for dinner. The valet took him to his room.

"Now," he said, "you must take your bath, so give me your clothes."

"Do I have to give up my clothes? I haven't taken off this suit in thirteen years, and I am not familiar with baths."

"You will soon become so," said the valet, "and I shall bring you a new suit." The valet brought the new suit, white tie, and tails.

"Do I have to wear that?" asked the poor prince. And finally he was ushered into the dining hall. Such an array of silver he had never before seen. How each tool should be used was beyond his ken. And as he endured the hindrances in trying to eat the best meal he ever had, he mumbled to himself, "all free—I knew there was some catch to it."

At any rate, the Christian life seems uncomfortable to those who are not Christian. The hindrance of dress and silver looms large, while the privileges of a prince go unappreciated. Adoption into God's family is all free, but there is indeed a catch to it. The Christian must be plunged into a cleansing flood that washes white as snow; he must put on the clothes that are suitable for the social circles in which he is now to move; and his diet and table manners will need revision. No longer may he fashion himself according to his former lusts in ignorance, but as his King who called him is holy, so too he must be holy in all the details of his life.

The lusts of the non-Christian life are all too frequently the literal, sensual lusts of the flesh. The divorce rate in the United States will not permit an informed person to shut his eyes to the sensuality of Americans. The people have rebelled against God's laws, and the legislators have followed their lead. A return to wholesome family life is needed as well as a return to God. Of course a return to God would result in an immediate lowering of the divorce rate and in the establishment of family worship. However, the lusts mentioned in the New Testament are not only those of the literal flesh. The flesh as an evil principle in Scripture refers to the depraved nature inherited from Adam, and this includes a depraved mind with mental lusts. Pride or inordinate ambition, any desire at variance with the law of God, is a lust. Much of the crasser vice is hidden, for people still feel some shame about it; but the sins of the mind, the pride of life, the superiority of race, and social position are widely regarded as virtues.

The tendency to excuse or to approve of mental sin is evident occasionally in Christian groups. There is a type of Christian who complains loudly and incessantly against certain overt actions that he regards as sin. Unfortunately he sometimes defines sin merely by his personal dislikes instead of by the law of God. But let us suppose he has hit upon something that is plausibly sinful. He will insist on telling everyone to avoid that sin. But not everyone needs to be told to avoid that one special sin, at least no everyone needs to be told every day. So far this type of Christian may be merely a minor nuisance. The serious damage occurs by his total silence on other sins that are far more heinous. There is a certain Bible teacher who hates smoking, the movies, and enjoys the victorious life. Yet his writings are full of blunders and contain even misquotations. He constantly repeats untrue, slanderous stories about other Christians, and has no objection to underhand tricks in business. Now obviously the movies are responsible for a great deal of marital infidelity, and tobacco smoke irritates the noses and throats of many who do not smoke. But—

In the same town is a man who is an earnest Christian and an unsuccessful evangelist. As an independent he is without the support of a denomination, and he does not have the ability to squeeze money out of audiences. Rather than go deeper into debt, he has taken honest, manual employment. He deserves the respect and prayers of his fellow Christians. Out of his somewhat unhappy experience he spoke words of wisdom when he said, "These victorious-life people are just ordinary Christians away from home."

What God requires is not merely obedience in one or two minor matters. God forbids us to substitute for his laws the commandments of men. He requires complete obedience: "These ought ye to have done, and not to leave the other undone."

The people to whom Peter addressed his epistle ought not perhaps to be classed with the Pharisees. The Pharisees were hypocrites. They had consciously devised external rules of conduct for the purpose of avoiding the obligations of sincerity. Christ frequently castigated them severely. Peter, however, speaks of his people as having sinned in ignorance. Probably, therefore, they were not pharisaical hypocrites but were just ordinary sinners. They may have taken without question the Pharisees' interpretation of the Old Testament and may have obeyed the law sporadically. Or they may not have had even this small amount of knowledge. Now Christ teaches that knowledge increases and ignorance decreases the amount of the penalty. Some will be beaten with many stripes because they have disobeyed a known command. Others, who have done wrong without knowledge, will be beaten with few. But they will be beaten nonetheless. Ignorance may lessen the penalty, but it does not abolish it. No doubt this is because no one is totally ignorant of God's commands. When God created man he wrote into his being a knowledge of his law. Sin has defaced the image of God in man and distorted his sense of right and wrong, but still the Gentiles, who had not received the special revelation granted to Noah, Abraham, and Moses, show the work of the law written on their hearts; and however vile they may become, they know the judgment of God that sin is worthy of death, yet not only continue in sin but take pleasure in sinners.

If the ignorance of the Gentiles in the time of Moses or David was not completely excusable, ignorance in America now is much less so. It is hardly possible that a single person exists in this country who does not have access to a Bible. The Indians on the reservations might have to walk a good distance to find a Bible, but even they can get to one if they really want to. Most other people can get one with very little difficulty. Ignorance under these conditions is willful ignorance. Or if a few of these, born in the slums and missing all education, or born in high society and raised without any reference to religion, do not know there is a Bible, and can therefore claim some slight consideration, what can be said of some terribly devout people who carry their Bibles to church every Sunday and shut their eyes to half of its message? Surely in their case, ignorance is no excuse.

The results of ignorance are the lusts; and when an obedient child learns the truth, the lusts are conquered. Peter urges the necessity of being holy. If we are children of God, we want to be like him; and if he is holy, we ought to be holy too. Ignorance prevents progress in holiness. Knowledge and truth, on the other hand, illumine the mind and bring our conversation into harmony with God's law. An unregenerate person may have some knowledge of God's law and not want to obey; but it is equally true that Christians often want to obey and fail because they do not know God's law.

Paul says the same thing as Peter (Ephesians 4:17–21), "This I say therefore, and testify in the Lord, that ye henceforth walk not as other Gentiles walk, in the vanity of their mind, having the understanding darkened, being alienated from the life of God through the ignorance that is in them, because of the blindness of their heart: who being past feeling have given themselves over unto lasciviousness, to work all uncleanness with greediness. But ye have not so learned Christ; if so be that ye have heard him, and have been taught by him, as the truth is in Jesus."

Some Christians are fond of pointing out that knowledge does not guarantee right conduct and that ignorance is not the cause of sin. There is a certain amount of truth in such a statement, if only it be restricted to its proper application. The last part is almost wholly incorrect. Nowhere in Scripture is ignorance called the cause of righteousness. Ignorance is never praised. If sometimes ignorance does not lead a man into heinous sin, surely it is not a reliable guide to obedience. On the other hand there is a certain sort of knowledge that does not guarantee right conduct. A man may know some of the Biblical revelation and consciously disobey it. Whether he knows it is true, whether he really believes it, is an exceedingly delicate question. But if one pays attention to the conditions Scripture lays down, one can avoid misapplications of plausible statements.

There is a verse of Scripture that non-Christians have frequently misapplied by neglecting to pay attention to the conditions. For example, a college might think it appropriate to use the device, "Ye shall know the truth and the truth shall make you free." But chiseled on the walls of a secular institution, the phrase is detached from its proper setting. It has been put to a naturalistic use that completely falsifies it. To see the difference in meaning that the same words can bear, imagine it first over the door of an atheistic school; and then read it in John 8:31–32: "Then said Jesus to those Jews which believed on him, If ye continue in my word, then are ye my disciples indeed; and ye shall know the truth, and the truth shall make you free." A knowledge of God's truth guarantees right conduct for some people. Let us make sure that we are that people and that we are continuing in the word and increasing in knowledge. Ignorance is not a virtue; it is a sin.

Putting off ignorance and lust, let us remember who called us. It is God who chose us, who elected us in Christ. God is a holy, righteous God. And if it is he that called us, we should strive to be holy in all our manner of life. Peter again refers to the Old Testament for support in what he is saying. The thought comes from Leviticus 11:44ff., 19:2, and 20:7. In these verses God made his holiness the compelling reason why the Israelites should obey his commands.

Holiness as an attribute of God in the Old Testament has a wider meaning than is common in colloquial English. Today we think of holiness as synonymous with righteousness or purity. In the Old Testament, however, holiness has a more profound meaning, from which righteousness follows as an implication. There is some reason to hold that the origin of the word *holy* meant *to be separate*. Thus Jehovah is the Holy One who stands in opposition to others, imaginary gods. He is also separate from the creatures. There is none like him. To use in a technical way a phrase that has almost become slang, God is in a class by himself. It is not Scriptural to say God and the world are two species of Being, and Being is a genus that includes them both. It is wrong to say Jehovah, Zeus, and Allah are instances of the class Deity. The living and true God is absolutely unique; he is truly in a class by himself. He in unique because of his attributes. No one else is omnipotent, and no one else is righteous. Because of man's sinful opposition to God's laws, because of his depravity, the point of contrast in God's revelation to man is the contrast between righteousness and sin. Thus holiness is often thought of as God's uniqueness in righteousness, and the other phases of holiness recede into the background. This is even more prominent in the New Testament than in the Old. And so in the verses under discussion, Peter connects the holiness of God with our obligation to turn from sin and to become holy. And the fact that some groups of Christians, referred to as holiness groups, distort the teaching of the Bible and introduce all sorts of human vagaries to the discredit of the term, is no valid reason for neglecting to emphasize our obligation to become holy. They may have wrong ideas and a lop-sided religion; but if we neglect the idea, we shall be no better than they.

Three Crucial Matters

1 Peter 1:17–21

And if ye call on the Father, who without respect of persons judgeth according to every man's work, pass the time of your sojourning here in fear:

Forasmuch as ye know that ye were not redeemed with corruptible things, as silver and gold, from your vain conversation received by tradition from your fathers;

But with the precious blood of Christ, as of a lamb without blemish and without spot:

Who verily was foreordained before the foundation of the world, but was manifest in these last times for you,

Who by him do believe in God, that raised him up from the dead, and gave him glory; that your faith and hope might be in God.

Reverence

To give further grounds for his exhortation to a godly life, Peter refers to the custom of calling on God as Father. At first sight this might seem to reflect the use of the Lord's Prayer as a part of the regular weekly worship. The Lord's Prayer was early introduced as a regular part of the service, and no doubt these people used it. But if the main body of readers were Jews, Peter is appealing to a usage of worship more ancient than that of the recently inaugurated New Testament church. The Jews for ages had called upon God as Father. Speaking of David, God said (Psalm 89:26), "He shall cry unto me, 'Thou art my Father.'" Again (Isaiah 63:16), "For thou art our Father," and (Jeremiah 3:19), "Thou shalt call me My Father."

But Peter probably had in mind something more particular than a general custom of calling God Father. Note that the verse combines the ideas of Father, without respect of persons, and fear. This particular combination of ideas occurs also in Malachi 1:6, 8, 9, from which it may be inferred that Peter again, as so frequently, is using the Old Testament. The passage in question is, "'If then I be a father, where is mine honour? And if I be a master where is my fear?' saith the Lord of hosts. . . . 'And if ye offer the lame and sick, is it not evil? Offer it now unto thy governor; will he be pleased with thee or accept thy person?' saith the Lord of hosts. 'And now, I pray you, beseech God that he will be gracious unto us: this hath been by your means: will he regard your persons?' saith the Lord of hosts." It is plausible therefore that Peter was thinking of this particular passage.

The notion that God is not a respecter of persons ought not to be hard to understand. In all ages there have been unjust judges, corrupt officials, and, what is worse, governments based on wrong principles. The unjust judge would condemn a poor man and overlook the offenses of the rich. Autocratic governments have granted privileges to nobles (whatever they choose to call noble) and have imprisoned common people without a trial. With such governments and with such officials, the main question is not, *What* did he do? but *Who* did it? The same act, be it murder or theft, would be a serious offense if one person did it, and a matter of little consequence if another did it. It depends on the person. God in his judgments is not a respecter of persons; he does not grant special concessions to the rich, the talented, or the noble born. He judges according to the act. Murder, adultery, and theft are murder, adultery, and theft, whether committed by publican or Pharisee, by Jean Valjean or by Buckingham. God's judgments are according to truth, and he "will render to every man according to his deeds: . . . to the Jew first and also to the Gentile: For there is no 'pull' with God" (Romans 2:6, 10, 11).

Like every other simple idea in Scripture, this too is capable of being misunderstood. Some have argued that God, because he is no respecter of persons, cannot be partial but must treat everyone alike. If he did not treat everyone alike, he would be unjust.

Before analyzing this argument in the light of Scripture, one might look around at people and nations. Does it seem that God has treated them all alike? Some people are wise, others stupid; some are energetic, others lazy. Some were born in Philadelphia, others in Tibet. It is more than obvious that God has not treated us all alike. He has not favored Tibetan children as he has favored those within the sound of the Liberty Bell. But, someone will reply, these are only external, temporal advantages. In the matter of salvation—the only thing that really counts—God cannot be unjust, he must treat everyone alike. Indeed? And do not more people hear the Gospel in Philadelphia than in Tibet? Does it make no difference in matters of salvation where one is born? Can bushmen of Australia accept Christ of whom they have never heard in the same numbers as those who were born where Whitefield preached? A glance at the peoples and their countries gives the answer. Scripture gives the same answer. God sent Paul into Asia but forbade him to preach in Bithynia. God has blessed the West with the Gospel; he has not so blessed the East. He has called some; he has not called others.

Does this make God unjust? Does this make him a respecter of persons? Not at all, for there is nothing in the person called that induces God to call him. There is no foreseen merit of any kind. Calling and salvation are matters not of justice but of grace. They are initiated by love. And who is such a fool as to think that love must treat everyone alike? Are men unjust when they give presents at Christmas time? Would you be unjust to all other beggars if you should give a coin to one? And if you should help a number indiscriminately, would you be a respecter of persons? God is not a respecter of persons; no one will escape his wrath because of personal position. But because God's wrath is impartial, it does not follow that his love and favor are shown to everyone alike. There is no conflict, logical or otherwise, between the principle of "no respecter of persons," and the principle of free grace. We need only to keep the concepts clear in our mind in order not to be confused.

There is then no pull with God. He judges according to every man's work. This needed some emphasis among the Jews, for they were tempted to depend for salvation on their national privileges. Although there is no support for the notion in the Old Testament, many Jews believed that it was impossible for any Jew to be lost. Gentiles might be condemned to hell, but Jews could be sure of heaven. Circumcision guaranteed it. It is true of course that the covenant privileges granted to the Jews as a people worked toward the actual salvation of many of them. But actual salvation requires more than birth and baptism in Philadelphia or in Rome. Someone may say, I was born there; but God judges him by what he does. Perhaps it is not only the Jews who have suffered from Pharisaism; on the contrary, it is a rather universal failing. And to those who rely on external privileges, God says, "Thou are inexcusable, O man, whosoever thou art that judgest: for wherein thou judgest another, thou condemnest thyself; for thou that judgest doest the same things. But we are sure that the judgment of God is according to truth (Romans 2:1)."

The fact of the coming judgment is something that needs emphasis in the world today. The unregenerate man does not like to think about such a possibility and tries not to believe it. Frequently, usually, he is successful. Then too, the minister of the Gospel is often tempted not to preach about it, for it is not a pleasant or popular subject. If he stresses it in the pulpit, the pews begin to empty. And it often seems that the more faithful a minister is, the smaller is his congregation. The unfaithful minister with a deceptive Gospel, with the dance music of popular choruses, with a program of entertainment rather than edification, can often draw crowds. And he is careful not to offend them with displeasing and controversial doctrine. The faithful minister must offend people—Christ did. And he certainly must speak of unpleasant matters, for God has spoken of them in his word. In fact God has frequently warned of judgment to come. In Acts 17:31 it is written, "God hath appointed a day in which he will judge the world in righteousness." This judgment is no mere show; it will make a great difference, for the outcome will be everlasting life for some and everlasting punishment for others.

In some fundamentalist circles it has been taught that Christians shall not come into judgment. But the fact that God will render to every man according to his deeds is true for the saved as well as for the unsaved. The warning of Peter in these verses was addressed not so much to the heathen as to the elect. It is the Christians who are urged to attend to their conduct and to pass their time in fear.

This is also what the apostle Paul teaches. In 2 Corinthians 5:10 he writes, "For we must all appear before the judgment seat of Christ; that every one may receive the things done in the body, according to that he hath done, whether it be good or bad." And in these words Paul is speaking mainly of Christians. And in Romans 14:10, 12, where he says, "we shall all stand before the judgment seat of Christ. . . . So then every one of us shall give account of himself to God," he is speaking exclusively for Christians. It is not true therefore that the Christian will escape being judged. All men will stand before God's throne. Hence it is the part of wisdom to gather information concerning the judgment and to prepare ourselves for it.

The subject matter of the judgment, as given both by Peter and by Paul, is the deeds done in the body. Imagine the thieves and the murderers who will be called to account, the adulterers, the profane, the slanderers. Pontius Pilate and Peter will be there; Plato and Augustine; Bishop Latimer and Bloody Mary; Hitler, Churchill—and you.

However, it is not only the big sinners and the big sins that will stand revealed in that day. God's judgment will be comprehensive and will take in sins that most people call little. It is written in Matthew 12:36 that "every idle word that men shall speak, they shall give account thereof in the day of judgment." This is a terrible thought: to be held accountable for every thoughtless expression. At the same time it may also have a consoling side if we have habitually cultivated kindness and righteousness, so that our unpremeditated conversation is somewhat in conformity with God's holy law.

The preaching of the judgment, then, should be directed to the saved and unsaved alike. That is what the Scriptures do. And we may well join in singing the solemn hymn:

Before me place in dread array
The pomp of that tremendous day,
When Thou with clouds shalt come
To judge the nations at thy bar,
And tell me, Lord, shall I be there
To meet a joyful doom?

To some who have been told by unfaithful ministers that Christians shall not stand before God's bar, this hymn and its solemn thought may occasion some surprise. Is it not the heathen who should fear, and is not the salvation of God's chosen people secure? Quite true. But the saints are secure through faith. They are elect unto obedience. They must persevere. Salvation was not completed at regeneration; those who think so may be tempted to heedlessness, carelessness, and presumption. They may be tempted to take their salvation for granted, as it were; to regard it as something common and of little value. Such an attitude is irreverent, and for this reason Peter sets forth his explanations so that the Christian may preserve the sense of fear and reverence before God, the just judge.

The matter of one's attitude before God is so important that it may be wise to consider fear and reverence at greater length than Peter's brief mention would ordinarily call for.

No one, and especially no Christian, when brought consciously to face the question, would assert that carelessness and indifference are proper attitudes in the presence of the almighty God. But unfortunately multitudes, and even some Christians, are not brought consciously to face the matter. The unregenerate give little thought to God; they neither glorify him as God nor give thanks; and since they are without excuse their condemnation is just.

On the other hand, though God and man's attitude toward him are nothing to the unthinking crowds which pass by, there are serious people, too few in number, who, instead of needing to be persuaded that such a view is folly, would welcome, in their genuine concern to please God, even a mediocre treatment of the subject. Now while these people are in no danger of ignoring God, it may yet happen that some of them are in slight danger of tending toward the opposite extreme of bold presumption. This does not mean that they consciously intend to impose on God; on the contrary they may be seriously seeking to please God and at the same time fail because they take him too much for granted.

If one suspects that one is failing, or if one wishes to engage in self-examination as a periodic precaution, no better method could be employed than the consideration of conspicuous Scriptural examples.

Undoubtedly the clearest early example is to be found in Abraham. In the fifteenth chapter of Genesis there is the description of a remarkable meeting of God and Abraham. Abraham had asked God for a sign by which he should know that God would fulfill his promise. That sign involved a vision in which Abraham saw God as nearly as any man can see God. What, then, was the instinctive reaction of Abraham? What effect did that vision have upon him? Was it the ordinary effect that good news has on most people? Did he shout? Was he vociferous? Or was the reaction more subdued? The text makes it perfectly clear: "and, lo, an horror of great darkness fell upon him."

The thoughtful worshiper may demur at taking the experience of Abraham as normative for his own. For, in the first place, it was a vision and visions are not in order today. Even if they were, it is not obvious that visions are safe guides for states of ordinary consciousness. Second, it was a sign which Abraham may have needed but which has no immediate application to common folk. And third, the revelation or presence of God was so definite and intimate that no one today could reasonably expect its duplication.

Now, although the first two of these three reasons are true enough in themselves, the third rather indicates, not so much *why* as *how* we may apply the experience of Abraham to ourselves. Even though we do not expect such a definite revelation in this life, the account in Genesis shows how man actually behaves when face to face with God. If the manner of others is more carefree, perhaps the reasons is that they do not know God as Abraham knew him; if others really knew God, they might conclude that Abraham's horror was justified. Therefore, we may ask ourselves the question: If God, when so personally revealed, elicits such a response, what should our present attitude be toward such a God? For he is the same unchanging God.

However, not to run the risk of misunderstanding a single illustration, one may turn to Exodus 3:6. Here Moses was confronted by the living God; what was his attitude? The text reads: "And Moses hid his face; for he was afraid to look upon God." The account of Gideon in Judges 6:22 is entirely similar.

Or, one may quickly turn the pages of the Bible and come to Isaiah 6:5. When Isaiah was brought into the presence of God, what did he consider the proper attitude to be? Did he rejoice and sing? Did he take it as a good fortune though somewhat as a matter of course? Did he feel at home? No, the text does not indicate that our common attitudes in our everyday life are appropriate, but rather the verse reads:

"Woe is me, for I am undone; because I am a man of unclean lips, and I dwell in the midst of a people of unclean lips: for mine eyes have seen the King, Jehovah of hosts."

Now it is easily imagined that someone, particularly if he has leanings toward liberal theology, will argue that these illustrations have all been taken from the Old Testament, and that therefore they do not apply to the present generation. Jesus has come since that time and has taught that God is our Father, that we should have confidence before him, and that we should no longer look on him as an oriental despot after the manner of the Old Testament.

This type of argument is such a confusion of truth, error, and invalid inference that it cannot be disposed of in one breath. The examples so far adduced do not indicate that the men of the Old Testament lacked confidence in God. In fact Abraham is the outstanding example of faith; and it is also recorded that God spoke to Moses face to face as a man speaks unto his friend (Exodus 33:11). And those who go so far as to use without modification the figure of an oriental despot are usually guilty of at least a semi-conscious misinterpretation. Of course, Jesus taught that God is our Father, and undoubtedly his teaching goes beyond that of the Old Testament; but it "goes beyond" in the sense of explanation. For the New Testament, as many passages indicate (Romans 1:17, 3:21, 4:6, Galatians 3:8) does not abrogate but rather completes the Old. It brings to light what was previously obscure, so that the Lord rightly says to us, "O slow of heart to believe all that the prophets have spoken. . . ."

The Christian who wishes to have an accurate understanding of the Bible must avoid two extremes. The first extreme deepens the colors of the Old Testament and fades out the colors of the New. It overestimates the severe aspects of the Old by forgetting what is said of loving-kindness and tender mercies, while at the same time it is voluble on the beauty of Jesus and silent on what he said about a generation of vipers, outer darkness, and gnashing of teeth. This lack of balance which is characteristic of liberal theology finally results in a rejection of the Scriptures as the very Word of God and in a conception of God as love to such an extent as to deny him sufficient righteousness to punish sin.

The other extreme to be avoided is less dangerous in that it is less attractive, for no one would wish to underestimate the clearer revelation of God as Father which we have in the New Testament. For we have not received the spirit of bondage again unto fear but the spirit of adoption whereby we cry, Abba, Father. To use an illustration from human affairs, there comes to mind two boys or young men, who in addressing their fathers always made frequent use of the word, Sir. With them it was always, Yes, Sir; No, Sir; I beg your pardon, Sir. Perhaps one who is accustomed to more tender language is not capable of passing judgment on such usage; but at first sight it might seem that respect had passed over into timid servility. The other extreme, however, in which a boy refers to his father as "the old man," is obviously worse. So then, the Christian must choose his course between these two, maintaining a proper reverence without a spirit of bondage to fear.

To discover by way of concrete illustration how the New Testament confirms rather than abrogates the Old, one may consider the disciples' relation to Jesus. At first it would seem that the fear of God had here disappeared into human familiarity. But we must remember that during the earthly life of our Lord his divine nature was veiled by his human nature. His glory and deity did not clearly shine forth. On one occasion, however, there was a difference. After Jesus had brought Peter, James, and John up into a mountain he was transfigured before them. Even so, Peter managed to sputter some well intentioned but utterly inappropriate sentences. But while he yet spake, God spoke from heaven, and the Scriptures record that the disciples were *sore* afraid. They had heard the voice of God.

Then, after the earthly ministry had been accomplished, one notes in the first chapters of the Acts the joy and freedom characteristic of the early Christians, and one is tempted to see in this a modification of the fearful attitude of the Old Testament. At the same time, the Holy Spirit, who gives the joy, is not to be trifled with. His joy is not a careless thoughtlessness nor a superficial emotion. The fear of the Lord forms its background. This fear need not be exactly the same kind of fear which Paul had in mind when he spoke of the spirit of bondage to fear. Paul was thinking of the fear of the extreme penalty of sin; but the fear of the Lord is something quite different. It is possible that the early Christians in the first glow of their new zeal momentarily forgot the lessons of the ancient Scriptures; but God ended their forgetfulness by a serious example. Ananias and Sapphira conspired to lie to the Holy Ghost, and they were on that account stricken dead. Then the apostle records that *great fear* came upon all that heard it. Fear rather than hilarity is the proper attitude when a man comes face to face with God.

But how may we tell whether we have the proper attitude; how may we know to avoid both a cheap familiarity and a state of abjection which argues lack of confidence in God? At first it may be a disappointment to find that the Scriptures spend very little time describing subjective feeling. Frequently, as in Exodus 33 and 34, the account is reserved and objective. But if the Scriptures give no psychological analysis, how may we judge ourselves? Fortunately there is, as it would seem, a very sure method, available to all who ask the question seriously. It is to be observed that Abraham, Moses, Isaiah, and the Christians in Acts did not study, fret, or figure how to attain the proper attitude. The response to God was instinctive, instantaneous, unpremeditated. It was not the result of introspection; it was the result of seeing God.

From this it may be inferred that if we wish to have a proper attitude before God, we should cease to study attitudes and, instead,  seek and study God. There is a certain gentleman, who, along with many estimable qualities, is constantly feeling his pulse and inquiring into the state of his stomach and other organs. He is a constant visitor to three or four doctors and regularly takes as many prescribed medicines. To be sure the state of his health requires a physician, but his constant attention to the least fluctuations of his heart is not doing him any good, and it is a marvel how his stomach can put up with so many drugs. Similarly the state of spiritual hypochondria is not desirable. Sickness may require examination; and occasional spiritual checkups are good; but as a regular thing the direction of attention should be healthy and objective. Subjectivity breeds morbidity. And the Scriptural examples cited substantiate this view.

The next question naturally suggests itself after the first. If our attention should be directed to God rather than to ourselves, how may we know that we are coming into contact with God and are not deceiving ourselves with vain imaginations? The answer is as easy as the question is natural, though first, the answer may be given negatively, using for concreteness and contrast an illustration from the Old Testament. The thirteenth chapter of First Chronicles shows that mere good intentions are insufficient to bring us into a blessed contact with God.

The chapter gives the account of David's first attempt to bring back to its proper place in Israel the ark of the covenant which the Philistines had previously captured. All the people were sincere in wanting to have again this symbol of God's presence in their midst. The first part of the chapter gives a joyous picture of a multitude desiring to please God. Their intentions were very good. But when God showed his displeasure at their attempt their joy was turned to sorrow, fear, and dismay. While their intentions were good, they had failed to ascertain how God wished to be worshiped. They thought that good intentions were a substitute for knowledge. So long as they meant well, so long as their feelings were acceptable to themselves, it made little difference what God had objectively commanded.

The situation has frequent parallels today. In the first place the religious liberal thinks he can come to God in his own way and can dispense with the blood of Jesus Christ, who is the only way to the Father. His intentions may be of the best, but they merit only God's displeasure. In the second place, those who have trusted in Christ, those who are truly regenerated by the Holy Ghost, also on occasion disregard God's commands and seek to please him in their own ways. The result can only be that instead of drawing nearer to God, they deafen themselves to his voice.

This unfortunate result can easily be avoided. There is no good reason for remaining in ignorance of what God would have us do. So to change from the previous negative answer, a positive and definitely certain way of coming into the presence of God may be stated. And the more definitely we see God, the less we need to worry about our attitude. That sure way of coming to know God is the study of the revelation of himself which he has made to us. Holy Scripture is the only infallible rule of faith and practice. In the Scriptures, and in them alone, do we have a clear and accurate concept of God. Our duty, then, is to study them diligently, carefully noting the attributes of God, the distinctions of his persons, particularly the person of the Son, and also all God's works of providence. When we thus come to know God, then we, like Abraham, will naturally have a proper attitude before him. It will not result from a subjective study of our emotions, but from an accurate knowledge of God himself. Fear God and keep his commandments, for this is the whole duty of man.

This digression on the fear of God has been longer than a single phrase in a verse ordinarily warrants. What perhaps is less excusable is the delay in emphasizing the reason Peter gives for inculcating fear of God. For the reason why we should fear God is the fact that we have been redeemed by the precious blood of Christ.

Morality

Verses eighteen and nineteen are familiar verses. They are often quoted. And that is good. Here and there throughout the Bible certain verses stand out, because, we might say, they are outstanding. They sum up in elegant phrase or in forceful emphasis some great truth. They strike us as a climax and summary of an important section. And so we quote them frequently. But when we quote them, do we always remember the context of which they are the climax? Undoubtedly such verses are great verses, but they lose much of their significance if we forget the setting in which they occur. We are redeemed with the precious blood of Christ, Peter says. Yes, but what of it? The "what of it?" is just the attitude of fear, reverence, and obedience that formed the subject matter of the less prominent preceding verses. The way in which Peter has written this section makes fear of God the main thought and redemption by Christ the reason or secondary thought. In thus subordinating redemption to reverence Peter is touching upon only one phase of Christ's work. There are other senses in which Christ's work is far from being subordinate to any human subjective attitude; yet as we now proceed to consider the significance of Christ's blood, let us not altogether forget the immediate purpose of Peter's paragraph.

In fact, since Peter so closely conjoins Christ's death with an appeal for holy living, it may prove wise to discuss first the relation of theology and the atonement in particular to the general subject of ethics.

We believe, of course, that Christianity is an ethical religion; in fact we hold that no other religion, no other system of thought, presents so accurate and so worthy standards of right and wrong; and further, it is true that however much individuals and groups have at times departed from those standards in actual conduct, Christianity has made notable progress in developing a better morality both within Christian groups and also among non-Christians. There are still discrepancies between creed and conduct in the Church, but few if any churches present so sorry a spectacle of moral turpitude as the converts Paul gained directly from heathenism. With a keen imagination of the horrors of war there is little desire to minimize the wickedness of the non-Christian world. We abhor the brutality and immorality that goes with armies on the march; we shudder at the deliberate cruelty of the Gestapo; and yet, though the Gestapo had been trained to hate Christianity, though they had been taught that they were a superior race and above "Jewish" morality, they still were probably less vicious than the Chinese Communists who never were under the influence of Christianity. Certainly the majority of Americans are not Christian; the humanists and Unitarians attack supernaturalism and the blood of Christ; but if the humanists show any tendency to be humane, it is the result of the Christian teaching of previous generations. At any rate, no one can seriously doubt that Christianity has had a tremendous influence on the morality of the western world.

To such an extent has the Christian ideal been accepted by all classes of people—in theory if not in practice—that it has been possible to argue: Since Christian ideals are best, the Christian religion must be true. And the defense of Christianity against its enemies has often rested on the assumption of its moral excellence. But suppose the moral excellence of Christianity is denied. There may have been a time and place when such a denial was unthinkable. Today, however, voices are raised in favor of other types of morality. This is true not only in atheistic Russia, not only in the recent National Socialism of Germany, it is true also in the case of respected theologians in Boston and New York who reject the blood of Christ. In fact, one of the basic attacks on orthodox Christianity is that it is immoral. To meet this criticism, the old argument must be recognized as inverted. One cannot argue the truth of Christianity on the basis of its ethics; one must defend its ethics, if at all, on the basis of its truth. The ethics is a logical consequence of the truth, not its cause.

No one with any Christian training would, I suppose, want to deprecate morality. Nevertheless, it is quite possible so to exaggerate its importance, so to misunderstand its relative place in philosophy, that only confusion both moral and theoretical can result. This overemphasis on morality, so it would seem, is an important contributory cause to the rise of modernism. The authority of conscience was insisted on, a moral consciousness was developed, ethical institutions were sought for. And as these aspects of human nature—indispensable as they are—were continually brought forward, they came to usurp the position of supreme judge. Thus we find statements of which the following two are typical. "Old theology is always becoming new in the vitalizing influence of ethics. . . . It is reason enough for doubting and for restudying any traditional teaching or received word of doctrine if it be felt to harass or to confuse the Christian conscience of an age. Nothing can abide as true in theology which does not prove its genuineness under the ever renewed searching of the Christian moral sense. . . . Christian ethics cannot consent to commit suicide in any supposed interest of theology."*

And in a chapter on "Punishment and Forgiveness," whose theory would have definite consequences for the atonement, we read: "Now as in the days of Plato it is a paramount duty of Moral Philosophy to lay down Canons for Theology. . . . the idea of substituted vicarious punishment would never for a moment be defended by a modern Christian except with a view to bolster up an obsolete theological tradition."†

One might also refer to current oral reports that the evangelical view of the atonement is a "butcher-house religion," and probably everyone who reads this has similar illustrations of his own.

It seems then that the Christian conscience has so developed that it is all conscience and no longer Christian. Moral sense has become the judge of truth and error. And moral sense turns out to be nothing but unadulterated mysticism. Now to some, mysticism has the connotation of piety and devotion. The hymns of Zinzendorf cast a holy halo about the word and after all no one dare slander the exemplary conduct of groups who studiously follow the Inner Light. But it is doubtful if their good points come from their mysticism. To the mystic, the final authority is a feeling or an emotion which no one but himself can experience. Its dictates are not open to verification by any other person. Truth, therefore, depends on one's emotions, and if two mystics contradict each other, there is no possible basis of reconciliation, for,

---

*Newman Smyth, *Christian Ethics* (New York: Charles Scribner's Sons, 1892), p. 11.

†Hastings Rashdall, *Theory of Good and Evil,* Vol. I (London: University Press, 1892), pp. 311, 312.

however much each of them might deny it, their theory makes them inhabitants of different worlds as much as Protagorean skepticism would.

Let us therefore face the question squarely. Should ethics determine our theology, or should theology determine our ethics? Nor permit it to be said that each influences the other. However true that may be in some sense of the words, one theorem or set of theorems cannot be both consequence and postulate. We may, to be sure, learn a theorem of geometry before having studied geometry. But because we learn the axioms last it does not follow that the axioms are based on the theorems. So too, our parents may teach us some very valuable morality long before we know anything of theology. The question which separates Rashdall and, as I conceive, evangelicalism, is the problem of logical dependency—a mere question of logic, of definition, of theory; yet vitally connected with our view of the atonement. Is theology or ethics logically prior?

Our answer depends on our general view of the world as a whole and particularly on our concept of God. To illustrate, we may summarily divide all philosophies very roughly into two types. The first type may be termed naturalism and be taken to include all systems which picture the ultimate as either law or fact. In antiquity Plato posited a World of Ideas above the Demiurge who made this world of ours. The World of Ideas was a pattern for the Demiurge to follow. It existed independently of him. In modern philosophy there is neither Demiurge nor World of Ideas. We must simply take things as they are, and while any particular thing, like a tree or an auto, can be explained by its antecedents, the world as a whole has no cause and cannot be explained. Facts or law are ultimate.

The second type of philosophy may properly be called Christian Theism. In this system facts and laws are not ultimate. God is ultimate—the only, living and true, triune, personal God. If then God is supreme and all facts and laws depend on his ordinance, it follows that no law, fact, or World of Ideas is superior to him. Most people find it easy to conceive God as creating physical law by divine fiat. He made water so that it would freeze at 32°F. He might have made some other world in which water would have frozen at 28°F. At certain temperatures water and bismuth expand upon cooling, but lead and other metals contract. God could have reversed all this. But as a matter of fact God chose to create the sort of world we actually live in. Now for some peculiar reason people find difficulty in applying the same consideration to ethical laws. Instead of recognizing God as sovereign in the moral sphere, they seem ordinarily to think of him as being compelled by some vague superior power to make morality what it is—a remnant of the Platonic World of Ideas. But it seems more reasonable to think of God as just as untrammeled in creating moral distinctions as in creating physical facts. Once then we are able thoroughly to grasp the absolute sovereignty of God in all realms, our initial moral problem is solved. Morality, like the physical universe and its laws, is what it is because God made it that way; and if we want to live a moral life we must determine what standards God has set up. Now it is possible to learn something of God from his works. We might, for example, learn that honesty is the best policy and conclude God is that kind of a God. But it is to be noted that the discovery of ethical principles by empirical methods is exceedingly difficult and never certain. This history of ethics, one of progressive skepticism it seems to me, can fairly well be summed up in the words of G. E. Moore: "We never have any reason to suppose that an action is our duty. . . . It is difficult to see how we can establish even a probability that by doing one thing we shall obtain a better total result than by doing another. . . . No sufficient reason has ever yet been found for considering one action more right or more wrong than another."

If this be not sufficiently serious, there is still another difficulty in establishing ethics and then passing on to theology. It is apparently a matter of experience that the consciences of men may be seared and their moral judgments warped. If it be true that God has given up some to a reprobate mind, their moral opinions are probably insecure bases for ethical theory. So one might almost expect the world in desperation to reverse its procedure and attempt to base ethics on theology. The view then would be that the nature of God is not to be determined by means of our consciences or intuitions, but these rather are to be corrected in the light of the nature of God. But in this case we must expect the objection to arise that if our moral judgments cannot be trusted, neither can our theological. To this the Christian has an answer not permitted to the Deist or Pantheist who may well have followed the position as so far stated. God has revealed himself, not only in nature, but much more explicitly in the Scriptures. Naturally there is little hope for evangelical Christianity if the Scriptures cannot be regarded as a divine revelation. But assuming this important point for the present, if the Scriptures teach vicarious punishment and our consciences don't like it, so much the worse for our consciences. In the determination of truth such personal subjective considerations are to be eliminated, else we too have taken the first step into mysticism and modernism.

At this point some very conscientious persons raise an apparently serious objection to the view here outlined. If this view were true, they say, honesty might not be the best policy. If morality depends purely on God's ordinance, just as the laws of physics, then possibly stealing would be right and right would be wrong. Unless such an objector has definitely aligned himself with Plato and Rashdall, it is not likely that he means God in creating the world was under obligation to suit his fancy in the matter. That we have become accustomed to given ethical standards is no reason for believing that God had to make the world that way. Even if our moral opinions are correct, it is no more a reason for so believing than our knowledge of physics is for putting God under the compulsion of physical laws.

If then the objector does not mean this, it is likely his objection arises from an emotion resulting from previous training respecting honesty. Certainly in this world honesty is best. But it is best precisely because God made the world that way. Anything God does is right, because he does it; and had we no knowledge of God we could not guess what sort of moral standards he might set up for some hypothetical world not now in existence. The reason we object to stealing or to any other sin is that we have learned that it is contrary to God's ordinance. We must learn God's plan first and develop our morality afterward.

To those who still have doubts about this way of stating things, it is recommended first to consider the attitude of some heathen man who, with a conscience as void of offense as was Paul's when persecuting the infant church, is sacrificing his child as a religious rite. If theology must be based on ethics and conscience, there is nothing to be said to such a heathen. From childhood he has been taught that it would be immoral to omit these rites. If you should force him or half persuade him to neglect them, he would suffer the pangs of conscience. The man who asserts that conscience is the final judge must accept the dictates of the heathen conscience—if not as a rule of his own conduct, at least as an inviolable rule for the heathen. He cannot argue that God does not want human sacrifice, because, on his theory, theology or knowledge of God depends on how one's conscience feels. In the second place, anyone who has doubts about God's sovereignty over the laws of conduct may consider the position of him who claims that orthodox Christianity is immoral. The same results follow. For him his anti-Christian conscience is basic, and the only god whom he can come to know is an anti-Christian god. It is thus clear that if conscience is made basic, there is no method left by which one can argue for a change of conscience. The burning of widows in India and the urbanity of a Unitarian are equally justified. Each is conscientious. In view of this the conclusion seems forced: We must adjust our ethics to our theology, not vice versa. We must argue, not from our moral standards to the truth of the Bible, but from the truth of the Bible to the morality it upholds. And this indeed is what Peter has done. ***Because*** we are redeemed by Christ, he says, we ought to fear God and be holy.

Redemption

The principles of morality therefore are logically secondary to the doctrine of redemption by Christ's blood; redemption in turn is logically subsidiary to the deity of Christ and to the whole doctrine of the Trinity. For if Christ were not the second person of the Trinity as well as man, of what avail would be his death? Nonetheless, though the doctrine of the Trinity is the most basic logically, redemption by Christ's blood receives the greatest emphasis. The Trinity may be basic, but Calvary is central. No one can well understand the significance of the crucifixion without some grasp of the nature of the person crucified; in fact it is doubtful whether any adult was ever saved who was totally ignorant of what some people call theory and theology. Even the thief on the cross had some idea, vague and inaccurate no doubt, but nevertheless had some idea that Jesus was Lord and ruled a Kingdom beyond the grave. Nor is it true that a sinner first accepts Christ as Savior and then at a later date with a second experience of grace accepts him as Lord. There are no such two groups of Christians, and there are no assurances in Scripture given to anyone who tries to accept Christ as Savior without recognizing him as Lord. And to know this is to know some very important theology. Nonetheless, in preaching the Gospel to the lost, it is not the Trinity nor even the person of Christ that receives the first emphasis. It is Christ's sacrifice, redemption by his blood, that composes the main subject matter.

The three most important ideas in verses eighteen and nineteen, all phases of the one thing, are redemption, Christ's blood, and the lamb without blemish. These three refer to major aspects of what we today call the atonement. In view of all that should be said on the atonement, the brief statement permitted within the present limits is pitifully inadequate. But however inadequate the following explanation may be, the omission of all explanation would be criminal.

To begin with the last of the three ideas: that Christ was a Lamb without spot. Also in the Gospels we read, "Behold the Lamb of God that taketh away the sins of the world" (John 1:29). The Jews understood such language easily. They were accustomed to sacrifices. When John, or Paul, or Peter told them that Christ was the Lamb of God, they might not believe, but they could not fail to grasp the meaning. It meant that Christ's death was a sacrifice for sin. Christ's death was not an unavoidable calamity, or the death of a martyr, it was rather the result of a deliberate purpose to offer a sacrifice for sin. The epistle to the Hebrews at great length compares and contrasts the sacrifices of the Old Testament with the death of Christ. Christ fulfilled what the Old Testament sacrifices foreshadowed. Now sacrifices, in any religion, are considered to be offered to God, or to some superior being; and their aim is not to produce a frame of mind in the worshiper so that that frame of mind makes the worshiper acceptable with God. The aim of a sacrifice is, as it were, to produce a frame of mind in God by a means acceptable to him, so that his anger toward the sinner is placated. Thus when anyone makes Christ's sacrifice his own, he is in effect offering the blood of Christ to God the Father with the hope that God will accept the offering and on the basis of the offering forgive his sins. The primary effect of a sacrifice is on God, not on man. It is essential to understand that Christ's death was a sacrifice, and the Jews, even the unconverted Jews, understood the meaning quite well.

It is interesting to note how all the doctrines of the Scripture fit together into one system. Here it can be seen again how the Trinity is presupposed by Christ's death. One day a young man who did not know everything there was to be known was engaged in conversation with a Swedenborgian minister. The young man had heard of Swedenborgianism, but knew few of the details and was asking for information. It was explained that Swedenborgians believed there was but one person in the Godhead. There was no Father, Son, and Spirit, but just one person. This one person came to earth as Jesus Christ. The young man, a Christian, then asked, if there is but one person in the Godhead, how can Christ be the Lamb of God? The Swedenborgian replied, "Oh, we have a symbolical method for explaining such passages." It would have to be very symbolical, and it would have to be a symbolism entirely unfamiliar to the Jews of apostolic times. That the apostles disguised their meaning in words the Jews would be sure to misunderstand is hardly reasonable. The apostles were Jews themselves, and when they said Christ was the Lamb that should take away sin, they were altogether conscious of the Old Testament meaning of their words. They intended to teach that Christ's death was a sacrifice.

The second idea that Peter mentioned was the blood of Christ. It was the blood that was the sacrifice. Again the Jews were sure to understand. In the Old Testament the blood of sacrifice cleansed the sinner of his sin. The sin was expiated and the sinner forgiven. In the Old Testament expiation is frequently expressed by the notion of covering. This is true both of the ritual sacrifices and perhaps more obviously at the Passover. Sin in man exposes him to God's wrath and curse; he needs to be covered or protected from God's justice. At the Passover the faithful Jews stayed in their houses under the blood, but the Egyptians who were not covered suffered the loss of their first born. "Blessed is he whose transgression is forgiven, whose sin is covered. Blessed is the man unto whom the Lord imputeth not iniquity" (Psalm 32:1–2).

The other phase of Christ's work in these verses is the notion of redemption. Christ has redeemed us. This shows that the expiatory sacrifice of Christ was vicarious. Christ took our place, became our substitute or representative, and paid the penalty for sin instead of us. The animal sacrifices of the Old Testament were vicarious: the sinner did not himself die, but a lamb or some other animal died in his stead. The Jews of the first century easily understood substitution—so ought we.

And this is the doctrine that so-called modern minds believe is immoral. Let us repeat: so much the worse for their minds. They need a change of mind, and change of mind in the New Testament is called repentance. God "commandeth all men everywhere to repent, because he hath appointed a day, in which he will judge the world in righteousness by that man whom he hath ordained," Jesus Christ, the Lamb of God, whose blood is more precious than corruptible things such as silver and gold.

There is a hypothetical possibility that a vicarious atonement could be immoral. If a sacrifice could cover one from sin so that one could continue in sin with impunity, that type of sacrifice might well be called immoral. But such is not Christ's sacrifice, as Peter has already explained in the immediately preceding verses. Christ's blood covers our sin, but not in the sense or for the purpose of allowing sin to continue to rule us. On the contrary,

He died that we might be forgiven,
He died to make us good,
That we might go at last to heaven,
Saved by his precious blood.
Oh dearly, dearly has he loved,
And we must love him too,
And trust in his redeeming blood,
And try his works to do.

The next verse returns to a thought similar to the notion of election that was found in verses one and two. But in this case the decree of God concerns the incarnation and work of Christ rather than the salvation of men. The King James version says that Christ was foreordained before the foundation of the world; while the American Revised version uses the more literally accurate phrase, "was foreknown," etc. The meaning of foreordination and foreknowledge will be discussed later. What will then be said of the election of men can be applied here to the original choice of Christ as redeemer.

All that is needed at this point is the reminder that the occurrence of sin in the world was no surprise to God. And the atonement was no afterthought. The question of the origin of sin has perplexed many people—Christians and non-Christians alike. And many of both groups have been led to queer speculations by the difficulties of the problem. Some have assumed the existence of two utterly independent and equally eternal principles or gods. Exponents of such dualism are

Zoroaster, Plato, and William James. This attempted explanation of the existence of evil and sin is clearly not Christian, for if the Old Testament teaches anything, it teaches that there is but one God, unique and sovereign. "I am the Lord, and there is none else, there is no God beside me. . . . I form the light and create darkness: I make peace and create evil: I the Lord do all these things" (Isaiah 45:5, 7).

Others have disposed of the problem in other ways. Many simply give it up and confess failure in their attempts to understand it. There is nothing dishonorable in such an admission. A great many problems are too difficult for a great many people. The invention of synthetic rubber was not within the ability of most people; and all the mathematicians in the world have not yet rediscovered the proof of the Fermat theorem. Instead of being a disgrace, it is a mark of wisdom to admit failure when there is failure. Others, however, are neither so wise nor so modest; for there are those who argue in effect: I have not solved the problem, I cannot solve the problem, and therefore no one else can solve it. And thus they transfer their own limitations to the whole world. Indeed they go still further. They argue that their failure to solve the problem results, not from their limitations, but from the nature of the problem itself. They assert that the problem is insoluble. In fact Barthianism now claims that not even God can solve the problem.

But the Scriptures teach that God has a complete understanding of this as of all other matters. There are no "problems" for God. And not only so, but in this verse some understanding of the problem is vouchsafed to us. Christ's death is the supreme example of that love than which none is greater; and his sacrifice becomes intelligible only against the background of sin. If redemption from sin was planned from the foundation of the world, sin must also have been included in the plan. To suppose that the irruption of sin in the world was some unforeseen, uncontrolled event is derogatory to the sovereignty of the only wise God our Savior.

No claim is made here that God has revealed to us all he knows about sin; but in view of the confusion in people's minds, it may well be that God has revealed to mankind more of the solution than most people think. Consideration and careful meditation is asked for the following inerrant words of God:

"The Lamb slain from the foundation of the world" (Revelation 13:8).

"But we speak the wisdom of God in a mystery, even the hidden wisdom, which God ordained before the world unto our glory" (1 Corinthians 2:7).

"Who hath saved us, and called us with an holy calling, not according to our works, but according to his own purpose and grace, which was given us in Christ Jesus before the world began" (2 Timothy 1:9).

"He hath chosen us in him before the foundation of the world" (Ephesians 1:4).

"Who works all things after the counsel of his own will" (Ephesians 1:11).

Contrasted with the eternal foreordination of God is the manifestation or fulfillment of the plan at the end of times. The manifestation, of course, includes Christ's incarnation, his life, death, and resurrection, and probably refers also to the preaching of the Gospel.

Christ was manifested "for your sake." Christ was not manifested to or for everyone indiscriminately. His saving benefits are limited to the faithful elect. When the angel before the birth of Christ explained the significance of what was about to happen, he said to Joseph, "Thou shalt call his name Jesus, for he shall save his people from their sins."

Here and elsewhere the Scriptures teach that in eternity God gave to Christ a special people. As John 6:37 states it, "All that the Father gives me shall come unto me." In the tenth chapter of John this people is pictured as flocks of sheep in danger of attack by wolves; and Jesus gives his life for his sheep. And in John 17:6 Jesus mentions those whom the Father gave him, and a few verses below he prays for them as he does not pray for the world.

There is of course a sense in which Christ died for all men. He is the propitiation for the sins of the whole world, as this same John tell us in his first epistle. No greater sacrifice would be needed even if all men were to be saved. But obviously Christ is not the propitiation for all sin in the sense that he saves all men.

Beyond this reference to all men, there is another sense, a much more precious sense, and a much more definite sense in which Christ dies for some only and not for all. In 1 Timothy 4:10 Paul says, "We trust in the living God, who is the Savior of all men, especially of those that believe." Christ died for these in the sense that on the cross he definitely intended to save just those and no others. For example,

Christ definitely intended to save Abraham and Moses; he did not intend to save those who were destroyed in Sodom.

How then can a widely read religious paper print the following? "If Christ died for all, he died for each; for no one more than another, and no one omitted." The untruth of the quotation is attested by Matthew, by John, by Paul, and by the whole consistent teaching of the Bible.

And why, may one ask, does any true Christian, even when emphasizing the general propitiation for all sins, wish to conceal or deny the particularizing grace and election of God by which God chose him specially and personally out of a mass of lost mankind? We who were chosen in Christ before the foundation of the world are his people whom he came to save. To God alone be all the glory.

We, his people, believe in God by him. Without Christ we can know little of God. His great majesty and our depraved faculties make saving knowledge altogether impossible. The unregenerate retain, as Romans 1:20, 32 indicate, some knowledge of the power and deity of God and some sense of the distinction between good and evil. But since they do not care to retain God in their knowledge and since God gave them over to a reprobate mind, they succeed fairly well in eradicating or at least in distorting their knowledge of God. The heavens declare the glory of God, but men are blind. Truly magnificent systems of human wisdom have been elaborated; but apart from Christ speculation on God is vain. How can it be other than vain, for Jesus Christ "is the image of the invisible God" (Colossians 1:15), and no man can come to the Father but by the Lord Jesus Christ? No man would want to come to the Father except for Christ. Man's sin requires a mediator. Without a mediator man would shun God in terror rather than believe on him with confidence. Certainly it is through him that we trust in God.

In the immediately following phrase descriptive of God, Peter gives a good reason for trusting God. God raised Jesus Christ from the dead and gave glory to him. The resurrection provides a solid basis for our confidence; the glory Christ received assures us that those in Christ will also be glorified. And thus our faith has a reasonable and intelligible foundation. Faith in God, saving faith in God, is more than the bare belief that God exists. The devils believe that there exists one God, and their belief makes them tremble. The Christian believes something that the devils cannot believe. The Christian believes that Christ died in his stead to save him. The Christian believes that Christ is his mediator. Without the resurrection and without a mediator, God would have remained God and we might have believed in God's existence, but there would have been no saving faith. "Seeing then that we have a great high priest, that is passed into the heavens, Jesus the Son of God, let us hold fast our profession. For we have not an high priest which cannot be touched with the feeling of our infirmities; but was in all points tempted like as we are, yet without sin. Let us therefore come boldly unto the throne of grace, that we may obtain mercy and find grace to help in time of need" (Hebrews 4:14–16).

The Incorruptible Word

1 Peter 1:22–25

Seeing ye have purified your souls in obeying the truth through the Spirit unto unfeigned love of the brethren, see that ye love one another with a pure heart fervently:

Being born again, not of corruptible seed, but of incorruptible, by the word of God, which liveth and abideth forever.

For all flesh is as grass, and all the glory of man as the flower of the grass. The grass withereth, and the flower thereof falleth away:

But the word of the Lord endureth forever. And this is the word which by the Gospel is preached unto you.

Once more Peter returns to emphasize the notion of obedience. We should learn God's requirements and obey them, whether they relate to external and overt acts or to the internal action of the mind. As Peter has already indicated in verse fourteen, a knowledge of the truth purifies, while ignorance causes sin. Probably there was some situation in the churches to which Peter wrote that made this emphasis necessary; certainly there is need of this emphasis today. The emphasis on truth is needed; the emphasis on obedience is needed; and the resulting purity is needed likewise.

The result of all this is unhypocritical love of the brethren. If among the brethren there is not enough love of the brethren, what is the cause? Maybe our thoughtlessness causes unnecessary hurt to others. Or we may intend to say a kind word and pass on a compliment, but—you know how it is—we just don't get around to it: laziness. Or it may be that not all the members of a denomination or local congregation are really brethren. True believers are children of God, as has been seen in 1:3, 14, and 17. But in many churches not every member is a true believer. And the result is unfortunate. When men and women agree in doctrine, they can easily cooperate; but when their doctrines are different, when their aims diverge, there is constant friction.

The modernists in churches have distorted the principle of brotherly love. When a true Christian opposes the introduction of unbelief, when he protests against the exclusion of sound doctrine from Sunday School literature and against the inclusion of unsound doctrine, the modernist is quick to complain of the lack of love toward the writers of the Sunday School material. If the true believer had love, so he is told, he would not be so cantankerous, always objecting to sweet-souled writers of innocuous platitudes spiced with denials of Scriptural truth.

What the modernists do not mention, and what they hope no one will notice, is that the "cantankerous" Christian is showing a sincere love to the children who are in danger of being poisoned. The pure food and drug law may not seem lovely to one who wishes to cheapen and to adulterate; to the consumer, on the other hand, it is the essence of brotherly love. Love of the brethren shows itself in one way when we deal with the brethren directly; but when we deal with the enemies of the brethren, our love takes other forms. It is love nonetheless.

In both cases our love must be unhypocritical, from the heart, and fervent. Let us ask ourselves again whether we have and whether we show such love. We are pilgrims through a barren land; there are fears within and fightings without; let us think of the enemies of our Lord and be closer drawn to each other. When we feel inclined to condemn a Christian, let us first put the most charitable interpretation on his acts. We all do stupid things; we all make mistakes of judgment; and if someone deliberately sins, let us be most kind in gently leading him to repentance.

The twenty-third verse may be taken as a reason for the command to love our brethren, and may therefore be translated, "love one another

. . . *because* you have been born again." Our new birth makes us the brothers of all who have likewise been born again. And this new birth is different from all natural birth. It is the result of an incorruptible sowing. Both English versions, the King James and the Revised Standard, speak of corruptible and incorruptible seed. But the word, which occurs only here in the New Testament, usually means sowing rather than seed. The sowing therefore is the begetting of God. It is the act of God, the work of grace, and this idea confirms John 1:13, "Which were born not of blood, nor of the will of the flesh, nor of the will of man, but of God." It is God's work, not man's; as James 1:18 says, "Of his own will begat he us with the word of truth." Anyone who looks to man's will as the source of regeneration will be led far astray. And the verse just quoted from James confirms Peter with respect also to the means God uses in this gracious sowing of a new life. James says, "with the word of truth"; and Peter says, "through the word of God."

This verse does not mean "through the word of the living and abiding God." The descriptive participles refer to the word, as the first phrase of verse twenty-five shows. Yet when Peter speaks of the living and abiding word, he does not mean Christ. He means the Gospel. Christ may very properly be called the living Word, the *Logos,* the Wisdom of God. But such is not Peter's meaning here. The different word for *word* in the first phrase of verse twenty-five shows that Christ is not meant. And the second phrase of the same verse conclusively and positively identifies the Gospel as the living and abiding word.

A smattering of philosophy or of Shakespeare may incline one to say: "words, words, words." The intended implication is that words are meaningless sounds and cannot accurately express thought. According to the view that disparages words, the phraseology of the Bible half-conceals, half-discloses the thought of God. Somehow we must grasp the thought that the words do not quite express. But who are these that limit the power of words? Or, rather, who are these theologians who limit the power of God? If God has some thought that is not expressed in the words of Scripture, by what means could a man grasp such thoughts? Let those theologians who disparage words refrain from using them. Show me thy thought without thy words, and I will show thee my thought by my words; for thought without words is dead. But the words of God live and abide. Accordingly, if the Bible is not verbally inspired, can it be said to be really inspired at all? Words, words, words; true words, blessed words, wonderful words of life.

Such at any rate is the insistent and uniform teaching of the Bible. In opposition to liberalism, modernism, and the so-called orthodoxy, the Bible stresses words and teaches verbal inspiration. Christ and the writers of the New Testament speak of the Old Testament as the Scriptures, and the term *Scripture* means simply what is written. Written words make Scripture.

Note this emphasis in the Old Testament. For example, consider Deuteronomy 18:15–19, particularly the last two of these verses in which the Lord promises a future revelation: "I will raise them up a Prophet . . . and will put my words in his mouth . . . and whosoever will not hearken unto my words which he shall speak in my name, I will require it of him." Also, Jeremiah 1:9 tells us that "The Lord put forth his hand and touched my mouth. And the Lord said unto me, Behold I have put my words in thy mouth."

It would be instructive though tedious to multiply these examples, but to show that they are not unusual, a few other references will be briefly indicated. "But I am the Lord thy God. . . . And I have put my words in thy mouth" (Isaiah 51:15–16). "And he said unto me, 'Son of man, go, get thee unto the house of Israel and speak with my words unto them'" (Ezekiel 3:4). And finally, "The word of the Lord that came to Micah" (Micah 1:1).

Corresponding to the prophets' continual claim of having received the words of God is the insistence of the New Testament that these words were written down. Christ said, "Had ye believed Moses, ye would have believed me, for he wrote of me; but if ye believe not his writings, how shall ye believe my words?" (John 5:46–47). On many occasions Christ appeals to what is written. At the beginning of his ministry, when after his baptism he was tempted in the wilderness by Satan, he said and repeated, "It is written."

Additional verses will enforce the idea of a revelation written in words: Christ reminds his audience that "It is written in the prophets . . ." (John 6:45). "It is also written in your Law . . ." (John 8:17). "And Jesus, when he had found a young ass, sat thereon, as it is written . . ." (John 12:14). In John 15:25 Jesus teaches that he pursued his ministry "that the word might be fulfilled that is written in their law." And these references could be still further multiplied.

A relatively recent objection to the idea of verbal revelation is that revelation is never a communication of truth. The contemporary use of this phrase—revelation is not a communication of truth—is not intended as a repetition of an older objection to the Scriptures. One of the older views was that God revealed himself in the great redemptive acts of the exodus, the crucifixion, and the resurrection (and of course he did), but that the Bible, instead of being a revelation itself is simply the record of the revelation. This older objection to the Scriptures is poor because it leaves us no assurance that the Bible correctly records or explains the events.

The contemporary use of the phrase, however, has a different meaning and leaves us with even less assurance of anything at all. The revelation intended, which is not a communication of truth, is not the redemptive acts of God in history either; but rather it is some sort of individual, subjective experience. Perhaps it is an experience similar to that of contemplating a great work of art. Beholding the majestic cathedral at Cologne, reading Keats' *Ode on a Grecian Urn,* or enjoying the pictures of Renoir and Cézanne may not communicate truth or add to our stock of information; but they produce an aesthetic response that cannot be put into words. Or, perhaps, again, this revelation may be a matter of formal rejuvenation. Without receiving any new truth, we regain a lost determination to strive for the right. And such subjective experiences are all the revelation this view will allow, for revelation is not a communication of truth.

Now, undoubtedly, there is a place for moral determination, enthusiasm, and even for aesthetic experience. But determination can be evil as well as good. Enthusiasm can lead in any direction. In each person, enthusiasm will lead in the direction his opinions point. The dictators of totalitarian states have enthusiasm and determination, but their ideas are wrong. And if God has not given us any truth, any directions to guide our enthusiasm, then, for all we know, we may be enthusiastically doing the work of the devil. At any rate, the Bible from beginning to end claims to be the written words of God—a communication of truth for our instruction and edification.

Of not so recent origin is a second objection to which more detailed attention should be paid because at first glance it seems more plausible.

The idea that God gave his words to the prophets seems to some unbelievers a mechanical and artificial theory of revelation. If God is not a man with a physical body, perhaps he just cannot speak in words. Or, if he could, it would nonetheless be undignified, and he did not. God is not like a boss dictating a letter to a stenographer, but rather, so it is said, he suggests thoughts and ideas to the prophets and they put these thoughts into their own words. Thus it is argued that God inspires the thoughts but does not control the words. Since this allows freedom and spontaneity to the prophets, it maintains their personalities inviolate, and avoids mechanical artificiality.

This theory of a conceptual but non-verbal revelation probably depends in large measure on a misunderstanding of the evangelical doctrine; and by all means the evangelical doctrine should be clearly understood. But before a short exposition of the orthodox doctrine is given, two consequences of this conceptual theory must be pointed out.

In the first place, if God inspired only the thoughts of the prophets and did not control their words, then no doubt Isaiah and Jeremiah received a revelation, but it does not follow that you and I have received any message from God at all; for on this theory we could never assume that the prophets' words bring God's thought to us. We would have no assurance that they accurately reproduced God's ideas in their writings. There is so little dictation in this theory and so much human spontaneity that the prophets may have misconstrued God's message at any point, and we today would have no means of deciding which verses are in harmony with God's thought and which verses are not.

Perhaps, even, there are no verses that correctly express God's thought. For in conjunction with this theory it may also be held that all words are inadequate representations of thought; and in particular God's thoughts are so high above our thoughts that they are totally incommunicable. God is infinite, and we are finite; and by our very nature we are incapable of comprehending or understanding even a single item of his mind. What the prophets wrote therefore are merely pointers, echoes, or symbols—echoes and symbols of a reality or truth forever hidden from human understanding. We could not even say that the words and ideas of Scripture are similar to the ideas of God; for obviously if we do not have God's ideas we cannot judge the prophets' words by them. One can judge that a newspaper reporter has given a fair and accurate account of a presidential speech, only if one has the speech itself to compare with the account. If a man has no knowledge of the president and no accurate copy of the speech, there is no way of discovering to what extent the newspaper reporter distorted it through bias or missed the point through ignorance. Similarly if God's mind and message are never accessible to human minds, then no matter what the prophets said, they have not disclosed God's mind to us.

These implications are, I believe, sufficient to discredit the theory that God inspired the thoughts but not the words of the prophets. The second thing that needs to be said before coming to any positive account of the evangelical doctrine is that the denial of verbal inspiration contradicts the numerous and uniform statements of Scripture.

The Scriptures nowhere describe a God who cannot put words into a man's mouth. On the contrary, in Exodus 4:11–12, the Lord explicitly argues with Moses to the effect that if he, the Lord, created man's mouth, surely he can speak through it. And that he not only could but did, is asserted over and over again. Several verses have already been adduced, and it would be easy to collect a page full of quotations in which the various prophets claim to have received words from God.

Therefore it must be necessarily concluded either that the Scriptures are in truth the very words of God, or else that they are so full of lies that it would be a waste of time to study them.

Whatever other motives lie behind the theory that God inspired the thoughts but did not control the words of the prophets, it is certain that its advocates habitually misrepresent the meaning of verbal inspiration. God,* they say, is not like a boss dictating letters to a stenographer, for obviously the books of the Bible, unlike the letters of stenographers, show differences of personal style. And thus an objection to verbal inspiration is based on the obvious fact that the language of Jeremiah sounds quite different from the style of Isaiah and that Paul's literary habits are not at all the same as John's. The stamp of human personality on the various books is so distinct, this argument maintains, that we cannot possibly believe the words to be the words of God. They are clearly the words of Jeremiah and of John. In this way verbal inspiration is often misinterpreted and caricatured as a dictation theory; and the facts of the Bible contradict such a theory. Of course, several

*Compare Paul Tillich, *Perspectives on Nineteenth and Twentieth Century Protestant Theology*, p. 139.

stenographers of one boss would turn out letters of the same literary style; they do not or should not improve on the boss's English. And if God dictated the words of the Bible, how could one account for the great literary differences?

Now, let us keep certain facts sharply in mind. In the first place, the differences of style—and they are so obvious that even a translation cannot hide them—show decisively that the Bible was not dictated as a boss dictates to a stenographer. There have been indeed a few orthodox theologians who have used the idea of dictation; but whether they all meant dictation in the sense in which it occurs in a modern business office, or whether some of them meant it in the more general sense of a command and authoritative imposition, we need not discuss. What is chiefly to the point is that the great majority of theologians who hold and have held to verbal revelation never accepted the dictation theory. One could easily suppose that unbelievers found it easier to ridicule dictation than to understand and discuss verbal inspiration as it is actually taught by evangelical theologians.

How, then, are the differences of style to be accounted for, and what does verbal inspiration mean? The answer to these questions, involving the relation between God and the prophets, takes us quickly away from the picture of a boss and a stenographer.

When God wished to make a revelation, at the time of the exodus or of the captivity, he did not suddenly look around, as if caught unprepared, and wonder what man he could use for the purpose. We cannot suppose that he advertised for help, and when Moses and Jeremiah applied, God constrained them to speak his words. And yet this derogatory view underlies the objection to verbal inspiration. The relation between God and the prophet is totally unlike that between a boss and a stenographer. If we consider the omnipotence and wisdom of God, a very different representation emerges. The boss must take whom he can get; he depends on the high school or the business college to have taught her shorthand and typing. But God does not depend on any external agency. God is the Creator. He made Moses. And when God wanted Moses to speak for him, he said, "Who hath made man's mouth? Have not I, the Lord?"

Put it this way. God from all eternity decreed to lead the Jews out of slavery by the hand of Moses. To this end he so controlled events that Moses was born at a given date, placed in the water to save him from an early death, found and adopted by Pharoah's daughter, given the best education possible, driven into the wilderness to learn patience, and in every way so prepared by heredity and environment that when the time came, Moses' mentality and literary style were the instruments precisely fitted to speak God's words.

It is quite otherwise with dictation. A boss has little control over a stenographer except as to the words she types for him. He did not control her education. She may be totally uninterested in his business. They may have extremely little in common. But between Moses and God there was an inner, spiritual union, an identity of purpose, a cooperation of will, such that the words Moses wrote were God's own words and Moses' own words at the same time.

Thus when we see God's pervading presence and providence in history and in the life of his servants, we recognize that business office dictation does not do justice to the Scriptures. God's control is far more extensive. It is all extensive. The Holy Ghost dwelt within these men and taught them what to write. God determined what the personality and style of each author should be, and he determined it for the purpose of expressing his message, his words. The words of Scripture therefore are the very words of God. No wonder Peter says they live and abide forever. No wonder believers find in them truth, blessing, and assurance of eternal salvation.

This is precisely the point Peter wishes to make by his quotation from the Old Testament. He contrasts the incorruptible sowing by the living words with the corruptible sowing that results in the ephemeral glory of a flower that fades.

In making the poetic contrast between the corruptible and the incorruptible sowing, Peter again brings to our attention a truth that needs emphasis today. He has been quoting the Old Testament, and the passage at the moment comes from Isaiah 40:6–8. These frequent references to the Old Testament, and the fact that Peter uses part of the Old Testament as an integral part of his argument, are a rebuke to those who say that the Old Testament was only for the time prior to the coming of Christ and does not apply to us. Some people go so far as to say that even the Gospels with the Beatitudes and the Sermon on the Mount do not concern us, but are passages to be applied only in a future Millennial Kingdom. For us in this dispensation the epistles must suffice. And perhaps not all of the epistles at that. This view is not in accord with Peter's procedure.

The dispensational exclusion of the Old Testament as inapplicable in our age was not one of Peter's worries. He expected that his readers would accept the word of the prophets as decisive. What was perhaps more of a problem in his day was the inclusion of the New Testament in the sacred canon. It was universally agreed among the early Christians that the Old Testament, as we now call it, was the authoritative word of God. Not to say anything more, Christ repeatedly sealed it with his approval. He rebuked the Jews for not having believed Moses (John 5:46–47); in his temptation and in disputes with the scribes, he settles the question by, "It is written"; in replying to a charge of blasphemy (John 10:34ff.), he not only asks, "Is it not written in your law?" but also adds as conclusive, "the Scripture cannot be broken." There was therefore no controversy in the early church about the authority and applicability of the Law and the Prophets.

But for us, how can we justify the New Testament? When the apostles speak of the Scripture, and say it is all inspired of God, does not this refer to the Hebrew canon and leave the New Testament without such authority?

This verse in 1 Peter is part of the answer to this question. Note very particularly that the word of the Lord, at first exemplified by the quotation from Isaiah, is immediately extended to the Gospel which is preached unto you.

Peter also in his second epistle (3:15–16) speaks of the writings of Paul. Here too it must be noted that Peter does not put Paul's letters in a class different from the writings of the prophets. On the contrary he classes them together. There are, he says, some unlearned persons who wrest Paul's epistles as they do the other scriptures to their own destruction. Very obviously it is as great a sin to misrepresent and misunderstand Paul as to wrest and twist Jeremiah.

Paul also in 1 Timothy 5:18 puts Deuteronomy 25:4 and Luke 10:7 on the same level as Scripture. In this way the books of the New Testament were imposed on the church by apostolic authority. Luke, of course, was not an apostle: but Paul insists that the church accept Luke's writings.

Accordingly, after Paul had identified Deuteronomy and Luke as equally Scripture, the verse which says, All Scripture is inspired of God, applies to the New Testament as well as to the Old.

Spiritual Milk

1 Peter 2:1–5

Wherefore laying aside all malice, and all guile, and hypocrisies, and envies, and all evil speaking,

As newborn babes, desire the sincere milk of the word, that ye may grow thereby:

If so be ye have tasted that the Lord is gracious.

To whom coming, as unto a living stone, disallowed indeed of men, but chosen of God, and precious,

Ye also, as lively stones, are built up a spiritual house, an holy priesthood, to offer up spiritual sacrifices, acceptable to God by Jesus Christ.

There is no particular break in thought between the first and second chapters. The chapter and verse divisions in the Bible were not made according to logical or grammatical principles. They are purely arbitrary divisions for convenience of reference, and in certain cases the suggestion of a more than arbitrary division has produced unfortunate results. For example, the mere fact that Romans 7 ends with verse 25 and that the next verse is in a new chapter obscures the fact that the "no condemnation" of Romans 8:1 is the conclusion of the argument that runs through the last half of Romans 7. The visual break on the printed page between the two chapters makes it appear that a new subject is begun, and in the Romans passage has given illicit support to doctrines of perfectionism.

Similarly here in 1 Peter, chapter two does not begin a new subject; it continues the thought of the previous verses.

Peter has just been contrasting the corruptible sowing of our natural birth with the incorruptible sowing of our second birth. A normal result of this new life is the putting away of all wickedness, all treachery, hypocrisy, envy, and all slandering. These are the sins that Peter thought it well to condemn. It is hardly to be supposed that the people to whom he wrote were noticeably worse than other people in these respects. Rather Peter knew by revelation that these sins would beset human nature until Christ returns, and we today do well if we heed his admonition. There may be some Christians, though we hope the number is small, who take pleasure in seeing others in misfortune. There are certainly and unfortunately more who are envious of the good fortune of their brethren. Let each of us ask ourselves, can we, do we, rejoice at the good fortune of other Christians? Not the good fortune of some Christian in China, but the success or special ability of someone in our own local congregation. It happens in secular circles and in Christian circles too: someone with ability starts to push ahead and gives promise of achievement; then small mediocre minds plot his downfall. Smear campaigns have not been confined to politics.

Then too there is a large group of Christians in the United States who prefer to substitute man-made sins for the sins emphasized in Scripture. Their motive was originally good. They wanted to grow in grace and be separated from the world. But whether it was because they found it so easy to avoid the sins the Bible mentions and wished to press on to new heights, or whether it was because they found it too difficult to follow Scriptural exhortations and had to invent some "sins" if they were to be successful in avoiding a respectable number, in any case they placed their emphasis on man-made sins.

There is a church that excludes from its membership anyone who plays cards, goes to the movies, or smokes. There is a college which prohibits attendance at the opera and at newsreels. But its track team has run a meet on the Lord's Day, its Gospel teams have been known to steal an auto when they could not find their own, and envy and hypocrisy are all too evident.

Let it be clear that most of the motion pictures today are filthy.

To take pleasure in them is a violation of the seventh commandment. And a person who spends an inordinate amount of time on any amusement is probably not discharging his Christian obligations. But if a man or any human agency prohibits us form seeing *Cinderella* or *Hamlet,* not to mention newsreels, that agency is usurping divine prerogatives. It is a mark of Pharisaism to teach for doctrines the commandments of men. The world at large may not know much of the Scriptures, but it recognizes misplaced emphasis and turns a deaf ear to perverted testimony. No Christian is required to attend the movies, the opera, or the ball games; but at the same time no Christian has the authority to make avoidance of these amusements a sign of a superior spiritual life. And when such externals are substituted for the internal virtues which are the contraries of the sins Peter here mentions, the result is disgusting.

In contrast with the wickedness and guile of the world, Peter urges us to imitate in a certain respect the conduct of new born babes. They desire milk for nourishment and they are conspicuously free from guile or treachery. Like them therefore the Christian should earnestly desire spiritual, guileless milk. The adjective guileless, which seems peculiar as a qualification for milk, may possibly be translated "unadulterated," but Peter chose the word deliberately in order to form a contrast with the sin in verse one. The King James Version is not technically correct in speaking of the milk of the word. As Romans 12:1 refers to a reasonable or spiritual service, so here we have the notion of spiritual milk, rather than milk of the word. But although the King James Version is not technically correct, it is substantially so. For the first nourishment of a new born Christian is the word. This is clear from the rebuke in Hebrews 5:12 addressed to some Christians who suffer from spiritual rickets:

"For when for the time ye ought to be teachers, ye have need that one teach you again which be the first principles of the oracles of God; and are become such as have need of milk, and not of strong meat.

"For every one that useth milk is unskilled in the word of righteousness: for he is a babe" (Hebrews 5:12–13).

Thus we may identify milk and nourishment with the study of God's word.

The quotation from Hebrews also shows that Peter's admonition here applies to some but not to all Christians. The members of these churches may not have yet made great progress in the things of Christ.

And for all such, milk is good food. Unfortunately for the progress of the church as a whole and for the growth of individual Christians, there is a strain of teaching today that would prescribe milk for everyone and deny the privilege of eating meat. Many popular Bible teachers, who themselves need milk, tell their audiences to avoid the deep things of God. These are guilty of disobedience. That they are disobedient may be seen, in addition to what has been said before, both from the verses in Hebrews just quoted and from the two verses that follow:

"But strong meat belongeth to them that are of full age, even those who by reason of use have their senses exercised to discern both good and evil.

"Therefore leaving the principles of the doctrine of Christ, let us go unto perfection" (Hebrews 5:14–6:1). To this may be added I Corinthians 14:20, which also returns us to Peter's exhortation against treachery.

The purpose of drinking milk, and of eating meat as well, is that we may grow to salvation thereby. Commenting above on the phrase, "the salvation of your souls," in 1:9, it was pointed out that the word "soul" is ambiguous. So also is the word "salvation." Here in 2:2 Peter says we grow into salvation. Frequently in colloquial English salvation is used as an equivalent of regeneration. Since regeneration is not a growth, but the absolute beginning of a new life, it is obvious that these two usages of "salvation" are different. And because what is true of one meaning is not true of another meaning, people are often confused by careless Bible teachers who dislike accurate definitions. It is of course impossible at this date to remake the English language, but each Christian for himself can avoid confusion if he will use the terms *regeneration, justification, sanctification,* and *glorification,* and refuse to use the term *salvation* except when intending to include all these phases of salvation under one concept. Then he can see that regeneration is instantaneous, but salvation is a process; justification is by faith alone, but salvation requires works, and yet salvation is all of grace, for God bestows the life and strength to do the works. After being thus particular for a while, one can again use colloquial language without the previous mental confusion.

Continuing his admonition to desire nourishment and grow in salvation, Peter adds a conditional sentence for emphasis: "if you have tasted that the Lord is good." The condition, the *if,* does not indicate any serious doubt as to the readers' having tasted Christ. Rather it means, I know you have tasted Christ and therefore I am assured you will seek the nourishment I mention. The word *if* is not always, perhaps not usually, a sign of doubt.

Sermons have been preached on the temptation of Christ in which it was said that the devil tried to suggest doubt as to Christ's deity: *if* thou be the Son of God, command that these stones be made bread. It is hardly likely, however, that the devil was so stupid or ignorant as to think that he could make Christ doubt his deity. Rather, the sense is, *since* thou art the Son of God, make these stones bread. The devil was appealing to Christ's admitted power. To suppose that the devil doubted Christ's power, or to suppose that the devil wanted Christ to doubt, makes nonsense of the temptation to turn stones to bread.

The same grammatical construction is found in Romans 8:9, "But ye are not in the flesh but in the Spirit, if so be that the Spirit of God dwell in you;" and in 2 Thessalonians 1:6, "Seeing it is a righteous thing with God to recompense tribulation to them that trouble you." In fact, in these two passages the word *if* is a stronger form of the word than that found in 1 Peter; it would therefore indicate still greater doubt; but especially in 2 Thessalonians 1:6, it is clear that the meaning is *since,* and expresses no doubt at all. Therefore the phrase in 1 Peter 2:3 is an expression of the assurance of salvation. Confidence, not doubt, is the idea.

The Lord is gracious, to whom coming—grammatically the sentence is becoming cumbersome. The participle "coming" is in apposition with the "you" that is the subject of the imperative in verse two and also in verse five. By omitting some of the dependent clauses the connection can be made clear: Desire the spiritual milk as you come to Christ and be built up. One should note that the coming is not a vague coming to God in an unknown or indeterminate way; on the contrary it is definitely a coming to Christ, for the Lord of course is Christ; and, as John says in his Gospel (14:6), Christ is the way. In fact, since there is salvation in no other name, Christ is the only way. "No man cometh unto the Father but by me."

This way is rejected of men. An insistence on only one way, a refusal to admit other ways to God, is called bigotry and intolerance by the darkened world. Worst of all it is undemocratic. Human pride would find some good in all religions and would scramble all churches into one ecclesiastical omelette. Men can come from the east and the west, Mohammedans, Buddhists, Jews, Romanists, and Protestants, and sit down at a round table to pool their religious resources. In this way a new, better, a more complete religion will be evolved.

Thus it is today that Christ is despised and rejected. He is set at naught by builders who wish to construct the temple of humanity without a cornerstone. His report is not believed, and like a root out of dry ground, we esteemed him not. So it had been prophesied, and therefore this dishonor is a sign of the Messiah. For God judged him otherwise. Held in dishonor by men, this divine cornerstone had been from all eternity chosen of God. He is preeminently God's elect, precious, held in honor and esteem.

Come to him, Peter says, and be built up into a spiritual house.

It is better to take "built up" as an imperative: Putting away wickedness, desire milk and be built up.

The spiritual house has Christ as the cornerstone; its foundation is the prophets and apostles; and each humble Christian is a living stone somewhere in the walls. If the blueprints are followed accurately the result will be a house that is suitable for a holy priesthood. In such a house acceptable spiritual sacrifices can be offered to God. But the blueprints must be followed if acceptable worship is to be offered. A house built of the wrong material will not do. The mere fact that visible organizations, the denominations, join in organic union does not ensure a spiritual house. The unity and strength of the building is obtained by means of living stones which resemble the cornerstone. The power and worth of the church is its life. Life is more important than organizational machinery; and, in fact, so long as the visible church contains some who are deluded and others who are hypocritical, great machinery and spiritual life will be almost incompatible. The spiritual house which is built of all believers as living stones does not derive unity from organization. The Scriptural injunction is to be of one mind. In Acts 2:46 the early church continued in the temple with one accord. And Peter will encourage likemindedness in the next chapter. It will be unity of mind in true doctrine that will make the church suitable for a holy priesthood, and any union lacking this truth cannot be holy. Such an organization may display gorgeous vestments, and it may offer sacrifices, but the sacrifices will more likely be through the Virgin Mary, or the saints, or through nobody at all, instead of through Jesus Christ.

A Precious Cornerstone

1 Peter 2:6–8

Wherefore also it is contained in the scripture, Behold, I lay in Sion a chief corner stone, elect, precious: and he that believeth on him shall not be confounded.

Unto you therefore which believe he is precious: but unto them which be disobedient, the stone which the builders disallowed, the same is made the head of the corner,

And a stone of stumbling, and a rock of offence, even to them which stumble at the word, being disobedient: whereunto also they were appointed.

A second time (if we do not count a few detached words) Peter quotes a verse from the Old Testament, and he will do so again in chapter three. On the previous occasion comment was offered on the doctrine of verbal inspiration. Emphasis was placed on the fact that God gave the prophets his own words.

At this point nothing much need be added; but the word *scripture,* which did not occur in the previous passage, makes explicit a thought that was presupposed and hinted at. The word *scripture* in Greek or English simply means something written. The Scriptures are the writings.

Now, this simple etymology is more important than might appear at first. For even though God indeed gave a verbal revelation to the prophets, it would have been of little use to us today unless the prophets had preserved it by writing it down.

And this obvious fact is in turn a reason for a verbal revelation in the first place. If God wanted to reveal himself, not just to Jeremiah, but to Jeremiah's contemporaries and to us, then either God would have had to speak his words directly to every individual, or else have his words recorded by one man for the others to read. Since then God did not speak to Zedekiah, and has not spoken to you or me, either we have no message from God, or the writings are that message. And only words can be written. When therefore Christ confounded the Tempter and the Scribes, he appealed, not so much to what was spoken; but his usual phrase was, It is written.

This has been a very brief account of verbal inspiration; but let us consider the particular passage and Peter's use of the Old Testament. As was mentioned previously, this quotation and Peter's constant usage show that the plan and message of God is a unity in both Testaments. Paul in Galatians 3:6ff argues that Gentiles receive salvation under the terms of the covenant with Abraham. The Gospel is not something new, preached for the first time by Christ and the apostles, but it was preached previously to Abraham; Noah also, as we shall see in the next chapter, preached the Gospel; and sinners in the Old Testament as well as now were regenerated and had their hearts of stone changed to hearts of flesh by the ministration of the Spirit.

In this passage from Isaiah 28:16 Zion, or Jerusalem, is typical of the church. Christ is the cornerstone, and believers in this age, when there is no longer a distinction between Jew and Greek, are the stones in the walls. Hence Peter's inspired understanding of Isaiah helps him to feed Jesus' sheep as Jesus had commanded him (John 21:15ff); and the same inspired understanding helps us to see Isaiah's meaning and to grasp the significance of Old Testament typology.

There is however a certain difference between the Gospel in the Old Testament and the Gospel in the New Testament. It is not a difference in principle, but a difference in amplitude. A tulip bulb, lying dormant through the winter, contains the whole beautiful tulip that we will enjoy in April. The bulb is really and truly a tulip—only its full development is not yet seen. So the Gospel in the Old Testament is really and truly the Gospel—only its secret or mystery in those earlier ages was not made known unto the sons of men in the full manner that is now revealed to his holy apostles (Ephesians 3:5–6). The secret or mystery is precisely the inclusion of the Gentiles in the benefits of the covenant; and this indeed was made known to Abraham, for it is written, "In thee shall all the nations of the earth be blessed" (Genesis 12:3, 17:4), and this Gospel truth was repeated a number of times through the Old Testament (e.g., Isaiah, 42:6 and Luke 2:32); but the details and the manner were not then explained as they are now revealed. One reason they could not be explained was that Christ would have to die first. Only after the Lamb of God had offered himself a propitiation to his Father could the full explanation of salvation be given.

This Lamb was slain from the foundation of the world. The events had been planned from all eternity. Christ was the chosen one. In the passage under consideration the choosing does not refer to his death, except obscurely in 2:7, but to his being the cornerstone of the church. Christ was elected or chosen in order that a holy priesthood could offer spiritual sacrifices acceptable to God. This is what Isaiah meant, and that is why Peter quoted him.

A temple of which Christ is the cornerstone will never never put the worshipers to shame. Peter uses a double negative for emphasis. It is not usually good English, but it is good Greek. Hebrews 13:5 has a double negative with one verb and three negatives with the next. These five negatives have been turned into excellent English in the line "I'll never, no never, no never forsake." So Peter says that believers on Christ will never never be put to shame. This does not mean that Christians will never suffer persecution—more of this later—and Peter himself (Acts 5:41) rejoiced that he was counted worthy to suffer shame for his name. Rather, the meaning is the same as in Romans 5:5 where it says that hope does not make ashamed. The particular hope, developed as indicated in Romans 5:1–5, does not disappoint. It will be fulfilled and satisfied in the end. The Bible and wise Christians do not limit their view to the immediate future. As others have said, God does not settle accounts every Saturday night. It is the final reckoning that counts, and when this building is completed, believers shall "not not" be ashamed of it.

Instead of shame those who believe shall receive honor. The idea of God conferring honor on his people was briefly alluded to under 1:7. Here it is better grammatically to translate the phrase, Honor belongs to you who believe; but with the parallel construction following, it is also possible to understand that Christ is honor for the believers and a rock of offence to the unbelievers.

The unbelievers are the disobedient. While the participle here is etymologically *unbelievers,* the King James Version is not incorrect in saying the *disobedient.* The verb has both meanings, for the very good reason that unbelief or distrust is an idea not far removed from disobedience. The man who distrusts Christ will not obey him, and the man who disobeys does not believe.

Sometimes the faith, belief, or obedience of Christians weakens, but here Peter is talking of the reprobate, the unregenerate who have no faith in Christ at all. Hebrews 3:18, 19 and 4:2, 3, 6 speak specifically of the unbelievers in the wilderness, of whom apparently there were many; but the principle is applicable to all unbelieving sinners, that God has sworn in his wrath that such persons should not enter his rest; the word may be preached to them, but without profit, for these people cannot enter heaven because of unbelief. For such, Christ is a stumbling block and a scandal. As Isaiah 8:14, 15 teach, though believers will use Christ as the cornerstone in building the church, the unbelieving builders, having left the stone lying around, will stumble and fall over it to their hurt and pain. Christ is an offense to them. By *offense* the prophet and the apostle do not mean merely some subjective vexation, such as people experience in the presence of a *persona non grata;* but it is objective ruin. Those who have rejected Christ will stumble and fall into a snare and will be killed like trapped animals. Such is Isaiah's use of the word offense, and such is Peter's.

These are the persons who stumble at the word, being disobedient; or, these are they who stumble, being disobedient to the word. Whichever way the phrase is translated, the people in question have refused to acknowledge the word of God, the prophecies of Isaiah, the epistle of Peter, the Bible as a whole. To this end they were appointed. The word of the Lord, though some do not believe and obey it, does not return unto him void; it always accomplishes what God intended and it always prospers in the thing whereto God sends it. He sends his word both to save and to condemn. Behold therefore the goodness and the severity of God. Some were elect unto obedience; others were appointed to an awful end (Romans 9:22 and 11:22).

Election

1 Peter 2:9

But ye are a chosen generation.

The idea that God would condemn unrepentant sinners to a fearful punishment has ordinarily seemed an understandable act of divine justice. A righteous God would naturally punish offenders. But in recent times a new and insipid notion of God has become popular, representing him as too "good," i.e., too good-natured to punish anyone for anything. According to this view, everyone gets to heaven, albeit by different ways.

Goethe's *Faust* is a literary expression of this view. The prologue, reminiscent of the first chapter of Job, is a scene in heaven as the Lord converses with Mephistopheles. But the characters of God, the devil, and Faust are profoundly different from the description in Job. At the moment Faust is a deeply dissatisfied scholar. His studies have revealed his ignorance and the ignorance of all the learned. Theology has left him without a belief in heaven or hell, and without peace of heart.

Then, I have neither goods nor treasure,
No worldly honor, rank, or pleasure.

Of this Faust, the Lord (Goethe's Lord) says,

Though now he serves me with imperfect sight
I will ere long conduct him to the light.

By themselves these two lines could express the mind of the true God, the God of the Bible, with respect to the earlier lives of Abraham or Peter. But the context in *Faust* shows a widely different meaning.

The light to which Goethe's Lord will bring Faust is merely the realization that life is worth living and that his present pessimism is unnecessary. The manner of accomplishing this "salvation" is not regeneration but the development of Faust's present abilities.

The gard'ner knoweth when the green appears,
That flowers and fruit will crown the coming years.

And anyway, Faust is a man. Only a man. He is doing his best, and

Man still must err, while he doth strive.

What he needs is a broader experience. Through this he will come to the light. And this experience which saves him includes heinous sin. In fact it would be possible to conclude that Goethe is advising young men to seduce innocent girls in order to be satisfied with life. Thus the paganism of Goethe and his unrighteous god.

But although sincere believers in every age have considered it to be just for God to punish sinners, some of them have shown a little reluctance to believe that God knew all the details ahead of time. The righteous God made man righteous; and it came as a surprise to God when man sinned; then God had to recast his plans and provide for a place of punishment.

It does not require much thought, however, to see that this is not Scriptural. The Lamb of God was slain before the foundation of the world. God saw the end from the beginning. And, known to God are all his works from the beginning of the world. If God from eternity intended the sacrifice of Christ on the cross, he surely intended that there be sinners. A plan for an atonement that did not include sin would have been an inconsistent and absurd plan.

Now, it should be noted carefully that the preceding verse does not say that the disobedient were appointed to punishment. It says something quite different, much more striking, and more repellent to the carnal mind that will not accept the Scripture. It says that the people in question were appointed to sin; they were appointed to be disobedient; they were appointed to reject the cornerstone. To be sure this involves their punishment, for their stumbling will ruin them like an animal in a trap; but the bulk of the verse stresses the sin and the disobedience to which they were appointed.

These are all disquieting thoughts that produce awe and reverence before God. God's ways are not our ways; his thoughts are not our thoughts. But there is a happier side to the same matter. It is, however, the same matter. Like the two sides of a coin, they must go together. Election and reprobation are heads and tails.

The happier side is that the people to whom Peter writes are an elect race. This is the fourth time that the word *elect* has been used in the epistle. It is at least the seventh time the idea has occurred, for it is a part of the main theme: Elect unto obedience.

There was a young Bulgarian student who came to this country for his education, both in liberal arts and in Bible, so that he might return to his own country and preach the Gospel. His Bible teachers told him—and of course he respected their advice—not to study the doctrine of election. In the first place, they said, it is too deep for the human mind; second, it is useless and impractical; and third, and worst of all, it is controversial.

As if anything in the Bible were not controversial; as if anything in the Bible were not profitable for doctrine, reproof, and instruction in righteousness; as if God had given us a revelation he did not intend us to study and understand!

The young man went to a mission in Chicago where some Bulgarian laborers had been gathered in. After all, if he expected to preach to the Bulgars, why not begin at once? Soon afterward he came back to me, amazed. This doctrine of election and predestination, which devout Christians avoid and which transcends human capacities, was precisely the matter in which these ignorant laborers were interested. They were asking him all sorts of questions; and, since he had dutifully avoided the subject, he could not give a reason for the hope that was in him.

Let it be clearly understood that anyone who advises not studying any part of the Bible is impugning the wisdom of God. In effect those

Bible teachers were saying that God made a mistake when he put the idea of election in the Bible. Undoubtedly there are more implications in the Bible than we can ever exhaust; but just because we do not understand all that is implied, it does not follow that we cannot understand some. It is all profitable.

Very likely Peter was writing to a congregation or to congregations that were largely Jewish in their make-up. Of them—not to the exclusion of Gentile Christians—but nevertheless of them he says that they are an elect race. Naturally these words do not apply to all the Jews who lived in Peter's day, but to the believing Jews only.

Speaking of the Jews, who had in large measure rejected their Messiah, Paul had written in Romans 11:2, 5, "God hath not cast away his people which he foreknew . . . there is a remnant according to the election of grace." Just previously (Romans 9:11), Paul was arguing, concerning a rejection of some Jews, that God loved Jacob and hated Esau before they were born and before they had done any good or evil, that the purpose of God according to election might stand, not of works, but of him that calleth.

This notion of election, which stands so closely related to the idea of grace in opposition to salvation by works, was not, or ought not to have been, an unfamiliar one to the Jews. And if it is unfamiliar to Christians today, it can only be because of unfaithful preaching. For way back in Psalm 65:4 David wrote, "Blessed is the man whom thou choosest, and causest to approach unto thee." If God did not call men and cause men to come unto him, no one would ever be saved, for "there is none righteous, no, not one; there is none that seeketh after God. So then it is not of him that willeth, nor of him that runneth, but of God that showeth mercy" (Romans 3:10, 11; 9:16).

There is an illustration told of a mature Christian who frequently testified, "I was saved partly by God's work and partly by mine." When his somewhat astonished listeners asked him what he had done, he would reply, "I resisted; God did the rest." How true it is, as the Psalmist says (3:8), "Salvation belongeth unto the Lord." And how familiar the doctrine of election should be to the disciples of Christ. For did not our Lord himself say, "Ye have not chosen me, but I have chosen you"? (John 15:16). This gracious note, like a clear tone in a great oratorio, is dominant throughout the New Testament: "He hath chosen us in him before the foundation of the world . . . having predestinated us unto the adoption of children by Jesus Christ to himself, according to the good pleasure of his will" (Ephesians 1:4, 5). And, "God, who hath saved us, and called us with an holy calling, . . . according to his own purpose and grace, which was given us in Christ Jesus before the world began" (2 Timothy 1:9). Could Peter have found a doctrine of more solid comfort for the theme or refrain of his letter?

Election to salvation is, in the next place, described as being in accordance with the foreknowledge of God. Someone who perchance is perplexed with the plain statements just quoted from the Psalms, Romans, Ephesians, 2 Timothy, and John may now think he perceives the solution. God, who can see into the future, knows ahead of time which people will be sufficiently wise and spiritual to make themselves disciples of Christ, and, foreseeing their conduct, God elects them to salvation.

It is of course true that God knows the future, and it is equally true that history unfolds just as God knows it will. Certainly all things happen according to the foreknowledge of God. But, as the Westminster Confession, Chapter III, section ii, so explicitly states, "Although God knows whatsoever may or can come to pass upon all supposed conditions, yet hath he not decreed any thing because he forsaw it as future." In very simple language, "according to" and "because of" do not mean the same thing. Consider a railroad schedule. The trains run according to the timetable (or should), but it is not the timetable that determines their progress. The type of engine, the weight of the load, the traffic, the stability of the roadbed, the purpose of the train—all these determine the schedule. Thus the train runs according to schedule, and if we know the schedule, they run according to our foreknowledge, but not because of it. Similarly with election. The mere fact that God knows ahead of time that a man will trust Christ is not the causal explanation of election. Election does not depend on God's knowledge of the future.

This popular confusion of phrases like "according to" and "because of" is also evident in a current interpretation of the Lord's Prayer. Some modern dispensationalists argue that Christians today should not use the Lord's Prayer because it says, "Forgive us our debts as we forgive our debtors." Since we are saved by free grace in this age, we ask forgiveness not on the basis of our forgiving others but on the basis of Christ's righteousness. So far so good. But then dispensationalism says that in the millennium people will be saved by works, and will then pray to be forgiven on the basis of their conduct. In opposition to dispensationalism the Bible knows only one way of salvation, the glorious way of the cross. And the Lord's Prayer does not request forgiveness on the basis of our forgiving spirit, but modestly and in a humbling fashion beseeches forgiveness from God in proportion as we forgive others. A little attention to words, to prepositions, would save a person from such absurd and sinful doctrinal error.

But to return to election: with respect to the notion that election is based on God's knowledge of the future, it must be understood that foreknowledge in the Bible does not mean merely knowing ahead of time. One must bear in mind that any author may use a colloquial word in a technical sense. One must also bear in mind that the meaning of words change somewhat through the centuries so that today a connotation may attach to a word different from that which it had in 1611, and certainly different from that which the equivalent Greek or Hebrew word had in antiquity. For example, owing in large measure to the philosophy of the seventeenth-century thinker, René Descartes, the word *soul* in modern languages means the conscious, immaterial principle in man distinct from his body. In the Bible, particularly in the Old Testament, we find another meaning. Genesis 2:7 states that God formed man of two substances: one was the dust of the ground, the other was the breath or spirit of life. This combination then became a living soul. Soul therefore is practically the equivalent of the word *person,* and usually it refers not to the immaterial element in man as distinct from his body, but to the whole man, material and immaterial. Other examples could be furnished of how Biblical terminology differs from colloquial English.

Likewise *foreknowledge* in the Scriptures means more than common English could lead one to believe. The verb *to know* itself has a special meaning. Consider Psalm 1:6, which reads, "For the Lord knoweth the way of the righteous, but the way of the ungodly shall perish." Obviously in everyday English the Lord knows the ungodly as well as the righteous. Being omniscient, he knows all things. But the contrast between *know* and *perish* shows that the Psalmist is using the word in the sense of *approve*. The Lord approves the way of the righteous; he disapproves of the ungodly.

Then in Hosea 13:5 and Amos 3:2, where God's knowledge is

restricted to the children of Israel, it is evident that the word *know* means *to choose*. When God says, "You only have I known of all the families of the earth," one cannot take the word as it is used in English today. Such a meaning would imply that God, being ignorant of the heathen, was not omniscient. The verse means that God chose Israel only and passed by all other nations.

Furthermore, in 1 Peter 1:20 the same word occurs. The American Revision translates it, "Christ, who was foreknown indeed before the foundation of the world," but the King James translation, if not so literal, gives the sense better when it says, "who verily was foreordained," etc. Acts 2:23 unites rather than distinguishes between foreknowledge and foreordination. It reads "Him, being delivered by the determinate counsel and foreknowledge of God, ye have . . . slain." Certainly God the Father planned redemption on Calvary and approved the plan; it was not something that God happened merely to know without having foreordained it.

Therefore when Peter refers to his readers as elect according to the foreknowledge of God, he does not mean that God merely knows ahead of time that they will exercise faith in Christ. The verse (1:20) does not say that God foresaw the faith or the works of these people: God foresaw *them*. It is the people themselves that are the objects of God's foreknowing. These people God chose to save. And he chose to save them without foreseeing any faith, works, or merit that would induce him to save them. The doctrine of grace requires the doctrine of election. The whole Bible, and particularly the New Testament, is quite clear that salvation is entirely of grace, based on the all-sufficient merit of Jesus Christ, "not of works, let any man should boast" (Ephesians 2:9). Election looks forward to obedience, "elect unto obedience," and since obedience is the result and purpose of election, it cannot very well be the cause or ground of it.

The uninstructed Christian, still perplexed by the proud thoughts of the natural man, may avoid or even try to deny election. But what more comforting and assuring doctrine is there? Suppose Christ died to save sinners—what is that to me? Can I in my own power accept this salvation? Do I have greater spiritual understanding than others that I should desire him and others not? Have I ever sought after God, when it says that there is none that understands, there is none that seeks after God? Can I, dead in sin, resurrect myself to newness of life? And supposing I could, am I sure that I am able to keep myself alive? Might not my strength fail so that I would sink into a second death?

The basis of salvation is emphatically the work and particularly the death of Christ. Redemption rests squarely on Christ's merit. But on what does our assurance rest? Surely not on Christ's death. No matter how sufficient Christ's merit may be, it will profit me nothing unless it is applied to me. The application of salvation to an individual is the result, not of human, but of divine choice. It is not of blood, nor of the will of man, but of God. And likewise assurance of salvation, assurance that he who began a good work in me will complete it, depends on the immutable decree of God. What more comforting doctrine could Peter find as the refrain of his epistle?

There is a great deal more to the doctrine of election, how it is carried out, what its various results are; and Peter gives some brief information that Christians ought to know. There is a Gospel song in whose several stanzas the author recounts the things he does not know; for example, he does not know how Adam's sin lives on in you and me, he does not know how God could lay our sins upon his Son, nor how on Calvary's cross, for us he perfect pardon won. But, the refrain continues (with decision), "But I read it in God's Word and I believe it." No doubt we should not ask a song writer to burden his verses with an explanation of how he can believe what he does not know anything about. One cannot trust a person one does not know, nor can one believe a proposition in geometry that one does not know. But even if the song writer could produce some plausible explanation of his paradoxical refrain, it would not be in accord with Scripture. God has been very gracious and has revealed to us in the Word an immense amount of truth. This revelation includes a great deal of explanation that the song writer does not seem to have appreciated. Long sections deal with justification, sanctification, imputation, adoption, and so on; and these outworkings of election are all profitable for doctrine. Undoubtedly many true Christians do not know these things, but it is their loss and their shame. Surely one should not in song praise one's ignorance of God's Word. Rather the true Christian should search the Scriptures so as to become thoroughly furnished to every good work.

Except in so far as every event finds its place in the divine plan and so all of the epistle is an explanation of how election works out, Peter does not press into the details of the doctrine. In 1:2 he spoke about foreknowledge, then he added that election is in the sanctification of the Spirit, to obedience and cleansing; in 1:15 he continued that the calling of the holy God is to holiness; in 1:20 that God's foreknowledge or foreordination determined upon the death of Christ, who in 2:4, 6 is called the elect of God, though he was rejected by the builders who were appointed to their role, whereas believers are elect to what follows in 2:9. There are at least four further references in 1 Peter to God's calling; but for the rest Peter leaves us to the writings of Paul, even if in some places they are hard to understand. One short reference (2 Thessalonians 2:13) must suffice as a sample of the New Testament teaching to which Peter alludes. Paul wrote, "But we are bound to give thanks always to God for you, brethren beloved of the Lord, because God hath from the beginning chosen you to salvation through sanctification of the Spirit and belief of the truth." One verse is not much, but it sheds at least a minimum of light on the agreement of Peter and Paul in their inspired description of God's methods. And it also enforces the previous and important point that God's foreknowledge does not center in any merit in man. Man's sanctification is the work of God's Spirit and is not the basis of God's choosing to bless any individual with saving graces.

The Priesthood

1 Peter 2:9–10

A royal priesthood, an holy nation, a peculiar people; that ye should shew forth the praises of him who hath called you out of darkness into his marvelous light:

Which in time past were not a people, but are now the people of God: which had not obtained mercy, but now have obtained mercy.

Not only are believers a chosen race, they are also a royal priesthood. In the wilderness of Sinai (Exodus 19:6) God promised Moses and the children of Israel that he would make them a kingdom of priests. This was not fulfilled in the Old Testament. Before the coming of Christ the priestly functions were limited to members of the tribe of Levi. Saul lost his kingdom because, though king, he arrogated to himself the rite and right of sacrifice. Jeroboam's sin of idolatry included the persecution and expulsion of the Levites from the Northern Kingdom and his appointment of the lowest people to fill their places. But God had not opened the priesthood to all people.

At first sight this might seem to justify the Roman Catholic hierarchy. Though the Roman priests are not an hereditary tribe, they and they alone are permitted to offer sacrifices. The people are not priests. The Old Testament arrangements might also seem to justify the position of the Pope as Pontifex Maximus.

But the Scriptures teach that the Old Testament sacrifices, the incense and lamps, the gorgeous temple, the priests and the High Priest were typical of better things to come. They have now all passed away because Christ fulfilled them. The sacrifices were ended by one all-sufficient sacrifice, offered once for all. The temple is heaven itself (Hebrews 9:24) into which our true High Priest entered. The incense is our prayers, and we are the priests. Thus it is that God's promise to Moses has been fulfilled in this dispensation. The shadows of the Old Testament Church have become the realities of the New Testament Church—one Church with two different forms of administration.

The fact that the Church today is largely Gentile bears no weight against the unity of the Church. God had foreordained that some branches should be broken off the good olive tree, in fact that only a remnant should remain (Romans 11:2,5,17), and that branches from a wild olive tree should be grafted in; but it is the same good olive trunk in both cases. And if at a later date God grafts back the natural branches, it will still be the same tree. Then Ephraim and Judah, Manasseh and Benjamin, as well as Levi, shall be priests. And their sacrifice will be acceptable to God, for it will be Christ's sacrifice.

In those times of refreshing we shall indeed be a holy nation. The Church is holy now in the sense that its members are set apart for God. It is holy also in the sense that its members are clothed in Christ's perfect righteousness. But in the regeneration when the Son of Man shall sit in the throne of his glory, the members of the Church will have become personally and subjectively holy and righteous. This is the future of the people who have been made God's own, a peculiar people, a preserved or acquired people.

God has made us his own people in order that we may show forth his virtues, powers, or excellencies. Two of these virtues or attributes that are closely connected with the idea of God's making us his people are omnipotence and mercy. Only an omnipotent power could contrive the plan of salvation, see it through the course of history, and apply its benefits to a rebellious people. And only mercy could do it, too. Omnipotence and mercy must walk hand in hand. If God were not merciful, we could hope for no benefit from his mercy. Certainly we are under obligation to show forth, to announce to the world these two excellencies of him who called us out of darkness into his wonderful light.

We had not always been his people; we had not always rejoiced in light. The light shined in the darkness and the darkness did not grasp it. In his mercy God said, "I will say to them which were not my people, Thou art my people; and they shall say, Thou art my God" (Hosea 2:23). Election and grace again. Those who had not obtained mercy, have now obtained it.

These past verses, from 1:13 to 2:10, have been a general exhortation to holiness based on the proper doctrinal foundation. Now, for quite a section, 2:11 to 4:6, Peter gives particular exhortations relative to specific situations.

Strangers and Pilgrims

1 Peter 2:11–12

Dearly beloved, I beseech you as strangers and pilgrims, abstain from fleshly lusts, which war against the soul;

Having your conversation honest among the Gentiles: that, whereas they speak against you as evildoers, they may by your good works, which they shall behold, glorify God in the day of visitation.

It is most unusual in the Scripture to find an exhortation to right conduct without a doctrine given as a reason. The popular distinction between what is doctrinal or theoretical on the one hand and what is practical on the other is not so sharply drawn in the Bible as it is in the minds of some people. Fundamentally, the distinction is not drawn at all. As has been said, obedience is both mental and internal as well as external and overt. And mental obedience, belief in the truth and authority of what is taught, normally leads to right conduct.

The doctrine or explanation on which the first exhortation here is based is that we are strangers and pilgrims in this world. Heaven is our home. When the children of Israel were to enter the Promised Land, they were commanded not to buy and sell land forever or in perpetuity, "for the land is mine, for ye are strangers and sojourners with me" (Leviticus 25:23). Thus they were taught that the journey through the wilderness was typical of earthly life, and they were warned thereby not to suppose that God's promises terminated in the land of Canaan. The Holy Land was heaven, and while they lived in the earthly Palestine, they were still sojourners and strangers. They and we are not to get too settled on temporal things. Real estate is not our aim, but we look for a city which has foundations, whose builder and maker is God.

Modern paganism ridicules this viewpoint as otherworldliness, or in slang as "pie in the sky." Some professing Christians have carried the idea so far as to become almost totally indifferent to temporal affairs and even to right conduct. But this antinomianism is an invalid inference from the Scriptural injunctions. Even as pilgrims we have a care for the affairs of the journey. We must gather our manna every day and twice the quantity before the day of rest. Property is indeed a concern of Christians, for we are commanded, Thou shalt not steal, Thou shalt not covet. Those who place their confidence in human potentialities overestimate the value of political and social reform. And the reforms spawned by enthusiasm sometimes turn out worse than what preceded. But to say that human ability and political reform can be overestimated is not to say that true and sober reform should not interest the Christian. The children of Israel were not prohibited from owning land and engaging in business. There was no controlled currency or ploughing under of little lambs. Business, making a living, and owning property were legitimate and respectable. It is proper to take interest in such things—always with the proviso that justice and morality are ever our concern. And this concern has largely to do with temporal affairs. We are neither to overestimate the importance of everyday details, as most people do, nor are we to underevaluate them, as antinomians do. Peter is here warning against the more usual defect and reminds us that we are pilgrims.

Therefore we should put aside, not all desires, but fleshly desires. Since the pollution of sin is transmitted from one generation to another, the flesh is used as a symbol for sin. The desires or lusts that Peter may have had in mind can be found in Galatians 5:19–21: adultery, fornication, uncleanness, lasciviousness—these first items on the list are particularly pertinent for a nation cursed with a high divorce rate—idolatry, witchcraft, hatred, strife, jealousy, anger, intrigues, dissensions, heresies, envyings, murders, drunkenness, revellings, and such like. Surely these war against the soul.

A sinner comes to Christ to escape not only the guilt and penalty of sin but also to escape sin itself. Our manner of life therefore should be noble, honest, or seemly among the unbelieving peoples, and for a specific purpose. The Gentiles look upon Christian conduct as strait-laced and puritanical; such conduct in fact seems evil to them and they regard Christians as lacking in humanity. The soldiers and sailors, who have suffered such terror in battle and have endured the hardships of the field—should they not be granted the pleasures of fornication as a reward of their services? Should they not be liberally supplied with liquor? To refuse them these comforts is inhuman and unpatriotic. So the Gentiles speak of Christians as evildoers. But there is coming a day of visitation when desolation shall come from afar (Isaiah 10:3). What will the Gentiles do then? Peter partially answers Isaiah's question. They shall be compelled to acknowledge the glory of God with respect precisely to these matters on which they now condemn the Christian life. They will be forced to admit that what they called good is evil and what they called evil is good. Such is the purpose—one of the purposes—of our good works.

Civil Government

1 Peter 2:13–17

Submit yourselves to every ordinance of man for the Lord's sake: whether it be to the king, as supreme;

Or unto governors, as unto them that are sent by him for the punishment of evildoers, and for the praise of them that do well.

For so is the will of God, that with well doing ye may put to silence the ignorance of foolish men:

As free, and not using your liberty for a cloak of maliciousness, but as the servants of God.

Honor all men. Love the brotherhood. Fear God. Honor the king.

This section is clearly an exhortation to obey the laws of the state. Such an exhortation was necessary in apostolic and subapostolic times for two reasons. The first reason grows out of the preceding paragraph. Christians are to walk honestly before men. And it was precisely the brotherly love so characteristic of the early Christians, and so invisible at the present time, that was regarded as a compact against the rest of humanity and the state. Such a suspicion is natural to the unbelieving mind when Christians are acutely conscious of the abyss that separates (to use Augustine's phrase) the City of God from the earthly city. The spiritual unity of the human race was destroyed by sin. Perhaps it is better to say that the spiritual unity of the race was destroyed by divine grace. God chose for himself a peculiar people and passed the others by. This forms a community that is in the world but not of the world, and the world naturally regards it with suspicion.

There is a second reason, a sort of converse, for exhorting Christians to obey the secular authorities. At times there have been groups of professing Christians, like the Anabaptists, who, believing firmly they were not of the world, forgot that they were in the world. Christians are a freed people, and, if so, they are not subject to secular ordinances. Why should a holy people submit to sinful rulers? In the twentieth century this tendency has taken the form of pacifism. In the name of Christianity we are exhorted to renounce war, to refuse to bear arms even if our country should be attacked; and some have deducted illegally from their income taxes the proportion that they think goes toward military expenditures.

But all this is thoroughly anti-Christian. When the Roman soldiers came in repentance to John the Baptist (Luke 3:13), he did not tell them to desert the army, but to be content with their wages. When Christ was tempted by the question about Roman taxation, he did not say that the part for military expenditures should be withheld; he said, pay it. And Paul teaches that the sword, the authority to wage war and inflict capital punishment, is a right that God himself has delegated to the state. If it be noted that the early Christians were averse to army service, it is not because they had scruples against war but because they had scruples against acknowledging the divinity and lordship of the emperor.

This last fact helps us to understand more accurately what Peter meant. If we read, Submit to every human law, we have a thought that is as contrary to Christianity as the Anabaptist view was. The word for law here is a strange one. It is used about nineteen times in the New Testament and usually means creation or creature. This makes no sense here; plainly it must mean a law. Liddell and Scott give the meaning, created or ordained authority. If this be an acceptable meaning, it hints that Christians are not under obligation to obey an authority that is not ordained. For surely Peter himself (Acts 5:29) teaches us to obey God rather than men. And was Moses' mother sinning when she disobeyed Egyptian law to preserve her son's life?

This hint that there are occasions when the Christian is obligated to disobey the secular law is made explicit in the phrase, *for the Lord's sake*. This phrase shows that secular obedience is a divine command and at the same time sets its limits. If and when a state commands anything forbidden by the Scriptures, then the state must be disobeyed and our allegiance given to God. In our day with the rise of Communism, the conflict between the state and God is evident. Similarly in Roman Catholic countries like Spain, the conflict is sharp. But for long periods of time there has been no clear-cut conflict, and even in Spain most of the laws are purely civil regulations, so that the usual emphasis should fall on obedience to the civil law. There are indeed exceptions, but they are exceptions.

The purpose of civil government is to preserve order, to punish violence, and to protect those that do well. Even as pilgrims and strangers we should cooperate in these aims. Civil government is a divine ordinance. "By me kings reign and princes decree justice" (Proverbs 8:15). And "he removeth kings and setteth up kings" (Daniel 2:21). It is the will of God that his children obey the constituted authority and so silence the ignorance of foolish men.

To be sure, the Christian is free and his citizenship is in heaven, but he is not to use this freedom as a pretext for evil. In all our daily lives we must remember we are the servants, the slaves of God. Free slaves. Free from the penalty of sin, justified by faith; God be thanked, that though we were servants of sin, we have heartily obeyed the doctrine of Christ and have become the servants of righteousness.

Therefore it is the Christian's duty to honor all men with the honor that is their due. Love the brotherhood, that is, the elect people, even though such love is a repudiation of the universal brotherhood of man. Fear God, and honor the king.

EMPLOYMENT

1 Peter 2:18–25

Servants, be subject to your masters with all fear; not only to the good and gentle, but also to the froward.

For this is thankworthy, if a man for conscience toward God endure grief, suffering wrongfully.

For what glory is it, if, when ye be buffeted for your faults, ye shall take it patiently? But if, when ye do well, and suffer for it, ye take it patiently, this is acceptable with God.

For even hereunto were ye called: because Christ also suffered for us, leaving us an example, that ye should follow his steps:

Who did no sin, neither was guile found in his mouth:

Who, when he was reviled, reviled not again; when he suffered, he threatened not; but committed himself to him that judgeth righteously:

Who his own self bare our sins in his own body on the tree, that we, being dead to sin, should live unto righteousness: by whose stripes ye were healed.

For ye were as sheep going astray; but are now returned unto the Shepherd and Bishop of your soul.

The first of the particular exhortations that make up this middle section of the epistle treats of faithful service to masters or employers. When Paul in Ephesians 6:5 gives a similar injunction, he uses the word that ordinarily means slave, and it is remembered how Paul sent back to Philemon the runaway slave Onesimus. Peter uses the word meaning household servant, but inasmuch as they were often maltreated, there can be no significant difference between Peter's sense and Paul's.

Slavery, both in its Roman and in its American antebellum forms, is largely a thing of the past. Even the oppressed workers under Communism, though the fruits of their labors are confiscated by the government, are not technically slaves. This does not mean, however, that Peter's principles no longer apply to our present society. They apply both to workmen and to those who control the workmen.

As for the former, workmen still loaf and cheat. At the present writing England is in a serious economic decline, at least partly and possibly mainly, because the workers demand pay for doing nothing. In the United States automobiles show evidence of sloppy assembly line deficiencies. And one carpenter working on our house told me that he had to charge me a high price because he botched some material on his previous job and had to make it up out of me. Featherbedding has been common; nor is it restricted to railroads—milkmen solidly entrenched in a union have been paid a thousand dollars a month for sitting around while their poorly paid helpers do all the work.

Those also who control labor come under Peter's injunctions. But those who control labor these days are not the bloated capitalistic bourgeoisie. On the contrary, the managers are so restricted that they can hardly manage at all. It is the unions who control the workmen. In the first place, men are forced to join unions under physical and economic compulsion. In a recent strike in Indiana a union agent at night crept up to the window of a workman's house and shot and killed his infant son in his crib because the man did not want to go on strike.

The unions berate the Taft-Hartley Act as a slave labor bill because it permits the states, if they wish, to protect a man's right to work. In a sense the Taft-Hartley Act may truly be called a slave labor bill, but for the opposite reason. The right to work should be guaranteed by the federal government; and instead of merely permitting some states to protect an individual's rights, it should prohibit any state from infringing upon those rights.

One might also mention the dictatorial, undemocratic constitutions of the unions which permit embezzlement of trust funds, unsecured loans to union officers, with the resulting tampering with juries to escape criminal penalties. Then for a final remark out of a long list that could have been included, the paid advertisements in the daily papers and the original material in the union papers display a form of statistics that forcefully recalls the adage that figures don't lie, but. . . . I have a sheet of one which compares the profits of a steel company with the pay of the workers. In that full page advertisement there is scarcely a single fraudulent statistical gimmick that has been omitted. Even if its basic figures are correct (and this I cannot check), its comparisons and deductions would rate an F in any college course. Mathematically it is ludicrous; economically and religiously it is the sin Peter condemns.

Those preachers who have repudiated the Gospel of individual salvation by the blood of Christ and who loudly tell the church to preach a social gospel, might at least take the trouble to find out what the social gospel is. Indeed the Church should preach social justice, and that is what Peter is doing; social justice requires a workman to do honest work. But when theological liberals show their definitely pink politics, economics, and sociology, it is clear that they have repudiated not only the Gospel of individual salvation, but also the Biblical social gospel. And this is not surprising, for Peter makes the social habit of honesty an implication of Christ's atonement.

Protestantism has been accused of being a suburban, middle-class religion, making no appeal to the laboring classes of the slums and tenements. Protestantism of course has tried and will continue to try to reach all classes, but it is no wonder that the Gospel of honest labor should lack appeal to the shiftless, the lazy, the cheats, and the labor racketeers. The Gospel is not intended to appeal to all men; in fact it does not appeal to the natural man at all, for it is a call to God and to righteousness, whereas men love wickedness. Only the omnipotent and irresistible Spirit can change a man's heart and mind so as to make the Gospel appealing. And the Spirit has indeed regenerated members of the laboring class. The early Christians were in very large measure found in the lower and lowest classes. They were often slaves. A few there may have been in Caesar's household, but not many mighty, not many noble, were called.

Peter addressed his letter to Christians, many of whom were slaves or servants. And we Christians today, we "middle class" Christians whose white collar salaries are lower than the wages of "lower class" people, are commanded to work honestly for our pay. Some employers are good and considerate; others are crooked and perverse; whichever type of employer we happen to have, we are to serve diligently.

There was a cabinet maker whose immediate superior was especially cantankerous. For twenty years the cabinet maker witnessed a good confession by his life. It did not seem to soften the foreman in the least; if anything it aggravated him. But if the obedient conduct of the subordinate did not bring the foreman closer to heaven, it must certainly have made him more inexcusable in hell. So far as I know, he went to his grave a bitter, cantankerous old man. The cabinet maker eventually retired to a farm for the last twenty years of his life and was one of the kindest and happiest men I have known.

This type of service is thankworthy—literally, this is grace. The same usage is found in Luke 6:32, "if ye love them which love you, what thank—grace—have ye?" When a man can conduct himself according to Christ's and Peter's exhortation, it is an indication that God has given him grace.

The believer is to serve even the hard master as if he were serving the Lord. It is our conscientious duty. In French the word *conscience* means consciousness; in German also conscience and consciousness are the same word; in English there may be two words with a difference in connotation, but reflection will discover them to be closely related. We are to give honest service to evil masters for conscience's sake, conscience toward God. But conscience toward God, as the English translations have it, is precisely a consciousness of God, as Peter wrote it. Because we keep thinking of God, because we know he sees us, because we recognize him as Lord and Sovereign, we are called upon to endure grief and suffer wrongfully.

But let us make sure that it is wrongfully that we suffer. If we do evil, if our labor is dishonest, the punishment is well deserved; but God is pleased if we suffer without having given any just cause for displeasure. The thought of the verse, however, seems to go beyond that of suffering simply without just cause. It is not as though an irrational boss takes out his ill humor on whoever happens to be around. The juxtaposition of the two participles, *doing good* and *suffering* gives a hint that God is pleased if it is our good works that provoke the ire of the unbelieving employer.

And why is this? Once again it is a matter of election. We were called to this sort of thing. Obviously this is not the ultimate purpose of our being called, but it is a part of the divine plan. And the more explicit doctrinal explanation follows immediately.

The believer in Christ has been called to suffer because Christ is his example, and this is made plain in the next verses. Those who speak of Christianity as being the religion of Christ in contradistinction to the religion about Christ, those who see in Christ merely an inspiring and worthy example, those who put Christ's power in his moral influence, are singularly blind to the teaching of the Bible. But in reaction to them another extreme, doubtless a less vicious extreme, so emphasizes the more important aspects of Christ's sufferings as to forget or at least minimize the fact that Christ is indeed our example. In what Christ is our example and in what Christ is not our example can be explained in a few lines.

The central point of Peter's allusion to Christ's example is that he suffered innocently and for doing good. On one occasion, true enough, the Jews protested, "For a good work we stone thee not" (John 10:33), but there may be a difference between their own explanation of their conduct and their real motivation; there surely was a difference between the confused mind of the ordinary Jewish citizen and the all too clear perception of priests like Annas and Caiaphas who saw that Christ's good works were powerful evidences of his claims. The raising of Lazarus from the dead certainly should be classified as a good work, but so stirred to frenzy were the chief priests that they wanted not only to kill Jesus but to murder Lazarus also.

At the same time, though we should follow in his footsteps and suffer innocently for our good deeds, the limitations on our ability to hold Christ as an example come quickly to view. Of Christ it is said, he did no sin. In Hebrew the word connotes particularly violence, but it also takes on the weaker and broader meaning of wrong in general; in the Septuagint the Hebrew translators rendered it *lawlessness;* and

Peter quotes it simply as *sin*. Christ did not sin. In a sense, here too, Christ is our example. We should strive to eradicate sin from our lives; as Christ loved righteousness, so should we also. But we do not succeed because we cannot. Christ's example is too much for us. Isaiah's prophecy is true of Christ alone; and the motions of sin that remain in the flesh, though they are being subjugated in the process of sanctification, never permit us to achieve perfect subjective righteousness. Even if sinless perfection were possible, still it would not be true to say of any one of us, he did no sin. And this is strange too, if Christ is only an example. What one man has done, some other man can do. Why should Christ be the only man completely without sin? Why, indeed, unless it be because he is not merely a man and not merely an example?

No guile was found in his mouth. This idea is appropriate because it was a constant temptation to slaves to deceive their masters, to be sly and crafty, to exaggerate their accomplishments and to minimize their failures. Likewise when Christ was reviled, he reviled not again. Proverbs 20:22 is, "Say not thou, I will recompense evil"; and Proverbs 24:29, "Say not, I will do so to him as he hath done to me." When Christ suffered, he threatened not. Christ indeed threatened the Pharisees and sharply rebuked them, but the terrible statements of Christ, for example, "Ye are of your father the devil; depart from me, ye that work iniquity; O generation of vipers";—these statements were not provoked by personal suffering. When Christ suffered, he prayed, "Father, forgive them for they know not what they do." So in his torture Christ committed his cause to the righteous judge. We too then are to "give place unto wrath, for it is written, Vengeance is mine, I will repay, saith the Lord" (Romans 12:19), "seeing it is a righteous thing with God to recompense tribulation to them that trouble you" (2 Thessalonians 1:6). In all this Christ is our example. Though we may not be able to duplicate his conduct, yet it is an example to follow and an ideal to approximate. But Peter, having come now to the end of this particular exhortation, and through it having his thought centered on Christ, goes on to praise the Savior for actions that can in no way be an example or ideal.

Christ himself in his own body bore our sins on the tree. Here is something we cannot imitate, cannot even approximate. The unregenerate will indeed bear their own sins in hell, but no one else than Christ can bear the sins of another. If the vicarious aspect of Christ's sacrifice was hinted at in 1:19, here it is inescapable. One person, Christ, is bearing the sins of someone else.

At the beginning of the modernist movement there were frequent attempts to reinterpret the Scriptures and water down their supernatural and orthodox theology. For example, Romans 9:5, "Christ who is over all, God blessed forever," instead of being understood to affirm the full deity of Jesus, was retranslated so as to say, "Christ who is over all; may God be blessed forever." The American Revised Version openly attacks the deity of Christ when in the footnote to John 9:38 it calls Christ a creature. And similarly the verses on the atonement have been misinterpreted so as to remove the notion of a vicarious, propitiatory sacrifice. The Revised Standard Version consistently mistranslates *propitiation* as *expiation. Propitiation* means the appeasing or placating of God's wrath; *expiation* means the putting away of sin without any hint as to how this result is accomplished. All of which stimulates the desire to have the Bible translated by Christians instead of by unbelievers. But in spite of the fresh help to the modernists in the Revised Standard mistranslation, it seems that through the years the unbelieving ecclesiastics have appealed less and less to God's Word; and this does not seem unnatural, for the evangelical doctrines of grace are so plain in the Bible that the reprobate lose face in trying to twist the Greek language as no Greek could ever have imagined. Can anyone make anything else of this verse other than, Christ himself bore our sins in his own body on the tree?

Peter says on the tree, rather than on the cross, because of Deuteronomy 21:23, "His body shall not remain all night upon the tree . . . for he that is hanged is accursed of God." The verse is quoted by Paul in Galatians 3:13; and other references to the tree are Acts 5:30 and 10:39.

Reinforcing the constant message of the epistle, Peter asserts that the purpose of Christ's dying for our sins is that we should live to righteousness. The line from the hymn was previously quoted: He died to make us good. Sin is a sickness unto death and it is the stripes of Christ which cure the disease and give us life and health. By his stripes, his welts, we are healed. This is language that the slaves could unfortunately understand. They had many times been beaten. Perhaps there were cases where the beating produced illness; but quite contrary to the ordinary effect of beating, Christ's welts give health—not to him, but to us.

We needed the healing bruises of Christ, for like lost sheep we all had gone astray, we had turned every one to his own way, and were by nature the children of wrath; but now we have returned, or, since the word may bear the meaning, we have been converted to the Shepherd and Bishop of our souls.

Marriage

1 Peter 3:1–7

Likewise, ye wives, be in subjection to your own husbands; that, if any obey not the word, they also may without the word be won by the conversation of the wives;

While they behold your chaste conversation coupled with fear.

Whose adorning let it not be that outward adorning of plaiting the hair, and of wearing of gold, or of putting on of apparel;

But let it be the hidden man of the heart, in that which is not corruptible, even the ornament of a meek and quiet spirit, which is in the sight of God of great price.

For after this manner in the old time the holy women also, who trusted in God, adorned themselves, being in subjection unto their own husbands:

Even as Sarah obeyed Abraham, calling him lord: whose daughters ye are, as long as ye do well, and are not afraid with any amazement.

Likewise, ye husbands, dwell with them according to knowledge, giving honor unto the wife, as unto the weaker vessel, and as being heirs together of the grace of life; that your prayers be not hindered.

Instead of continuing with an exhortation to masters to treat their slaves in a considerate manner, as Paul does in Ephesians 6:9, Peter next takes up the duties of wives to husbands. It is entirely possible that there were no Christian masters in the communities to which this letter was going, so that the balancing exhortation could be omitted.

Wives are to be in subjection to their own husbands. Peter is here applying the seventh commandment. Adultery and fornication are sins that have darkened human history through the ages and have brought untold misery in their wake. Some ages seem to have been noticeably worse than others; cynics might say, not worse, just more open and less hypocritical. But is not this itself worse? A hypocrite at least shows some fear of being known as immoral; the open sinner has lost all sense of shame. The much maligned Victorian age, the age of calm and peace before the brutal, warlike twentieth century, may have had its share of hypocrites, but the open acknowledgment of Christian standards is a deterrent. Is this not a better condition than the open vice of the Hollywood era?

At any rate Peter's time was evil; the Romans themselves joked about the prudent men who loaned their wives but not their money. And Christians are tempted and dragged down by the intellectual and moral climate that surrounds them. High scholarship can flourish only in a community and within a tradition that honors it and keeps it alive by personal contact. Alcuin and Rabanus Maurus in the darkness of the sixth and seventh centuries may well have been as intelligent and capable as Augustine before them or Thomas after them. But the light of a living tradition had been extinguished by the barbarian invasions, and they could only lift themselves by their own bootstraps. So too with Christian morality: It is easier to live a moral and spiritual life in a community that openly approves and to some degree practices Christian principles. Some Christians have been fortunate to live in such times and places, but others are called upon to rise from the mire that sucks them down. In such a situation Peter's addressees found themselves.

The wives were to submit to their own husbands—not to some other woman's husband. The word *own* in this verse probably should receive some emphasis, though it does not seem to have the same emphasis in verse five below. The need of emphasis may have arisen from the circumstance that some of these Christian women were married to unbelievers. They had been converted and their husbands had not. It was therefore a temptation to associate with some Christian man. What at first might even appear innocent, would quickly not appear so, and could in time not be so. Paul had taught that if an unbelieving husband (or wife) should become disgusted with the Christianity of his wife (or husband) and desert her, the believing wife is to let him depart. But the Christian is not to desert the unbeliever. The reason for this that is mentioned by both Peter and Paul is that the unbeliever may be converted by the good conduct of his wife.

When Peter says that the unbeliever may be converted without the word, he should not be understood as teaching that conversion can occur without the preaching of the Gospel. In order to believe on Christ for salvation, one must know who Christ is and what he has done. The unbelieving husbands of this verse had already heard and had proved disobedient. They had heard the Gospel at the same time their wives were converted. And perhaps continued hearing of the Gospel irritated them. There comes a time then when it is best not to preach the word. They had heard it; nothing more can be said. From this point on, only subjection and chaste conversation can avail. Only, it must be borne in mind, "conversation" means behavior and not talking. Nor is the chaste behavior in fear solely or even mainly conjugal; it is quite general and most likely refers mainly to holy behavior and fear of God.

Fear of God would involve the more immediate and daily duties, even the relatively trivial matters of dress. Ornate or indecent decoration is to be avoided. Loud dress proclaims the type of person a woman is. On the other hand some devout people misunderstand the verse by a literal interpretation of some phrases coupled with a blindness to the sentence as a whole. There is a very honest and commendable group of Christians who make a point of using hooks and eyes instead of buttons on their clothes, of using horse and buggy instead of autos, or, if they use autos, of painting the chrome black. They dress in the fashion of long ago. Would that other Christians were as industrious and dependable; but their peculiarities of dress are not required by this verse. If the verse were an absolute prohibition against plaiting the hair and wearing a piece of gold, it would also be an absolute prohibition against wearing clothes. The three items, hair, jewelry, and clothes are all equal parts of the same grammatical construction. What is said of any one is equally said of the other two.

The thought of the verse concerns the adornment of women. What adorns a woman? What makes her attractive? Some women are attractive only in the sense that they attract attention. Their adornment is external. The Christian woman depends on an inward spiritual attractiveness. Let her plait her hair, let her wear gold jewelry—a wedding ring would come under this classification—and of course let her wear clothes; but let her not depend on these for her personality. The verse does not stress the objects worn so much as it stresses the manner of wearing them; and it stresses still more a different source of attractiveness. The adornment of the Christian woman is to come from the hidden personality of the heart—an adornment that never goes out of style and that becomes more and more attractive as the years pass by.

One of Rodin's famous pieces is a statue of an old hag. With all his marvelous skill Rodin pictured the repulsive ugliness of a withered woman. It would not be a bad idea to have curvaceous blonds study the statue. See, we might say, this is your end. The boys whistle at you now, but sooner than you realize people will avoid you. Old age comes to us all, perhaps more feared by women than by men. But it need not be repulsive. When the adornment is not corruptible, when charm comes from a meek and quiet spirit, instead of from a loud mouth, it is in the sight of God of great price.

The exhortation is supported by an appeal to previous examples, especially Sarah. If Peter's first readers were largely Jews, this example would carry great weight. Sarah was a very beautiful woman; she was also an exemplary wife; and she had long been a sort of heroine in the eye of Jewesses. To be called a daughter of Sarah was a high compliment. Not that Sarah, any more than the virgin Mary, was sinless. On the occasion that Sarah called Abraham "my lord," she was laughing at God's promise of a son (Genesis 18:12). But all in all she was a good wife, not being afraid of sudden fear (Proverbs 3:25) or terror. Peter's word for terror is the same as that in the Septuagint, from which it may be inferred that the reference is to trust in God. The good wife, though Proverbs speaks of a son, shall not be afraid when she lies down, her sleep shall be sweet, and she shall not be afraid of the desolation of the wicked, when it comes. Perhaps—we cannot be sure—these Christian wives of unbelieving husbands were terrified at the thought of desolation striking so near them; they feared for their husbands; they may even have feared for themselves as somehow involved in the desolation. Whatever their particular fears might have been, Peter counsels them to trust in God.

The position of women in the East, in the past, and in non-Christian countries generally, has been lower than in the Protestant nations. Husbands therefore needed and still need to be reminded of their duties also. This was necessary even though the husbands were believers—for Peter was not writing to unbelievers. While the Jewish women enjoyed a manner of life distinctly superior to that of heathen women, still the fuller revelation of Christ was to place them in an even better position. Christ not only did away with the distinction between Jew and Greek, bond and free, but between male and female also. The Jews of course never regarded woman as a soulless creature, but the Old Testament gives the privileges of religion more fully to men. One instance of this is that the sign of cleansing from sin and of entrance into the covenant was given to the male infant only. Now both boy and girl babies are baptized. There is still a subordination of sexes in accordance with their natural functions. The wife is the weaker vessel, and the man is the head of the woman as Christ is the head of the man. The husband is therefore to act with a knowledge of the relationship. He is to remember that his wife is the weaker vessel; she needs his care and protection as well as he needs her ministrations. But though the man occupies the higher office in the institution of the family, he must render honor to his wife because they are equally heirs of the grace of life. God's lot or choice has fallen upon both. They have been chosen together to inherit life. In heaven where they neither marry nor are given in marriage, the natural functions of husband and wife cease, and they shall be as angels. The earthly offices shall have fulfilled their usefulness, and no distinction due to sex will remain.

The man therefore is to give honor to his wife and dwell with her according to knowledge. In this way their prayers shall not be hindered.

Happy Sufferers

1 Peter 3:8–17

Finally, be ye all of one mind, having compassion one of another, love as brethren, be pitiful, be courteous:

Not rendering evil for evil, or railing for railing: but contrariwise blessing; knowing that ye are thereunto called, that ye should inherit a blessing.

For he that will love life, and see good days, let him refrain his tongue from evil, and his lips that they speak no guile:

Let him eschew evil, and do good; let him seek peace, and ensue it.

For the eyes of the Lord are over the righteous, and his ears are open unto their prayers: but the face of the Lord is against them that do evil.

And who is he that will harm you, if ye be followers of that which is good?

But if ye suffer for righteousness' sake, happy are ye: and be not afraid of their terror, neither be troubled;

But sanctify the Lord God in your hearts: and be ready always to give an answer to every man that asketh you a reason of the hope that is in you with meekness and fear:

Having a good conscience; that, whereas they speak evil of you, as of evildoers, they may be ashamed that falsely accuse your good conversation in Christ.

For it is better, if the will of God be so, that ye suffer for well doing, than for evil doing.

In somewhat different wording and with a little additional material, these verses are to an extent a repetition of previous thoughts, here supported by another quotation from the Old Testament. In his constant reference to the ancient Scriptures, Peter shows as clearly as any New Testament writer how the full Gospel grows out of the earlier revelation.

All Christians are to be of one mind, to have the same thoughts, the same purposes. Accepting the same revelation they should believe and preach its message; acknowledging the same authority, they should obey the same commands and work toward the same end. The text does not say, "belong to one organization." If, after doctrinal unity has been established, and mistranslations and reinterpretations no longer eviscerate the Gospel; if after a single purpose has been accepted and the social implications of the Gospel are put in opposition to humanistic socialism and arrogant bureaucracy; if, after the explicit commands of the Bible have been sufficiently obeyed; if after all this Christians prefer to unite in one ecclesiastical body, there is nothing in the Bible to forbid them; but it would be better to devote present energies to accomplishing what is commanded instead of distracting any minds with unspiritual ecclesiastical politics.

The more Christians are of one mind and purpose, the more they will be mutually sympathetic and compassionate, loving the brethren, tenderhearted, and humble. Peter's words contrast with the scramble for position and power in denominational mergers.

What was directly recommended to slaves in 2:23 is here extended to all: Not repaying evil for evil or reviling for reviling; but on the contrary, blessing one's detractors. And the reason is election. To this end we were chosen. Not that it is the final end. Beyond the blessing we give to our enemies is the blessing we inherit from God.

Such is the teaching of the Old Testament, Psalm 34:12ff. Verse

10 and the first half of verse 11 are rather negative. They stress the avoidance of evil. The last half of verse 11 speaks positively and urges active goodness. And as a general rule engaging in active goodness is a fairly efficient method of avoiding evil. It may not be a foolproof method, for of course we may blunder in our Christian work; but nonetheless for the great majority of church members and in most situations activity in the Lord's service prevents us from falling under the power of the devil. The Pharisee who thanked the Lord that he had not committed the sins other men had may indeed have had cause to thank God; for it is something to avoid adultery and extortion. But though it is something, it is not enough. If the Pharisee's negative goodness enabled him to avoid the grosser and more obvious sins, his pride and inner disposition left him without active goodness. He may even have kept himself from rendering evil for evil, but surely he was not a blessing to others and he did not inherit a blessing for himself. And today also one of the enervating factors that sap the life of the church is a widespread negative respectability.

The reason why we all should be actively engaged in doing good, in seeking and pursuing the peace of God, in being a blessing and not a headache to our associates, is that the eyes of the Lord are over the righteous and his ears are open to their prayers; but the face of the Lord is against them that do evil. The Gospel of grace should never be distorted so as to suggest that good works do not matter. God deals with man on a principle of justice and he "will render to every man according to his deeds: to them who by patient continuance in well doing seek for glory and honor and immortality, [he will render] eternal life." In man's present condition sin has so depraved human nature that man is totally unable to do any spiritual good, unless by the grace of God he is born again. An exhortation to good works does not, or at least should not, deny the principle of grace, but presupposes it. If we have been born to newness of life, we should live that life. The eyes of the Lord are over us.

Quite parenthetically it is interesting to note how the *eyes* of the Lord are contrasted with the *face* of the Lord. And also it may be noted that the word *over* and the word *against* are in the original the same word. In interpreting the Scriptures, as in reading any book, we should avoid grammatical blunders; but grammar alone is insufficient. Grammatically "over the righteous" and "over them that do evil," could mean exactly the same thing. But obviously they do not. The context makes this clear. And to go further, in interpreting a verse, a paragraph, or a thought in the Bible, we should bring to bear on it, not only the immediate context, but all the passages throughout the Bible that bear on the subject at hand.

But to return to good works: who will harm us if we seek what is good? In all ordinary cases the world will possibly commend us or at worst ignore us. Bent on their own devices, our unregenerate neighbors will be too occupied to go out of their way to injure us. And we, by doing good, may soften hard hearts and gain them as friends. But the question of verse 13 does not imply a universally negative answer. Who will harm us if we are zealous for the good? A number of people may suffer injury because of the very fact that we are zealous for the good. He who demands civic righteousness, who tries to clean out gambling and racketeering, may be slandered, beaten up, or even killed. People who have opposed the liquor interests have been framed and jailed. And from time to time and from place to place preachers of the Gospel, ordained and unordained, have suffered persecution. Doing good, opposing evil, is not a sure way of avoiding financial, social, or physical evil. But if ye suffer for righteousness' sake, blessed are ye. According to ordinary modes of speech and the superficial judgment of those who pass by, the Christian martyr is more miserable than happy. A missionary who was asked whether he really wanted to return to his work in Korea answered, "I am a man of some sensibilities and of course I don't like the fleas and the filth." Even though this man escaped the North Korean invaders in 1950 and did not suffer brutality, his daily life was not one of comfort. He suffered inconveniences and hardship for Christ. Others have suffered much more. And yet, though not superficially happy, they are blessed. Give them the happiness of the crowd and they would be profoundly unhappy. There are indeed people and powers who will do all they can to injure those who are zealous for good; but, Peter tells us, quoting Isaiah 8:12, "Be not afraid of their terror, neither be troubled." This is a hard exhortation to those who are actually suffering persecution; and we who live safely sheltered lives should pray that the members of that noble army who meet the tyrant's brandished steel and the lion's gory mane may be able with eagle eye to pierce beyond the grave, to see the Master in the sky, and climb the steep ascent of heaven through peril, toil, and pain: O God, to us may grace be given to follow in their train.

Peter is well aware of the sufferings that Christians are called on to undergo, but he urges us, instead of being troubled, to sanctify Christ as Lord. We are to set him apart in our hearts. We are not to set him aside and forget him, but set him apart and above all other interests as Lord of all.

It is important to understand the term *Lord*. Christians should never allow the indifferent world and its unfaithful ministers to forget that the Greek term *Lord* designates Jehovah in the Old Testament. One need not know much Greek, and need not search through all the Septuagint; but, if only one can distinguish the letters *Kurios,* one will see in Exodus 20 that the Lord spoke all these things and that Jehovah in giving the Ten Commandments began by saying, I am the Lord. Peter could not have failed to know this; nor Paul, nor John, nor hundreds of the early Jewish Christians. It is clear therefore that the earliest Church, and the men who had seen Jesus in the days of his humiliation, recognized him to be the Jehovah of the Old Testament. It was Christ who brought the Israelites out of Egypt, and it was Christ who followed them through the wilderness (1 Corinthians 10:4).

There may be many ways of sanctifying Christ, of setting him apart, of honoring his name. But Peter, thinking of the opposition that his people must face, recommends one particular procedure. When anyone asks us for a reason, an account, an explanation of our Christian hope, we must be ready with an apology. Apology, of course, in colloquial English, is nothing like what Peter meant. The verse could better be translated: Be ready to give the inquirer a course in Apologetics. The inquirer has asked a reason, or, we may say, he has asked for the logic of our hope; and we are to be prepared to give logic and reason. Not only is such a reply in keeping with the sacred dignity and importance of the Christian message, but the asking gives us an opportunity that should not be bungled. Unfortunately many Christians bungle their opportunities. They are not ready. At work, in a restaurant, on a train, a question concerning Christianity is asked, and the unprepared Christian must reply, I have wondered about that myself, or, I had never thought about that—I must ask my pastor. Indeed in this day of decline a good many pastors would not know.

And this includes the fundamentalists as much as the unbelieving modernists. A large segment of the professing Christian populace, particularly among those who sing catchy choruses with great gusto, has a fear of giving a reason. They distrust logic. They fear that knowledge will spoil their zeal.

In a Christian college, where one might expect academic standards to be upheld, an attempt was made by a part of the faculty to remove Theism from the curriculum. The uncompromising president, who stood so staunchly against all forms of unbelief, had just been fired; and now those who had engineered his dismissal wanted to remove the course he had taught. Theism was to be replaced by World History. The professor who led the debate argued, "Theism never converted anybody." Whether he thought World History would, I cannot say. The same professor was on a committee to award honors to alumni. He was terribly perturbed to hear that an alumnus of some distinction smoked cigars—no honors for him; but the fact that another denied the vicarious sacrifice of Christ troubled him not at all, for, he asserted with finality, the Bible nowhere uses the word vicarious. If Christians generally were ready to give the logic of their hope, a professor in a Christian college would not talk such nonsense, or perhaps he would not have been employed in the first place.

And it is more than likely that God uses good courses in Theism as a means in conversion. Perhaps the students who take such courses are already Christian: they will not be converted. But with their faith strengthened and their understanding enlarged, they will be ready to give an answer to someone who asks. And the answer, depending on time and circumstance, could be long enough to include a clear statement of the plan of salvation. This is personal work; this is preaching the Gospel; and therefore theism or apologetics is well worth studying.

But, some say, the Bible will defend itself. No need of our defending it. In a sense it is true that the Bible will defend itself. Cases have been reported of people who, though they never heard a sermon preached, have yet been converted by simply reading the Bible. But just because there are such cases is no reason for our not defending, expounding, and proclaiming the Bible. The Westminster Shorter Catechism in answer to the question, "How is the Word made effectual to salvation?" replies, "The Spirit of God maketh the reading but especially the preaching of the Word an effectual means of convincing and converting sinners, and of building them up in holiness and comfort through faith unto salvation.

This preaching of the Word may be a sermon from the pulpit or a conversation in a restaurant: in either case it is not merely a repetition from memory of several Bible verses. There ordinarily should be exposition and explanation. There ordinarily should be an application to the situation in which the hearer finds himself. If he is inclined to question the existence of God because he is troubled with mechanistic science, then the Christian does well to say something pertinent. If it is a matter of humanism, behaviorism, or if the hearer is under the delusion of Christian Science, Ethical Culture, Mormonism, or Unitarianism, the Christian preacher cannot take full advantage of his opportunity without previous study of the subjects.

To be sure, it is somewhat difficult to become omniscient; and most Christians cannot take the time to become expert on all these subjects. Yet knowledge and not ignorance is the aim and ideal, for the verse calls us to answer every man. Could it be that we should say, "So, you are a behaviorist, or a Unitarian; now, my friend, I am not an expert on those topics and accordingly I am absolved of preaching the Gospel to you; you had better speak to some other Christian."

Some people might wish to turn this caricature into an argument against solid education and sound apologetics. It is so easy to see that no one can learn everything and only a few can learn very much. Let it be so: the point is that a theological education is desirable. And in the great crises of spiritual conflict, God chose as leaders of his people men with great minds: Paul, Augustine, Luther, and Calvin. But he also used unlearned and ignorant Peter. And sometimes the answers of the unlearned are as pertinent and even more so than erudite answers. Each one of us has his own responsibility to discharge. The uneducated faithful, such as those to whom Peter was writing, need not be cast down because they do not know as much as Augustine or Calvin. The lazy and unfaithful, who have the opportunity to study but neglect it, can find no comfort in God's approval of the humble. And the learned Christian is under obligation to make full use of his learning. Thus everyone who asks a reason may receive one.

The reasons are to be given in meekness and fear. A parade of learning on the one hand and a smart-aleck reply on the other are equally uncalled for. People are not always altogether logical, and they will often judge the value of our reply by the manner in which it is given. And among those who ask a reason are some who will seize any opportunity for ridiculing the Gospel. To this end they will use our evil conduct or even any legitimate conduct which can be put in a bad light. We cannot always at the moment defend ourselves against such prejudice. If we act in good conscience, if we have faithfully tried to obey God's commands, then we have done all we can to make these enemies of Christ ashamed of their false accusations. Fail though we may to impress this particular person, the contrast between his evil words and our good conversation in Christ may very well produce an effect in those who are watching us.

No doubt we cannot escape all tribulation. The enemies of the Gospel will succeed in causing us some harm. But if we are to suffer, at least we can suffer for good conduct rather than for bad. We shall suffer, but we need not be guilty. The mind of the world argues in a different fashion. It says, one might as well be hanged for a sheep as for a lamb; or, I should not take this affliction so hard if I had deserved it. But Peter says the opposite. And he gives as his reason the example of Christ.

The next few verses are the basis for Peter's admonition to us. Christ's life and sufferings show us how to accept tribulation, how to speak in meekness and fear, how to suffer for doing good works. But since perhaps enough has been said on this point, the following section will not repeat this lesson but will center attention on what Christ actually did, for the next five verses are rich in explanation of the work of our Lord.

A Complex of Ideas

1 Peter 3:18–22

For Christ also hath once suffered for sins, the just for the unjust, that he might bring us to God, being put to death in the flesh, but quickened by the Spirit:

By which also he went and preached unto the spirits in prison;

Which sometime were disobedient, when once the long-suffering of God waited in the days of Noah, while the ark was a preparing, wherein few, that is, eight souls were saved by water.

The like figure whereunto even baptism doth also now save us (not the putting away of the filth of the flesh, but the answer of a good conscience toward God) by the resurrection of Jesus Christ:

Who is gone into heaven, and is on the right hand of God; angels and authorities and powers being made subject unto him.

A Single Sacrifice

That Christ died once is hardly a startling statement. Neither the ancient Pharisees nor the modern Unitarians would deny it. But frequently a verse or phrase becomes important with reference to some false doctrine. If the doctrine had not been invented, the phrase would have remained in obscurity; but once the error is broadcast, the neglected phrase comes into its own.

The Roman Catholic mass is a denial of the phrase that Christ died once. The word *once* means *just once,* or *once for all.* When Christ died, his work was finished; he did not have to die again. The merit of his death is sufficient for all time, and nothing more need be added.

But the Roman Church teaches that the mass is a sacrifice, a repetition of Christ's death on the cross. The sacrifice is offered by a priest, and the priest transforms the bread and wine into the actual body and blood of Jesus.

The Canons and Decrees of the Council of Trent (Twenty-second Session, September 17, 1562, Chapter II) states:

> *[I]n this divine sacrifice which is celebrated in the mass, that same Christ is contained and immolated. . . . [T]his sacrifice is truly propitiatory. . . . [W]herefore, not only for the sins, punishments, satisfactions, and other necessities of the faithful who are living, but also for those who are departed in Christ and who are not as yet fully purified, is it rightly offered.*

It is to be noted that the mass is said to be a propitiatory sacrifice, and is rightly offered for sin and satisfaction, or atonement. And the same Christ dies every time the mass is celebrated.

But all this is far from the teaching of Peter and the other apostles. It is an eloquent testimony to the apostasy of the Roman church that the Pope and the Councils should be able so violently to wrest the word of God to their own destruction.

The epistle to the Hebrews is particularly explicit in this regard. Not only does it speak of Christ's sacrifice as more excellent than the Jewish rites, but it expressly contrasts the *many* previous sacrifices with Christ's *one* sacrifice that does away with all others. "Nor yet that he should offer himself often . . . for then must he often have suffered . . . but now once. . . . So Christ was once offered . . ." (Hebrews 9:25–28).

Christ suffered for sins; and the significance of his suffering is clarified in the next phrase: the just for the unjust. In the Old Testament sin barred the way to God, and in order to worship God a man had to offer a sacrifice. An animal without spot or blemish had to die for the sinful man. Christ died as the Lamb of God, the true sacrifice of which the Old Testament sacrifices were but anticipations. Christ, without spot or blemish, Christ the just one, died for the unjust. If anyone should say that the word vicarious is not found in the Bible, it means only that a Latin word is not found in a Greek text. Whether a given word is used or not is of minor importance; what counts is whether or not the idea or doctrine is found there. Here we have the substitution of the just for the unjust; instead of the sinner's suffering for his sins, Christ suffered for his sins. And thus God is propitiated and our sins are expiated.

Propitiation, expiation, and *substitution* are blessed words, for they sum up so much of Biblical teaching. In Leviticus, chapters 4 and 16, the sacrificial rites show that a penalty for sin was exacted and how remission and forgiveness were obtained. Christ fulfills these sacrifices. As the vicarious or substitutionary nature of the old sacrifices is clear, so the New Testament shows the substitutionary nature of Christ's sacrifice: "If one died for all, then all died" (2 Corinthians 5:14), and "Christ hath redeemed us from the curse of the law, being made a curse for us" (Galatians 3:13). Here we have the very central and most essential part of the Gospel. This is indeed the Good News, and there is no Good News without it. When this idea is absent from preaching, the preaching is no longer Christian. This does not mean that a minister can never preach on Abraham or Moses, on election or sanctification. It does mean that the significance of Moses and sanctification depend on Christ's sacrifice, and unless the full and finished work of Christ permeates the message, the message is not worth preaching. For otherwise it is impossible that we be brought to God. No one cometh unto the Father but by Christ; there is no other Name, and there is no other message.

The next pair of phrases is a little puzzling. The idea that Christ was put to death in the flesh, or with reference to the flesh, is altogether obvious; but the parallel phrase, made alive in his spirit, or with reference to his spirit, does not seem to make sense. Each phrase consists of three words that correspond to each other. The two verbs are "put to death" and "made alive"; the two particles are "on the one hand" and "on the other hand"; and the two nouns are "in the flesh" and "in the spirit." Since the construction is obviously parallel, the grammar does not seem to mean, as the King James Version indicates, that Christ was resurrected by the Holy Spirit. It does not seem so because if we translated it word for word, we would have to use the same words both times; and therefore if Christ was resurrected *by* the Spirit, he would have to be put to death *by* the flesh; or, if he died *in* his flesh, he rose *in* his spirit.

However, this confusion is only a seeming confusion, and in fact the King James Version is correct. The confusion arises from a schoolboy's method of literal or word for word translation. In English we make a distinction between *in* and *by*, and if we should wish to construct two contrasting phrases we would ordinarily choose one or the other preposition and use it in both places. But in Greek the ideas of *in* and *by* can be expressed by the same word, either by a preposition, or as in this case by the same case of the noun. Accordingly Peter writes his parallelism, contrasting the dative of the noun "flesh" with the dative of the noun "spirit," probably without ever being conscious that a poor student of Greek could misinterpret it.

The correct interpretation is obtained by attending to the meaning of the phrases. If either *in* or *by* is used both times, one of the contrasting phrases loses sense. Obviously, being put to death *by* the flesh has little meaning. Similarly there is hardly a good sense to be attached to the assertion that Christ was made alive *in* his spirit; but that Christ was resurrected *by* the Holy Spirit is a perfectly clear idea. That the Holy Spirit is meant is also borne out by the analysis of the next few verses, even though they are perhaps harder to understand than the phrase in question.

Noah's Gospel

Verses 19 and 20 have puzzled a great many people, and they have tried various devices to explain how Christ preached to the spirits in prison. In general there are two types of explanation. First, the verses are taken to mean that Christ used Noah to preach to the wicked that were about to be drowned in the flood. Second, the verses are interpreted to mean that Christ in person preached to spirits in the realm of the dead. This second interpretation is divided on the identity of the dead: the dead to whom Christ preached might be the righteous dead, or they might be the wicked dead. Let us examine this second interpretation first.

This is an old and widely accepted interpretation. Irenaeus, Tertullian, both the Greek and Roman churches, and also Zwingli and Calvin hold that Christ announced salvation to the Old Testament believers and brought them from the realms of death into heaven. In accordance with this idea John 3:13, "No one has ascended into heaven but he that came down from heaven," is said to mean that no Old Testament saint could precede Christ into heaven. They had to wait for Christ's ascension. The prison is the abode of the dead, and the preaching is the proclamation of Christ's victory.

As further support of this view Acts 2:27, 31 are taken to mean that Christ's soul went to hell or at least to the abode of the dead, though of course God would not permit his soul to be held there. Some have also appealed to Philippians 2:10 by taking the things under the earth that bow at the name of Jesus to be either the righteous or wicked dead. More plausible is the use of Ephesians 4:8, 9. "When he ascended up on high, he led captivity captive. . . . Now that he ascended, what is it but that he also descended into the lower parts of the earth?" These lower parts of the earth are supposed to be the realm of the dead, and the idea is repudiated that this descent is the Incarnation or Christ's descent to earth.

Before adopting this ancient view certain problems must be faced and solved. In the first place Peter's text does not mention anything about preaching to the saints. The spirits to whom Christ preached are explicitly called disobedient. This fact must be taken as a fixed point of interpretation. There is no reference to Old Testament saints. So, if Christ preached in person to anyone between the time of his death and resurrection, it would have to be the wicked dead, and whatever captivity Christ led captive, it could not be the Old Testament saints considered as held in prison.

In the next place the only disobedient people that Peter mentions are those who lived in the days of Noah. This time reference is another reason for refusing to think that Christ preached to Abraham, David, and the prophets. Not only is it wrong to call these men disobedient, but further they did not live at the time Peter mentions.

This time reference also militates against the view that Christ preached to all the wicked dead. From what Peter actually says, we could only conclude that Christ preached to those who were disobedient in the time of Noah. But without pressing this point too far at the moment, let us consider other aspects of the idea that Christ preached personally to the wicked in hell, and that the preaching, of necessity, is the announcement of their condemnation.

As for the notion that Christ announced the damnation of the wicked in hell, it is hard to see how it ties in with the context. The main idea that Peter wants to enforce is that Christians should be willing to suffer for Christ's sake and to suffer unjustly. Preaching to the wicked in hell does not advance Peter's main purpose. Or, if attention be centered on the nearer idea of Christ's being raised from the dead by the Holy Spirit, it still is not clear how this announcement of damnation adds to the theme. And it will hardly do to say that Peter just had to fill space to make his epistle long enough, and so was driven to insert something true but irrelevant.

But the decisive objection to understanding these words to refer to the announcement of damnation is that the verb, to preach, ordinarily means to preach the Gospel. It does not mean a judicial sentence, nor in the New Testament does it refer to sundry announcements. The regular meaning is the announcement of the Gospel.

Because this is so obvious, some interpreters have tried to hold to the general view while modifying it to make Christ's work the preaching of the Gospel instead of the announcement of damnation. While this maneuver escapes these immediate objections, it must face others.

Since the Bible does not teach that there is a second chance to be saved, a chance in the next life, but teaches that man's destiny is irrevocably fixed in this life, there would remain no reasonable purpose for preaching the Gospel to the wicked in hell. And, to return to a previous point, all these attempts fail to explain the mention of the antediluvian unbelievers. Any preaching in hell should be directed to all, and not to just a few. But the text specifically mentions those who lived in the days of Noah.

This view therefore, though adopted by many and held for so long a time, must be set aside. Perhaps the other view, held by Augustine and Beza, will prove better. According to this interpretation Peter is thought to say that Noah spoke by the Holy Spirit to his disobedient contemporaries, and that the flood which destroyed them is a type of baptism.

This interpretation must also face objections. For one thing, it is pointed out that Peter makes the subject of the verb Christ. Christ went and preached, and hence Noah cannot be the preacher. However, this objection is not so serious as it might seem at first. Peter actually says, Christ was made alive by the Spirit, by whom also he preached. This preaching therefore was done by Christ through the Spirit. What this might mean can be seen in chapter one verse eleven. In the first chapter Peter speaks of the Old Testament prophets. These prophets had received a message from God, and they studied the message to see what God meant. The words are, "searching what . . . the Spirit of Christ which was in them did signify when it testified beforehand. . . ." Now, obviously, if the Spirit of Christ spoke through the prophets, then too Christ through the Spirit could very well preach in the person of Noah. To suppose that the Spirit of Christ is not the Holy Spirit and could not therefore inspire Noah is a supposition contrary to Peter's thought and contrary to other New Testament passages. For example, Paul in Ephesians 2:17 virtually says that it was Christ, through his missionaries, that preached the Gospel in Ephesus. So far as this point goes therefore, this interpretation stands up under scrutiny.

If the preaching was Noah's testimony to his contemporaries, then one must ask the question, What is the prison? The other interpretation assumed that the prison must be hell or hades. But could it be hell, if Noah was preaching to living people? There are two answers to this question. First, one might assume that the prison is the prison house of sin. It is as reasonable to speak of the bonds of sin as it is to speak of the bonds of hell. The notion of a prison therefore does not rule out the idea that Noah was the preacher. But there is a second and a better answer to the question. The prison may still be hell and Noah still the preacher. For the verse can be interpreted to mean "the spirits (now) in hell." That is, the men to whom Noah preached are now in Peter's day suffering their just recompense. This is not just a guess, but is based on Peter's manner of speech. In 4:6 we shall see that the Gospel was preached to certain people who are now dead. The preaching had been done previously; when Peter wrote, they were dead. Further, that Noah was the preacher is supported by 2 Peter 2:5.

Another argument is that the participles *died, made alive,* and *went,* and the verb *preached,* indicate a temporal succession, and hence the preaching must have occurred after the death of Christ, and not in the time of Noah. But in the first place, if this were so, the preaching would have had to occur after Christ's resurrection, and not between his death and resurrection, as is usually supposed. Furthermore, the mention of the preaching is not so clearly connected with any alleged temporal succession as it is with the reference to the Spirit. Of course the resurrection had to follow the crucifixion; but the thought of the passage is not on the time element, but on the significance of these events in bringing sinners to God.

Thus the several objections that are raised against the personal preaching of Noah do not make this interpretation impossible.

Now, positively, this interpretation is the only one that can explain the mention of the wicked at the time of Noah, and the mention of Noah is motivated by Peter's desire to show that the flood is a type of baptism. In the larger connection Peter is explaining the work of Christ, the turning away from sin, the salvation of believers out of an ungodly world, and their tribulations during their lifetime. Peter thinks he can make his ideas clear by an Old Testament example, and Noah is more suitable than any other. For this reason Peter can confine his thought to one group of men. Had he been thinking of a personal preaching by Christ in hell, he could not have restricted his attention to this one group.

The reference to the time of Noah is of course explicit and obvious; and the statement that eight souls were saved in the ark is a plain matter of fact; but the connection between the flood and baptism requires a little explanation.

The Flood and Baptism

First it is to be noted that the eight souls are not said to have been saved from the waters of the flood. In truth they were saved *from* the water, but this is not what Peter sees fit to mention. Peter says they were saved *by* the water. And if they were saved *by* the water, it is evident that the peril *from* which they were saved was not drowning.

The Bible is a book with a spiritual message. Words are not always used in their literal senses. When the Gospel writers speak of life, it is not mere biological existence that they have in mind; and when they speak of death, they may include physical death, but their attention is centered on spiritual death. So too when Moses delivered the children of Egypt from bondage in Egypt, and when the blood of the lamb on the door posts turned aside the angel of death, the significance was not restricted to physical slavery and physical death; it was rather deliverance from the paganism of Egypt that this people might prepare for the coming of Messiah. The significance is spiritual. Thus it is also with Noah.

In Noah's day "God saw that the wickedness of man was great in the earth . . . and it repented the Lord that he had made man; but Noah found grace in the eyes of the Lord . . . and God said unto Noah . . . I even I do bring a flood of waters upon the earth to destroy all flesh . . . but with thee I will establish my covenant" (Genesis 6:5–18). Apparently Noah was saved from the corruption around him. The original revelation of God to man and the promise of a redeemer had been having less and less effect on human hearts. The godly line was almost extinct. And plausibly it would have become entirely extinct within one or two more generations. Noah and his family are saved from this disaster by the flood. The wicked were wiped off the face of the earth and God's covenant was re-established.

This line of thought ties back into verse eighteen. The plan of salvation, the covenant of the Lord, the preaching of the Gospel has as its purpose the bringing of some to God. For this purpose God controls all history. And thus it was that Noah was saved by water. One might picture Noah before the flood as a man immersed in a bog of iniquity. Going in and out among men he could find no one clean. The flood cleansed him. These ideas lead most naturally to the mention of baptism. Baptism and the flood are similar in that both are a sort of salvation from sin by means of water. The words can be translated: eight souls were saved by water, which also saves us now in its antitype, baptism.

On occasion I have enjoyed poking my good Baptist friends in the ribs by an apparent implication of these verses. Reflection on the situation discloses that while the wicked were immersed, Noah was only sprinkled.

More seriously one may ask whether baptism really saves us. The text says that the eight souls of Noah's day were saved by water, and that now in our day baptism saves us also.

This raises questions as to the efficacy and the necessity of baptism and connects with theories of baptismal regeneration. The Romish church in the Council of Trent asserted: "If any one saith that baptism . . . is not necessary to salvation, let him be anathema." The Synod of

Jerusalem (1672) in which the Greek church agreed with Rome in condemning Protestantism asserted: "Without it [baptism] no one can be saved, as the Lord said, 'Whoever is not born of water and the Spirit shall by no means enter the kingdom of heaven.'" The article goes on to list the effects of baptism, including the forgiveness of original and all actual sin, escape from eternal punishment, and conferment of immortality. Lutherans and Anglicans also hold to theories of baptismal regeneration.

The point in dispute is of more importance than one might at first think. And as Peter's words seem to assign a power of salvation to the water, a short survey of other Scriptural passages is in order.

The disciples were commanded to go to all nations and to baptize them. At Pentecost Peter told those convicted of sin, "Repent and be baptized." These facts are not here brought into question—it is clear that the sacrament of baptism is a command and should be obeyed, if possible.

But what if it is not possible? Is baptism absolutely essential to salvation? Is baptism the indispensable means of regeneration? Those who answer affirmatively depend largely on John 3:5, "Except a man be born of water and of the Spirit, he cannot enter into the kingdom of God." And is not this verse a clincher? Does it not say that the water is as essential as the Spirit? How then can anyone suppose that unbaptized persons ever reach heaven?

The verse occurs as Jesus was explaining the puzzling idea of the new birth to Nicodemus. To be born of God (John 1:13), to be born again (John 3:3), and to be born of the Spirit (John 3:5) are all the same thing. But what about the water without which one cannot enter into the kingdom of God? Does this water mean baptism?

Some zealous Bible believing Christians hold that the whole Bible should be taken literally. They deplore what they call "spiritualizing." But it is possible to accept the Bible as infallibly true and still understand certain phrases as metaphorical. And even those who insist on the literal truth of the the Bible, when they come to these passages, take them as figures of speech. Outside the possible exception of a textbook on mathematics there is probably no book of any size that can be taken literally throughout. We do not speak or write that way. For example, when John the Baptist said that his mightier successor would baptize with the Holy Ghost and with fire (Matthew 3:11), few people have understood him literally. Fire is a symbol of cleansing. Malachi 3:2 says, "But who may abide the day of his coming? and who shall stand when he appeareth? for he is like a refiner's fire" (compare Isaiah 4:4).

The following considerations bear on the question whether the water of John 3:5 is literal water, and thus refers to baptism, or whether there is another meaning.

Note in the first place that Nicodemus was a Jew who was honestly seeking the truth. He recognized that no man could have done the things Jesus did except God were with him. Therefore Jesus in explaining things to him would appeal to what Nicodemus ought to have known; that is, he would appeal to the Old Testament. Jesus would not assume that Nicodemus knew something foreign to the Old Testament. This principle of explanation is not mere surmise, but is the clear meaning of John 3:10, "Art thou a master of Israel and knowest not these things?" It is therefore obvious that Jesus is basing his teaching on the Old Testament which Nicodemus ought to have known. And if this is so, it follows that the meaning of the word "water" must be determined by its Old Testament usage.

To us who live in the Christian era water suggests baptism, but in the historical circumstances the preceding usage is what is meant—not something later of which Nicodemus was necessarily ignorant.

Evidence to support this point is found in the phrase "the Kingdom of God." That God is a King and has a kingdom is an Old Testament idea. (Compare 1 Chronicles 29:11; Psalms 22:28; 45:6, etc.) And if the kingdom of God figures in the Old Testament, we might at least hope to find in the Old Testament the conditions of membership in that kingdom.

And indeed we do. In the Old Testament we find repentance, faith, trust, sacrifice, redemption—all the Gospel terms. We find the new heart and the Spirit. Then why should we not also look there for the meaning of water?

We shall not be disappointed. As a matter of fact the Old Testament connects water with regeneration and uses it as the symbol for the Spirit. The first ten verses of Psalm 51 interweave the washing from sin, the creating of a clean heart, and the renewing of a right spirit. Isaiah 44:3 makes the pouring of water a parallel or symbol of the pouring of the Spirit. Joel 2:28 uses the familiar thought of *pouring* out the Spirit; and obviously this is a figurative expression taken from the pouring of water. Zechariah's fountain (13:1) may have eventually turned out to be a fountain filled with blood, but the figure again comes from an ordinary fountain that gives water. In Ezekiel 47:1–12 there are the waters that flow from the temple.

But most important of all is Ezekiel 36:25, 27. "Then will I sprinkle clean water upon you. . . . A new heart also will I give you. . . . And I will put my Spirit within you. . . ." This passage is so appropriate to the theme that Jesus wished to explain to Nicodemus that we may well believe that Jesus mentioned water for the express purpose of causing Nicodemus to bring to mind these words of Ezekiel. Water symbolizes cleansing from sin, the giving of a new heart—regeneration, and this is what it means to be born of the Spirit. All this Nicodemus ought to have known. And if the verse in John is a tacit allusion to Ezekiel, it also explains why water is omitted from verses 6 and 8: the allusion had been made and only the reality needed repetition.

To look at the whole matter from the opposite direction: baptism, especially Christian baptism, is not found in the Old Testament, and therefore Jesus could not have expected Nicodemus to know anything about it. If Christ had meant baptism, he would have had to go into a lengthy explanation, for otherwise such a reference would have confused Nicodemus rather than enlightened him. In this case Jesus could not have reproached Nicodemus for his ignorance. The reproach, "Art thou a master of Israel and knowest not these things?" shows clearly that Christ could not have been speaking of Christian baptism.

The conclusion is that Jesus was talking about cleansing from sin and not about a visible sacrament. Therefore it is not true that a person who for some reason has failed of baptism loses all chance of being received into heaven. Baptism is no more essential to salvation than the Lord's Supper; and the thief on the cross entered Paradise without celebrating either sacrament.

Peter in this passage gives as little support as John to the doctrine of baptismal regeneration. It is not the literal application of water and the washing away of dirt on the skin that Peter is talking about. Baptism is a symbol; it is not the reality. The Romanists have confused them; they identify the sign and the thing signified, and hence make the sacrament essential to salvation. Others, however, go to an opposite extreme. Some individuals and some groups do not administer baptism at all. They argue that the sacraments are mere symbols and are unnecessary. Whereas the Romanists absorbed the reality into the sign, these others absorb the sign into the reality. But though baptism is merely a sign, still the Lord commanded baptism; and we must obey. We must obey with a sufficient knowledge of what we are doing. The washing with water is a visible sign of a spiritual reality. It represents the washing away of sin. And accordingly Peter insists that it is not the literal washing that is effective to salvation, but the answer of a good conscience toward God.

Unfortunately this phrase from the King James Version is most likely a misinterpretation. Although the word Peter used can sometimes mean an answer given in interrogation by a higher authority, the usual and root meaning is not answer but conquest. And in this particular case there is no hint that God is interrogating a good conscience; nor does the idea of giving an answer fit with what Peter has been saying.

The Revised Version attempts to insert the notion of interrogation while omitting any reference to an answer. But if the grammar of the sentence forbids an interrogation by God, the structure of the argument forbids an interrogation of God by the good conscience. The Revised version therefore seems to have made complete nonsense of the phrase.

The Revised Standard Version gives a better sense by speaking of an appeal to God for a good conscience. This looks like a confession of sin and a plea for pardon and justification. And since such a plea would presuppose regeneration, the idea fits not too badly with what Peter has been saying. Liddell and Scott's *Greek-English Lexicon* (1940 edition) suggest the pledge of a good conscience to God; but perhaps the best is simply the request for a good conscience, the prayer for peace with God.

In this sense baptism saves us, more accurately *you,* by the resurrection of Jesus Christ. Christ was delivered up for our offenses and raised again for our justification. And if Christ be not raised, Christianity is vain and we are of all men most miserable. But thanks be to God: Christ has gone into heaven, is seated at the right hand of God, while angels and authorities and powers are subjected to him.

Sobriety, Persecution, and Service

1 Peter 4:1–11

Forasmuch then as Christ hath suffered for us in the flesh, arm yourselves likewise with the same mind: for he that hath suffered in the flesh hath ceased from sin;

That he no longer should live the rest of his time in the flesh to the lusts of men, but to the will of God.

For the time past of our life may suffice us to have wrought the will of the Gentiles, when we walked in lasciviousness, lusts, excess of wine, revellings, banquetings, and abominable idolatries;

Wherein they think it strange that ye run not with them to the same excess of riot, speaking evil of you:

Who shall give account to him that is ready to judge the quick and the dead.

For for this cause was the Gospel preached also to them that are dead, that they might be judged according to men in the flesh, but live according to God in the spirit.

But the end of all things is at hand: be ye therefore sober, and watch unto prayer.

And above all things have fervent charity among yourselves: for charity shall cover the multitude of sins.

Use hospitality one to another without grudging.

As every man hath received the gift, even so minister the same one to another, as good stewards of the manifold grace of God.

If any man speak, let him speak as the oracles of God; if any man minister, let him do it as of the ability which God giveth: that God in all things may be glorified through Jesus Christ, to whom be praise and dominion for ever and ever. Amen.

The break between this chapter and the previous one is not abrupt. Peter had foreseen that his charges would be called upon to face persecution, organized and unorganized; he wished therefore to prepare them for suffering for righteousness' sake; and to this end he held before them the example of the Lord. The reference to the work of Christ included the reference to Noah and the figure of baptism. Now that all this has been sufficiently set forth, Peter returns to the immediate matter of strengthening his people against the vicissitudes and temptations of their circumstances.

Accordingly, since Christ suffered in the flesh, he says, arm yourselves also with the same mind, the same ideas, the same determination. Ideas are weapons. Belief is armament. The notions that Christ entertained will aid each Christian in his struggle against the enemy. Even in the extreme case of martyrdom, the mind of Christ is a sure defense, because he who has suffered and died has ceased from sin. His trials and temptations are over.

The words "he that hath suffered" refers in the first instance to Christ, and secondarily to us. Since it is so closely connected with Christ, repeating the idea of suffering mentioned immediately before, it is best to take the suffering as indicating death. Peter by no means asserts that every Christian who suffers (present tense) persecution is sinless. On the contrary, it is the Christian who suffered (past tense) who has achieved rest from sin. This thought is to be a comfort to the dying martyr. Even in his shame and agony he knows that the struggle with sin will soon end and that heaven is at hand.

The purpose clause, *in order that,* connects, not with *ceased from sin,* but with *be armed.* Obviously we do not have rest from sin in heaven in order to live the rest of our time in the flesh. Rather, we arm ourselves with the ideas of Christ in order that the remainder of our lives shall not be given over to lust, but shall be in the will of God.

Human lusts or desires are not to be the norm of our lives. As the Prayer Book says, we have followed too much the devices and desires of our own hearts. Instead of this type of life the servant of God should govern his conduct by the revealed will of God. Sin is any want of conformity unto or transgression of the law of God. Obedience is what God requires, and a neglect of the Bible's commands is sin. And regenerated as we are, the remainder of our life, all too short as it may well be, should be spent in doing the works of righteousness.

The time previous to our regeneration is quite sufficient for the works of darkness. Too much time has already been squandered. The sins Peter lists seem to be Gentile sins rather than typically Jewish. Of course, although Peter may have been writing mainly to Jews, there were no doubt Gentile Christians among his immediate readers; and of course some Jews may have been guilty of the sins listed. Then perhaps, further, Peter is giving some common sins their plain names. He calls a spade a spade. Today people may speak of divorce, but they do not often call it lasciviousness. Lust may be disguised as glamor. But contrary to modern movies and novels, the Bible puts these things in their proper light. They are abominable wickedness, deserving God's wrath and curse in hell forever.

How like the ancient people are the people of today! They are positively bewildered when a conscientious Christian refuses to join in their sociability. Why, what is wrong with a little whiskey? Why shouldn't husband leave wife or wife leave husband if either finds a more appealing partner? Why be careful to attend church regularly? As our neighbors said to us once in amazement, before they knew us very well, "You are not going to church this evening, are you? Why, you went to church this morning!" And when the Christian prefers cleanness to filth, righteousness to sin, the people of the world speak evil of him. He is anti-social. He is a blue-nosed Puritan. We may reply that in that case, he is at least not an impuritan.

Let us not be dismayed at the bewilderment, the scorn, and the slander of the world. They are to be pitied, for they must give an account of themselves to him who is ready to judge the living and the dead. This is no laughing matter. When Paul reasoned of righteousness, temperance, and judgment to come, Felix trembled. Corrupt judge as he was, soliciting bribery, he still retained a sense of God's wrath. The people of today are more depraved than Felix was. Their accounting will be severe.

For to this end the Gospel was preached to the dead. At first sight this is a hard passage. Does it mean that the Gospel was preached in order that God might be able to judge the dead? And how was the Gospel preached to the dead? And who are the dead that Peter has in mind?

At first sight the dead of verse six might seem to be the dead of verse five: all the dead. Those who advocate the doctrine of a second chance say that the Gospel will be preached to all the dead, and since the wicked dead will be in actual torment, they will then be only too happy to accept Christ. Accordingly, everybody will be saved, for the dead, all the dead, whatever may have happened to them in the flesh, will, on this interpretation, live according to God in the spirit.

Aside from the indisputable fact that the Bible teaches neither a second chance nor universal salvation, this interpretation cannot explain the meaning of being judged according to men in the flesh. In coming to an understanding of this verse, one must give full value to the emphatic antithesis: judged according to men in the flesh *versus* live according to God in the spirit. Judgment and life, men and God, the flesh and the spirit, all concur to form a contrast.

We must therefore suppose that the dead of verse five and the dead of verse six are not identical. Peter named God the judge of all the dead for the obvious purpose of indicating the penalty for sin. But in verse six his mind continues the earlier thought of the Christians who have suffered death. The dead of verse six therefore are the martyrs. Furthermore, the judgment of verse five is not the judgment of verse six. The former is a judgment by God, whereas the latter is explicitly a judgment by men. If we take the reference to the final judgment in verse five as parenthetical, verse six will tie in with the thought of the whole passage.

The ideas revolve around suffering and a judgment by men, or martyrdom. This is made still more prominent in verse twelve; for which reason we need not be in doubt as to what was in Peter's mind when he wrote this chapter. In verse seventeen also there is the idea of judgment, and it is a judgment by men upon Christians. The passage therefore does not at all refer to any preaching by Christ in hell; there is no mention of hope for the wicked after death; on the contrary in verse eighteen it is plainly indicated that there is no hope.

Perhaps it will not be too far wrong to paraphrase the verse in this way: The reason why the Gospel was preached to the martyrs before they died was that they might indeed be martyred according to God's plan, and after martyrdom receive a far more exceeding and eternal weight of glory.

Now, the end and purpose for which all things have occurred is near. There is no need of anxiety or despair. Rather maintain a sound mind and be sober in order that you may be powerful in prayer. Above all, have constant love toward each other, because love covers a multitude of sins. Psalm 32:1 shows that to cover sin means to forgive sin. Mutual love stimulates forgiveness, and so sins are hidden. Romanists try to find human merit in this verse by supposing that God covers a man's sins on the basis of the man's love for his fellow Christians. A similar though not identical situation is found in the Lord's Prayer. Here some professing evangelicals of the dispensational variety repudiate the Lord's Prayer on the assumption that it asks God to forgive our sins, not because Christ paid their penalty but because we forgive those who have sinned against us. But the Lord's Prayer cannot be relegated to a future age by such a misinterpretation unless the dispensationalist is also to excind Ephesians from our Bible for today. Ephesians 4:32 reads, "Forgiving one another, even as God for Christ's sake hath forgiven you." In the case of Peter's statement, the misinterpretation is all the more unwarranted because no reference is made to God's forgiving us. The idea is not that our love to others covers our sins with God, but that our love to others covers their sins with us. And how needful this is in church work! There are so many annoyances, and sometimes the most faithful workers annoy us the most. The stupid blunders they make! And the weak Christian may in his heart begin to question their motives; or he may say he doesn't have to put up with such conditions—he can go somewhere else to church, or not go. But Christian love covers a multitude of sins.

Be hospitable to one another without grumbling. In time of war this is particularly appropriate with respect to refugees; at any time it applies with respect to the poor, the sick, and the aged. Tertullian noted that hospitality is hindered by mixed marriages. When a husband brings someone home to dinner, he ought to have forewarned his wife. Hospitality is a family affair; and if one spouse is not a Christian, there may be grumbling and less hospitality.

Each one has received some gift or talent from God. The gifts are not the same. Accordingly the service is not to be identical. We must minister to others the particular grace we have received. A young man who cannot learn German or Greek is hardly fitted for the mission field where he would have to speak a still more difficult tongue; he had better stay at home and be the Sunday School secretary: It is a useful service. In any case we must be good stewards. We must do the best with what we have. And since there is so much to do, so many tasks, of all sorts and types, it is good that God's grace is manifold, variegated, and many colored.

One of the greatest gifts and greatest responsibilities is that of preaching God's word. Now, if any man speak, let him speak as the oracles of God speak. The minister of the Gospel is to minister the Gospel. He is to preach God's Word—not something else. As a good steward he must dispense the Word, the whole Word, and nothing but the Word. Do sermons today measure up to Peter's standard?

If any one serves, if any one is a deacon, he should serve out of the strength that God supplies. And the purpose of these actions according to these rules is that in all things God may be glorified. No satisfactory reason can be given for glorifying God in some things only. And insofar as we disobey our instructions, we fail to glorify God. But if we are good stewards and faithfully follow these precepts, we shall glorify God in all things through Jesus Christ; and glory and power belong to Christ for ever and ever, Amen.

More Persecution

1 Peter 4:12–19

Beloved, think it not strange concerning the fiery trial which is to try you, as though some strange thing happened unto you:

But rejoice, inasmuch as ye are partakers of Christ's sufferings; that, when his glory shall be revealed, ye may be glad also with exceeding joy.

If ye be reproached for the name of Christ, happy are ye; for the spirit of glory and of God resteth upon you: on their part he is evil spoken of, but on your part he is glorified.

But let none of you suffer as a murderer, or as a thief, or as an evildoer, or a a busybody in other men's matters.

Yet if any man suffer as a Christian, let him not be ashamed; but let him glorify God on this behalf.

For the time is come that judgment must begin at the house of God: and if it first begin at us, what shall the end be of them that obey not the Gospel of God?

And if the righteous scarcely be saved, where shall the ungodly and the sinner appear?

Wherefore let them that suffer according to the will of God commit the keeping of their souls to him in well doing, as unto a faithful Creator.

Peter continues with the theme of persecution and martyrdom. Does it not seem strange that the very people who are bringing the greatest blessings to their fellowmen should be despised, tortured, and put to death? But Peter tells us not to think it so strange after all. Mankind, being depraved by sin and at enmity with God, automatically reacts against the preaching of the Gospel. They naturally oppose and persecute God's messengers.

And aside from this natural reaction of the non-Christian to the Christian, we should not think the tribulation strange because we too are sinners, and God uses the wicked for the good purpose of purging the righteous. The suffering is a fiery trial that will separate the pure metal from the dross.

Accordingly we are to rejoice if we are persecuted for righteousness' sake. Not only did unbelievers so persecute the prophets that were before us, but also these trials and afflictions make us partakers of the sufferings of Christ. And, if God has chosen us to share more fully in the experiences of Christ, even to the extent of death, we ought all the more to rejoice because of his evidenced favor. Let us therefore rejoice now in order that we may rejoice and be glad also when his glory shall be revealed.

If Peter wrote this epistle from the city of Babylon (compare 5:13) and not from Rome, the selection of the image of a fiery trial might have arisen from the memory of the three Hebrew children in Nebuchadnezzar's fiery furnace. To them the glory of the Lord was partially revealed as one walked with them whose form was like the Son of God. What those three saw in such a partial manifestation, we shall see fully when the Lord returns to execute vengeance on his enemies and to establish righteousness on earth.

If anyone suffers reproach for the name of Christ, he is indeed blessed; for such a reproach indicates that the Spirit of glory and of God rests upon him.

However, let us make sure in all our conduct that we never suffer as a murderer, or as a thief, or as an evildoer, or as a meddler. It may sometimes happen that devoted Christians suffer or are reproached not for their faith but for their foolishness. No doubt we are to have a concern for the souls of men, but we are not called upon to meddle in their affairs. The French novelist Balzac wrote an excellent piece,

L'histoire des treize, to show the calamities that can fall on innocent people when a busybody pokes his nose where it does not belong.

But if anyone suffer as a Christian, let him not be ashamed. The term Christian was originally a term of reproach, and it must still have carried that connotation when Peter wrote, especially among the Jews. In this age the term is not so frequently a reproach, but the reality for which the term stands often is. But whatever the sneers of the crowd may be, and especially whatever nastiness Christians must bear in the putrid morality of military life, there is no cause for being ashamed. On the contrary, we are to glorify God by this very name of Christian.

The suffering must be endured, for it is time that judgment should begin at and from the house of God. This Old Testament principle is a principle for all time. Judgment and tribulation begins with the church. Babylonia and Assyria were wicked heathen nations, but their punishment was postponed until the Jews had first been punished. "Wherefore it shall come to pass that when the Lord hath performed his whole work upon mount Zion and on Jerusalem, I will punish the fruit of the stout heart of the King of Assyria and the glory of his high looks" (Isaiah 10:12). So too we all must through much tribulation enter into the Kingdom of God (Acts 14:22).

Peter says it is time for the judgment to begin possibly because he is writing just before the siege and destruction of Jerusalem, where Christians suffered along with the others until their chance of escape came (Luke 21:20–24), and the Jews who had rejected Christ, who cried, "Let his blood be upon us and our children," perished horribly.

The suffering and martyrdom of Christians is terrible, and if God uses such severe methods to purge his saints, what shall the end be of them that obey not the Gospel?

Here again we recur to an earlier emphasis: elect unto obedience. The Gospel is to be obeyed. And to obey is better than sacrifice (1 Samuel 15:22).

The words of these texts are easy to understand; they are not so easy to put into practice. At least they are not easy to practice perfectly. Two tackles went out for football at college. They both admired the coach and both enjoyed the game. They both obeyed a good number of the coach's instructions. In fact, each of them had but one fault. One would not memorize the plays, and the other skipped practice too often. Both made the squad, frequently played in the games; but neither ever made the most of his athletic talents.

Is there not a class of Christians who resemble these students? They are willing to own Christ as Lord, they strenuously insist that only through the shed blood of Christ is salvation possible, and they hope for his return. They even obey fairly well, and are a welcome contrast to the wickedness of the world. Perhaps they are obeying all the precepts of which they are conscious. But perhaps also they are dimly aware of other precepts which they do not care to learn more accurately. They feel that such knowledge would entail an obligation to more obedience.

First Peter, not to mention other books of the Bible, has a wider notion of obedience than the common one. Obedience involves, not merely external conduct, like honesty, veracity, church attendance, and personal work, but it also involves internal, mental, intellectual action. It involves belief. In 1 Peter 2:7–8 the opposite of disobedience is belief, and those who refuse to believe are disobedient. In 4:17 the connection between obedience and accepting the Gospel is again indicated. Compare also 1:22 and 3:1.

Belief and external action are of course closely related. Sincere belief produces action, and actions are an indication of a person's belief.

But a typical Christian in the United States might reply in a hurt voice, "Do I not believe the simple Gospel of Jesus Christ? Does not my action show that I believe the blood atonement?" That is true, and that is commendable, but yet does the Bible teach us to limit our belief to the blood atonement? Are not Christian ministers commanded to "Go . . . and teach all nations, . . . teaching them to observe *all things whatsoever* I have commanded you?" (Matthew 28:19, 20).

How far, then, will the Christian obey the word of God? Will he study the doctrine of the Trinity or dismiss it as hair-splitting theology? Will he profess love to Christ and object to the preaching of the doctrine of election because it is "controversial"? Will he continue to support by money and personal membership an apostate denomination that requires sinful acts as tests of loyalty? Will he support an independent church when Acts 15 teaches that all local congregations should be subject to a general council? Or will he earnestly try to remain in ignorance for fear that that obedience may become too onerous?

And yet the purpose of election is obedience.

Obedience must be rendered to all of God's commands. We are not at liberty to pick and choose. The disobedience of dispensationalists who repudiate Peter's application of the Old Testament to our age has previously been mentioned. Others, apart from a dispensational scheme, mutilate the Scripture in a more haphazard but equally reprehensible way. They wish to soft pedal some of the Bible. Either God did not know his business and revealed some things we are not supposed to understand, or there are some very important people nearby who do not like to hear some particular doctrine. Some ministers therefore pride themselves on avoiding "controversial" topics—as if any part of Christianity were not controversial. But consider the following not altogether fictitious parable of the disobedient missionary.

Of course he did not begin by being disobedient. On the contrary, he was full of zeal for Christ and the Gospel. He took as a personal command to himself the words of Christ, "Go ye into all the world, and preach the Gospel to every creature" (Mark 16:15).

The almost imperceptible beginning of his disobedience came from the very zeal with which he was impelled to obey this command. It was a mere matter of emphasis, of Greek grammar if you please, although (or because?) he knew no Greek at the time. The imperceptible beginning of his disobedience came from his emphasis on the phrase, "Go ye into all the world."

It was when he was in college and the Christian students were discussing the merits of two organizations. One organization made its aim somewhat complicated: It wanted to build up the faith of Christian students, particularly of those in godless institutions; it also wanted to preach the Gospel of Christ's redeeming blood to the non-Christian students; and further it wanted to encourage the Christian students to enter the ministry or to go to the foreign mission field. The other organization had no such complex aim: Its sole purpose was to recruit foreign missionaries.

Because of its singleness of aim, this second organization seemed to him much more zealous than the other. Had not Christ said, "all the world," and obviously that did not mean the home field. Christians who stay at home are cowards. Only foreign missionaries are obedient to the heavenly vision. So he helped to vote the first organization off his campus and to establish the second. It was an almost imperceptible step of zealous disobedience.

The second step in disobedience came from the same cause. Not knowing much Greek, he emphasized the verb, "Go." He failed to notice that the going was incidental and the preaching and teaching were essential. So zealous was he to go, that he began to forget what he was to do as he was going. He had always preferred Mark's form of Christ's command above that of Matthew. Mark emphasized where to go, while Matthew was annoyingly specific as to what to do. Not only did Matthew command teaching and baptism, but he pointedly required Christians to teach all things that Christ commanded.

In Matthew's Gospel Christ had forbidden his disciples to edit the Gospel. They were not to omit any of the doctrines. But the disobedient student had Christian instructors who knew better. From their wider experience they told him that many doctrines were controversial. To preach them in the churches or on the mission field would stir up dissension. It would be the part of wisdom therefore to reduce the Gospel to its barest minimum. Whatever he could get along without, he should omit. Did not Christ's own experience prove it? When Christ tried to preach that men were unable to come to him except the Father enabled them, "many of his disciples went back and walked no more with him" (John 6:66). Certainly a modern missionary should learn from Christ's failure.

A little while later the student went to hear a well advertised missionary speaker. The gentleman, venerable in appearance, had been a missionary for many years; he had preached on five continents. If he had not stayed long in any one place, he had surely gone into all the world. In the face of such wide traveling, the student was impressed. The retired missionary spoke of his loyalty to Christ, and urged the audience to think only of Christ and to forget all theory and theology. It is not theology that saves, it is Christ himself. The student listened with rapture. He was so impressed that he forgot to ask how a missionary could be loyal to Christ and at the same time disregard what Christ said. He never stopped to think of what Christ taught, even of what Christ taught about himself. Person, not creed, rang in his ears. Second person of the Trinity, and one person with two natures, became "mere" theology. And so he resolved to follow the Person, and neglect what the Person taught.

The student graduated in time and went to the mission field. He would not preach perseverance because it was controversial; he omitted total depravity because it was Calvinistic. He found he could get along without the notion of a vicarious sacrifice to satisfy divine justice: how impractical theology is! He had indeed gone to the mission field, but in going he had become a disobedient missionary.

"As ye go, therefore, teach all nations . . . to observe all things whatsoever I have commanded you." The Gospel is the whole Bible. No mutilated Bible, no defective Christianity can replace the original.

Judgment therefore must begin at the house of God; and if a righteous man scarcely escape destruction, what do you suppose will happen to the impious sinner?

This thought should comfort us where we see the wicked exalted on every hand. The proud Assyrian was riding high as he came down like a wolf on the fold. How could God so forget his people? Why does God permit such men as Hitler and Stalin to cause so much misery? Why must Christians suffer? Such questions as these soberly considered ought to be a remedy for the disease of liberalism. Universal salvation would mean that there would be no hell for Hitler. Lenin and Stalin would accompany Peter and Paul at God's right hand. This is not the type of world, this is not the concept of justice, that the Bible presents. The Bible offers no hope to the ungodly and the sinner.

Wherefore let the suffering Christian take comfort. What appear to be the unalleviated evils of the world are according to the will of God. We cannot change the pain into pleasure, we need not pretend that we really enjoy it, but we can and should commit our souls to God, being careful to obey his commands, ever striving to do good and not evil; and in so committing our souls to God, we acknowledge that he is a faithful Creator who has planned the world from beginning to end and will see it through according to his promises.

The preceding material has dealt largely with the Christian's relation to the heathen. What follows will treat of relations among believers.

Church Government

1 Peter 5:1–5

The elders which are among you I exhort, who am also an elder, and a witness of the sufferings of Christ, and also a partaker of the glory that shall be revealed:

Feed the flock of God which is among you, taking the oversight thereof, not by constraint, but willingly; not for filthy lucre, but of a ready mind;

Neither as being lords over God's heritage, but being examples to the flock.

And when the chief Shepherd shall appear, ye shall receive a crown of glory that fadeth not away.

Likewise, ye younger, submit yourselves unto the elder. Yea, all of you be subject one to another, and be clothed with humility: for God resisteth the proud, and giveth grace to the humble.

The reference to elders is a reminder that the New Testament not only teaches the basic elements of salvation by the blood of Christ, but also gives instructions on how to organize a church. Christians are not left to their own inventions on matters of church government. Popular preachers, usually of the dispensational variety, sometimes assert that the Church is an organism, not an organization. This biological analogy is in some respects unfortunate. If by the church is meant the invisible church, the true body of Christ, consisting only of the elect, then the Church is not an organism. It cannot be an organism because it has neither parent organisms nor does it reproduce. All organisms reproduce other individuals of the same species, but the body of the elect is one Church, and it does not reproduce a second and distinct invisible Church. Christ has only one body, only one Bride. If, however, by Church is meant the visible groups who do in a sense reproduce and spread—in that new local congregations are formed—then it is false to deny that it is an organization. It may not be one organization, but at least it consists of several organizations. And the type of organization is prescribed in the New Testament.

From the verse under discussion it is clear that a church obedient to the divine plan has elders. This is the New Testament development of an Old Testament arrangement. Originally the elders were the heads of the twelve tribes. They are mentioned in Exodus 3:16, 18. Later, because of the burdens that had been imposed on Moses, it became necessary to appoint many more (Exodus 18:13–26). In the New Testament (Acts 14:23) the elders were ordained by the apostles, and Paul left Titus in Crete for the purpose of ordaining elders in every city. This does not mean that only ministers are to officiate in the ordination of elders. In the first place, when the church began, only the apostles were commissioned to ordain. In the nature of the case they had to act alone in setting up the first organizations. But it was not their intention to set up what today is called an episcopal government. For, in the second place, Paul reminds Timothy (1 Timothy 4:14) that he was ordained by the presbytery. Hence our rule should be that all elders should be ordained by the presbytery, in the sense that no presbyter, i.e., no class of elders, may be debarred from putting his hands on the head of him that is being ordained.

First Timothy 5:17 implies that there are two classes of elders, since they who especially labor in word and doctrine are to be honored, it follows that there are also others who do not labor in word and doctrine.

Although Peter does not allude to it, yet in order to avoid the misunderstanding that this is the only regulation concerning church organization, it is well to refer to the office of deacon, instituted in Acts 6. And Acts 15 shows that local congregations are to be subject to a general council. Note well that this council was not a mere conference whose decisions might be accepted or rejected as the local churches saw fit. The local churches were under divine obligation to obey, for it says clearly (Acts 15:28) "it seemed good to the Holy Ghost and to us. . . ." Obviously therefore the decisions are not mere resolutions whose fate is left to the discretion of the constituent delegates.

For the sake of a measure of completeness mention might also be made of the judicial function of the church as it was outlined by Christ himself. After private remonstrance with an offending brother, if the offense is not confessed and repented of, the offended party may tell it to the church. Presumably the witnesses of the sin, whom the offended person took with him for the private interview, are to give their testimony to the church. And then the Church may declare the offender a heathen and a publican.

The phrase, Tell it to the church, does not mean, tell it to some indiscriminate group of Christians. The Church is not some chance group of Christians; nor is it a special group selected by the offended party to hear his complaint. Evidently it is a group regularly in existence before the sin was committed. And it is a group with judicial functions because witnesses are required and a decision is given.

If this procedure were not judicial, then any few men selected by a person who fancied himself aggrieved could, on Christ's authority, pronounce a man a heathen. This would be entirely unjust and cannot be what Christ intended. Christ also gives other indications of church organization; so that it is clear that the church is not to be managed as the majority may think expedient, but as Christ has commanded. Christ is the Lord, and he must be obeyed.

The office of elder is a spiritual honor, as well as a responsibility, and Peter was happy to count himself one. He was also a witness of the sufferings of Christ; he could speak as competent witness about things that were not done in a corner. And likewise he would participate in the glory yet to be revealed, by which hope his readers also may be comforted in their tribulations.

Speaking specifically to the elders, Peter tells them to feed the flock of God. The flock requires good pasture, not book reviews on Sunday evening nor pink political propaganda. Sermons, if they are not strong meat, should at least be unadulterated milk. It is not the elder's flock, to be fed as the elder may arbitrarily choose; but it is God's flock, and its care must be according to God's specific directions.

The elders are to shoulder this burden not by constraint. Did the early church have to compel and force men to be elders? Or, is Peter addressing his exhortation to those who, discouraged, wish to quit the ministry? At any rate the elder is to serve willingly, voluntarily—should we say enthusiastically?—according to God's directions.

Apparently even in Peter's day, when the sincerity of professing Christians was tried in the fire of persecution, some elders thought that the office brought easy money. Or possibly Peter, prophesying by the Spirit, saw future ages when ecclesiastical offices would be worth buying and selling. Today ministerial students sometimes choose a seminary on the basis of the prestige and preferment it can bring, rather than on the basis of orthodoxy and scholarship. The worthy motive, however, is eagerness to serve the Lord.

Nor is the minister to look on himself as a boss. His calling is not to order people around. It might be thought that a minister who bossed people would soon become unpopular and would have to leave his congregation. But while that may frequently be the case, there are some domineering personalities who run one-man churches. The Lord's direction is to be not a boss but an example to the flock. No doubt the minister must lead; but he must not drive. Athanasius said, "The life should command, the tongue persuade." Peter was no pope.

And when the chief Shepherd shall appear, the reward will not be money, earthly honor, or ephemeral popularity, but a crown of glory that fadeth not away.

On the other hand, while the elder is not to be a boss, the congregation must submit to his legitimate authority. The session is charged with the spiritual discipline and development of the congregation. It has the authority of reproof, censure, and even of excommunication. Christ has not left his church without a visible government: even though that government is to be carried on in a different spirit from the spirit of those who exercise lordship over the Gentiles.

And for that matter, not only is the congregation to be subject to the elders, but all, elders and laymen alike, are to be subject one to another. Humility and not pride is to characterize the church member. All should serve in submission to God and in deference to one another. And again Peter quotes the Old Testament.

ELECTED TO GLORY

1 Peter 5:6–14

Humble yourselves therefore under the mighty hand of God, that he may exalt you in due time;

Casting all your care upon him; for he careth for you.

Be sober, be vigilant; because your adversary the devil, as a roaring lion, walketh about, seeking whom he may devour:

Whom resist steadfast in the faith, knowing that the same afflictions are accomplished in your brethren that are in the world.

But the God of all grace, who hath called us unto his eternal glory by Christ Jesus, after that ye have suffered a while, make you perfect, stablish, strengthen, settle you.

To him be glory and dominion for ever and ever. Amen.

By Silvanus, a faithful brother unto you, as I suppose, I have written briefly, exhorting, and testifying that this is the true grace of God wherein ye stand.

The church that is at Babylon, elected together with you, saluteth you; and so doth Marcus my son.

Greet ye one another with a kiss of charity. Peace be with you all that are in Christ Jesus. Amen.

Although Biblical editors make a new paragraph begin at verse six, there is no sharp break here at all. The thought flows smoothly on. But as the epistle is coming to a close, Peter adds some particular exhortations in a quicker and more disconnected fashion. However, verse six continues the theme of humility.

The previous verse had begun with the idea of humility among men, and with respect to one another; the reason for this humility within the church organization is the divine principle that God resisteth the proud and will bring down high looks. Therefore we are all to humble ourselves, not so much before one another, but under the mighty hand of God. This is probably an echo of 4:17. God sends tribulation upon his own people. So it was in the days of old. The Assyrians were the rod of God's anger, and he sent them against his own hypocritical nation; but after Assyria had done God's bidding in bringing wrath on Israel, God punished the stout heart of the King of Assyria and the glory of his high looks (Isaiah 10:12).

God's principles do not change, and the lessons of Old Testament times apply forever. Today also God will punish his people for disobedience, and he may use a wicked nation to bring the punishment, Russia perhaps; but when his people turn from their sins and seek his face, God will exalt them in due season.

Now punishment or correction, while in progress, is not pleasant but grievous. However, it works to our own good. In all the tribulation, God cares for his own, and the devout heart can cast its cares upon him.

Lack of anxiety, however, does not mean apathy and indifference. There is no need to become hysterical in the vicissitudes of life, and yet we must watch and be sober. While we pray, "Lead us not into temptation," we must use the powers God has given us to avoid courting temptation. Just because the Spirit of God dwells in us is no reason for ceasing all effort. Rather we are to work out our own salvation in fear and trembling. Of course God works in us both to will and to do; but though God works in us, or rather because God works in us, we must do the willing and we must do the doing.

Lie down on the job, and the lion will soon find us and start devouring. We will meet him even if we do not lie down on the job: no one escapes the struggle with Satan. But though this world with devils filled should threaten to undo us, we will not fear. . . . The prince of darkness grim . . . one little word shall fell him. Our duty is to resist the devil, and we have God's promise: "Resist the devil and he will flee from you" (James 4:7). Satan cannot devour the sober and watchful.

We may be comforted too by the apparently unhappy fact that all other Christians face the same adversary. There hath no temptation taken you but such as is common to man: But God is faithful, who will not suffer you to be tempted above that ye are able, but will with the temptation also make the way to escape, that ye may be able to bear it (1 Corinthians 10:13).

Tribulation is the common lot of Christians, but after we have suffered a while, the God of all grace, of undeserved favor, who apart from any worthiness of ours has called us unto his eternal glory by Christ Jesus, will make us perfect and establish us forever. Here almost at the end of the epistle we have again the note on which the epistle began: God has called us; we are his chosen, his elect. (And even this is not the last reference to election.) There may be many reasons for finding comfort in our adversities, but they are all based ultimately on God's electing grace. The doctrine of election is the doctrine of comfort and hope. The return of Christ is said to be a blessed hope, and so it is. But it is a blessed hope only to the elect. To the non-elect his return is a day of vengeance and wrath, and who may abide the day of his coming, and who shall stand when he appears? He shall sit as a refiner and purifier of silver: and he shall purify the sons of Levi, and purge them as gold and silver; that they may offer unto the Lord an offering in righteousness. We, Christians, are the sons of Levi; we are the children of Abraham; because if we be Christ's, then are we Abraham's seed and heirs according to the promise. These are not matters of physical but of spiritual descent.

In view of God's election by which we have been chosen in Christ before the world began, what is more appropriate than Peter's ascription of praise? To him be glory and dominion for ever and ever, Amen.

Silvanus or Silas possibly wrote at Peter's dictation or more probably carried the letter to its addressees. He was their faithful brother. The message is one of assurance: Peter's readers stand in God's true grace.

Then comes an interesting mention of Babylon: She, that is the church, in Babylon, salutes you. This indicates the place from which

Peter wrote and sent the letter; but there is a question whether Peter was actually in Babylon, the city on the Euphrates, or whether this is an apocalyptic expression for Rome. There can be little doubt that Babylon, the mother of harlots, in the book of Revelation, is Rome, the city that sits on seven hills. Is this Peter's meaning also?

This would of course please the Roman Catholics who wish to have Peter the founder and first bishop of the church in Rome. And there are Protestants who, without assenting to the Roman theory, still believe that Peter wrote the epistle from Rome and was later martyred there.

But there is one strong, almost conclusive reason against this interpretation. Peter's epistle is not an apocalyptic book and does not use apocalyptic language. Peter's style is quite matter of fact, and his metaphors are familiar, non-apocalyptic figures of the Old Testament. To inject a strange note at the end of the epistle, as a part of a plain matter of fact greeting, would be discordant and inexplicable. It would have neither preparation nor sequence. And if John wrote the Revelation after Peter died, or so soon before that Peter had no opportunity to read it, there would be no basis for calling Rome by the mystical name of Babylon.

On the other hand, if Peter was the apostle to the Jews, and if he wrote chiefly with the Jews in mind, then Babylon on the Euphrates is a possible place for the composition of this epistle because there were still large numbers of Jews in Babylon at this time. Peter may have gone there to evangelize them.

However, there is no good reason why Protestants should strain themselves in trying to prove that Peter was never in Rome. Even if he was martyred there, that fact would not substantiate the Romanist claim that Peter was for twenty-five years the first pope and bishop of Rome. It is not necessary to depend on tradition or archaeology to dispose of such a claim. The New Testament itself contains the evidence. From its infallible pages we can construct enough of Peter's travels to know that he did not spend twenty-five years in Rome. After his first labors in Jerusalem, he was imprisoned in A.D. 46 in Jerusalem. In A.D. 52 he was attending the Jerusalem Council. The next year he was with Paul in Antioch. About the year 58 Paul sent greetings to twenty-seven persons in Rome, but Peter is not mentioned. In A.D. 61 Paul arrived in Rome as a prisoner, and some Christians came to meet him, but not Peter. The next year Paul wrote to the Ephesians, the Philippians, the Colossians, and to Philemon; other Christians are associated with him, but not Peter. In A.D. 64 all men forsook Paul (2 Timothy 4:16); did this mean Peter also, or was not Peter there? Paul indicates (2 Timothy 4:11) that only Luke was with him. This period covers the last twenty years of Peter's life, and it all points to the falsity of the papal claims.

Only a few more words of the epistle remain. And here in the next to the last verse is the echo of the theme that was begun in the first verse: election. The church in Babylon was chosen or elected together with you. The blessed doctrine of God's sovereign, electing grace; alas, how this essential note is missing from the disobedient preaching of the twentieth century!

Missing or caricatured—which is worse? A certain school prided itself on its faithfulness and evangelistic zeal. Its students gave out great numbers of tracts. One day I took a tract from the tract rack. It dealt with election. Its heading of bold type was **ELECTION,** and the sheet was printed in the form of a ballot. Three persons were to vote in this election, and two had already put their marks in their chosen squares. The devil was one of the two, and he had voted against me. God was the other one and had voted for me. God and the devil had tied. Their equal votes had nullified each other, and I was to vote and break the tie. I was to elect myself to salvation. Thus God and the devil were made equal, and I was the equal of both. Man, God, and Satan on a level. Democratic perhaps, but not at all Christian.

It is God alone who elects, not you or I; and, praise the Lord, not the devil. And the God who has chosen us will keep us by his almighty power.

Here in the doctrine of election, the church at Babylon, the elect of the dispersion, Peter and his son Mark, and you and I can find assurance of salvation.

Greet one another with a kiss of charity. Peace be with you all that are in Christ Jesus. Amen.

SECOND PETER

Preface

The second epistle of Peter, like the first, has a message for the present age. In fact, it is more obviously pertinent to our present age than it has been to some of the centuries intervening since its original date of publication.

For example, Peter found it necessary to emphasize knowledge. Today also this emphasis is needed. The New Testament is regarded as mythology, whose language cannot be taken literally, and which therefore must be reinterpreted to agree with the anti-intellectualism of French existentialism. Now, the Middle Ages also had some anti-intellectualism. The influence of Dionysius the Areopagite, who preserved all the bad and discarded all the good of Neoplatonism, contaminated many minds, not only Eriugena, but even Aquinas. Yet the mention of Aquinas and especially the work of Anselm show that the Middle Ages were not anti-intellectualistic. Anti-intellectualism is a very contemporary disease. And Peter both begins and ends his epistle with an emphasis on knowledge.

In the second place Peter describes the baneful results of heretical teachers. Denial of the truth produces immoral conduct. Again this is a contemporary evil. Back in the twenties, when Harry Emerson Fosdick was preaching on the *Peril of Worshipping Jesus,* the liberals could claim that by shucking off the historical husks of Christianity, they were preserving its essential moral values. Today they have shucked off the moral principles as well, as is clear in Joseph Fletcher's recommendation to break every one of the Ten Commandments. One should read and ponder what Peter says about false teachers.

Then again, naturalism or humanism, historicism, and positivism reject every eschatological interpretation of history. Providence, a divine purpose, foreordination, a final righteous judgment are anathema to them. This twentieth century orientation plagued Peter's churches too. According to some modern scientists the sun will die and only a lifeless universe will remain. According to others the sun will explode and we shall all meet fiery destruction. Peter indeed predicts fiery destruction, but unlike modern scientism Peter is depicting a righteous judgment in which some only will be destroyed by the fire, while God's elect will find an abundant entrance into the heavenly kingdom.

But was it Peter who wrote all this? Maybe this letter was written by an impostor. Does anyone know the date of its publication? Peter, you know, died about A.D. 64. Was the epistle written after A.D. 125? A preface must say something about these questions.

Although this small epistle of only three chapters has not stimulated the writing of so many commentaries as the majestic and profound epistle to the Romans, the questions of authorship and date, which occasion so little trouble in the case of Romans, have been canvassed at great length.

The greatest work on 2 Peter is Joseph B. Mayor's *The Epistle of St. Jude and the Second Epistle of St. Peter* (London, 1907). This volume of ccii plus 239 pages is an incomparable triumph of detailed scholarship. In it linguistic usage is set forth by parallels from all Greek literature. It seems as if every word in the epistle is traced from Homer to the Hellenists. I want to make clear my admiration of Mayor's labors, particularly because I shall disagree radically with his main conclusions. His massing of detail is incredible, but I shall try to show that the arguments he constructs with it are fallacious.

In 1960 E. M. B. Green delivered and published a lecture entitled *Second Peter Reconsidered* (Tyndale Press). As the title indicates, it combats the prevailing liberal view that 2 Peter is spurious. An admirable exposition of original scholarship, although short, it is indispensable for serious study of this epistle.

Donald Guthrie has a *New Testament Introduction* (InterVarsity Press, 1962), in which one chapter surveys the problem of authorship. Fairly comprehensive, it is useful for elementary study.

Feine and Behm in their *Introduction to the New Testament* (Abingdon Press, 1965), who also declare that Jude is spurious, repeat parrot-like the usual liberal objections. They pay no attention whatever to conservative scholarship. The present small volume, no great triumph of scholarship, meets nearly every one of their assertions.

Of course there are also commentaries that include critical material; for example, Bigg in the *International Critical Commentary* and Strachan in *The Expositor's Greek Testament.*

The present commentary aims to stress Peter's message. Yet the critical questions concerning authorship cannot be ignored, for if the message is not apostolic and authoritative, it cannot be of much importance. Some of these matters are best discussed in the exposition of the verses where the difficulty arises. But a Preface can well contain other more external points. To give some idea of the controversy to non-scholars, I shall here repeat a few items from Green's lecture.

Second Peter is the most meagerly attested book in the New Testament, but it is incomparably better attested than any of the non-canonical books. Origen (c. 225) accepts it by name and quotes it six times, though he admits that some doubt it. Eusebius (c. 315) classes 2 Peter with James, Jude, 2, 3 John as *antilegomenon, gnōrimon d' homos tois pollois:* "spoken against, nevertheless well-known by the majority." Other books, such as the *Gospel of Peter,* are non-canonical, *notha.*

Second Peter was accepted by Cyril of Jerusalem, Gregory Nazianzus, and Athanasius, as well as by the councils that rejected the epistles of Barnabas and Clement of Rome.

These Councils are one evidence, and there are other evidences, that the early Christians, far from being unconcerned about forgeries, as the present day liberals so uniformly describe them, did not unthinkingly accept false writings. The sub-apostolics distinguished themselves and even Apollos from the Apostles. They deposed the author of *Paul and Thekla* for his imposture. Serapion banned the *Gospel of Peter* from his church on the particular ground that it was a forgery: he had taken pains to trace its history.

Eusebius and Photius say that Clement of Alexandria (c. 185) wrote a commentary on 2 Peter. Clement could hardly have been duped by a recent fraud. Other external evidence will be mentioned at the appropriate verses.

Mayor admits that "if we had nothing else to go upon in deciding the question of the authenticity of II Peter except external evidence, we should be inclined to think that we had in these quotations [including many not given by Green] ground for considering that Eusebius was justified in his statement that our epistle *pollois chrēsimos* . . . " seemed useful to many and was seriously studied with the other Scriptures (Mayor, p. cxxiv; Eusebius III, iii). For his liberal conclusions Mayor does not depend on independent, external evidence, but on the message itself and its relation to Jude. Therefore an intelligent Christian, even though he knows no Greek, is not so largely at the mercy of a professional scholar as he would otherwise be. A knowledge of Greek is of course indispensable to the scholar, and the external evidence is in other cases set forth at great length in the standard *Introductions*. But if all or almost all the evidence is found in four short chapters (three in 2 Peter and one for Jude), an intelligent Christian with a little time and attention can come to a well-founded conclusion.

In my opinion such time and attention is well spent, both for the preliminary but essential decision on authorship, and also, and more so, for an understanding or knowledge of the apostolic message.

Since commentaries search for the exact meaning of every phrase and word, the reader runs the risk of missing the main message by attending to the details. The details, of course, are necessary. Unless someone has already investigated the minutiae, there could be no assurance that an outline or summary is accurate. There must be trees to make a forest and leaves to make a tree. At the same time, if the reader does not want to be so thorough, if he merely wants some help in teaching Sunday School, or if, one step further on, he has just decided to study the Bible a little more carefully than those who skim over the surface, some provision should be made to prevent him from losing his way in the morass of profundity. Therefore an outline and summary make a proper beginning for a commentary.

Even so, the inexperienced student should be encouraged to see, not a morass of profundity, but a mine whose depths, if at first dark, yield great wealth to patient methods of extraction.

Outline

I. The Address, 1:1–2.
II. Knowledge Confirms Election, 1:3–11.
III. This Knowledge Is Revealed by God, 1:12–21.
IV. God Punishes Those Who Teach False Doctrine and Lead Evil Lives, 2:1–22.
V. The Lord's Return Will Bring both Punishment and Heaven, 3:1–18.

This outline will be expanded into short summaries at the beginning of each section.

Chapter One

Summary of 1:1–2: Simeon Peter, writing to those whom God has blessed with faith, wishes them grace, peace, and knowledge.

1:1 Simeon Peter, a slave and apostle of Jesus Christ . . .

As was customary with ancient authors, this epistle begins with the writer's signature: Simon, or Simeon, Peter. He describes himself as a slave of Jesus Christ, but a slave whom Christ had sent on a mission. He was an apostle. Although the first epistle, addressed to Jewish Christians, does not have the name *Simeon,* yet if the second epistle is also addressed to Jews, the *Simeon* would not be out of place.

Those who deny that 2 Peter is genuine face a difficulty here. If a later writer wished to imitate Peter, he would have been more likely to use the form of signature in the first epistle than to adopt one that Peter himself had not used. Only Peter himself would be completely free to sign as he wished. It is surely wrong-headed to say, "It is evident that the whole title given to St. Peter is carefully chosen by a process of reflection. There is therefore a presumption that another mind is at work here" (*The Expositor's Greek Testament,* Vol. V, p. 98). The presumption is quite the reverse.

The same expositor objects to Westcott, who said, "The Second Epistle of St. Peter is either an authentic work of the Apostle, or a forgery." The commentator does not like this introduction of a moral judgment on a forger. He says "It is in effect an attempt to browbeat the judgment into the acceptance of such books as genuine. . . ." Such a reaction simply shows the force of the evidence on the mind of one who insists on finding the epistle spurious. Reflection will show no despicable attempt to browbeat anyone. Why should a modern liberal, who wants to reject the epistle, think it necessary to defend the morality of the unknown second century impostor?

Perhaps there is a hidden reason; and it may be connected with the Roman Catholic view of the church and the Scripture. On the next page the expositor continued, "The standard of genuineness applied to the early Christian writings and especially in the formation of the Canon was their conformity to the teaching of the Church" [and not their apostolic authority]. This argument is essentially the Romish view that places the church above the Scripture: The church decides what right doctrine is and then canonizes books that agree. On the contrary, the doctrine of the church and the faithfulness of the church are decided by comparing it with the apostolic writings. The second century congregations determined what was and what was not canonical by investigating the authorship. What an apostle wrote (Romans, Galatians) or what he approved of and imposed (Mark, Luke, Hebrews) was for this reason canonical. The congregations after long and careful investigation decided that 2 Peter was genuine. They decided that it was not a forgery. But as Westcott says, it must be one or the other, "for in this case there can be no mean." So much for the signature at the beginning.

Besides the wish to defend the morality of an impostor and the desire to exalt the church above God's word, there is another twist to the liberal mind. Why should a scholar with such views write a commentary at all? There are ten spurious Platonic dialogues. No one pays them more than a passing glance. Similarly, if 2 Peter is a forgery, why bother with it? There is some scholarly point in studying the pseudo-Dionysius. One can respect Koch and Stiglmeier in their attempt to show that Paul's immediate convert in Athens was not the author of the *Divine Names*. But 2 Peter, if not genuine, is of less importance than Dionysius. Nevertheless one could admire a book of half the size in its attempt to show that 2 Peter is a later production. Such a book has been written, and some note will be taken of it. As a book for scholars who read Koch and Stiglmeier, J. B. Mayor's volume, more than half the size, also has its place. But devotional commentaries? Why write commentaries on three little chapters from the late second century? But if these three chapters are the Word of God, as the signature implies, then we are interested in every word.

1:1b to those who have obtained a faith equally honorable with ours

This address follows immediately upon the signature. Peter sends the letter to those who have faith, a faith of equal privilege and rank. This idea calls for some exegesis.

The connotations of the adjective *equally-honorable* (one word, *isotimon*) center around nobility. With the following participle, *obtained by lot,* or, better, *assigned to a post,* Peter describes a king conferring privilege on one of his choice. Accordingly Peter is addressing his fellow nobles. The contrast between nobility and slavery is striking and can hardly have been unintentional.

These people are noble because they have obtained the rank by lot, or, better, by allotment. The verb *lagchano* is sometimes contrasted with *exaireisthai, to choose* (compare *Odyssey* XIV, 233; *Iliad,* IX, 367). The idea of a man choosing something is different from the idea of a man receiving something by lot. Here his choice plays no role. The verb occurs in Luke 1:9, John 19:24, and Acts 1:26. In all of these instances, and there are no others in the New Testament, drawing lots is the paramount idea. The verb, however, does not necessarily emphasize, either in classical Greek or in Peter, casting lots; it can mean merely *obtain as one's portion.* Classical Greek uses it for the result of a deity apportioning goods (or evils) to a man and protecting him. The verb also refers to a military post being assigned to someone. The idea that Peter's addressees obtained their faith by drawing lots hardly fits New Testament theology; but the notion that God, prior to human choice, assigns faith to certain individuals cannot be deleted from the verb and is besides consistent with Ephesians 2:8.

Even if the word *faith* is objective rather than subjective—the doctrines believed rather than the psychological act of believing—this reference to God's election is not weakened. God decides which people to whom he will entrust his doctrine. In fact, the objective sense fits the text better. It is indisputable that the objective faith has equal honor, no matter to whom given. It is not so evident that all acts of believing are equally noble. In some sense they may be, but the objective meaning spares us the trouble of discovering what sense.

One commentator's remark that this line indicates that Peter was writing to Gentiles, rather than to Jews as he did in his first epistle, has no good support.

The New English Bible translates verse one as, "From Simeon Peter, servant and apostle of Jesus Christ, to those who through the justice of our God and Saviour Jesus Christ share our faith and enjoy equal privilege with ourselves."

This translation hardly gives the sense of the passage. In the first place, the verb share is ambiguous. Two students can share the same dormitory room: they use or have it in common. In this sense faith may be shared: two persons may have the same faith or doctrines in common. But in some evangelistically minded groups today, people speak of sharing their faith as they would share an apple pie: they pretend to give someone else a share of their faith. Objectively or subjectively this is completely unscriptural, for only God can give a man faith.

In the second place the Greek verb simply does not mean *share*. The New English Bible eliminates the notion in the text that faith is graciously assigned by God. Some commentaries also submerge the idea of God's dispensing faith to those whom he chooses. For example, R. H. Strachan in *The Expositor's Greek Testament* makes no reference to the word in the text. It is as if Peter never wrote *lachousin*. The poor translation continues, for, in the third place, the New English Bible seems to misconstrue the remark about the righteousness or justice of God. It makes Peter say that God's justice is the cause of people's having faith. Joseph B. Mayor, *The Epistle of St. Jude and the Second Epistle of St. Peter* (p. 181) says, "Choice does not mean favoritism. Israel was chosen to be a blessing to others, and at the same time to suffer more than any other people. God wills that all should be saved and come to a knowledge of the truth. This impartiality marked the determinate counsel of the Father no less than the redemptive work of the Son. Salvation is for all, not as the degenerate Jews supposed, a peculiar privilege for a peculiar people."

In this quotation, which can be taken anachronistically as a defense of the New English Bible's substitution of justice for grace, Mayor makes several mistakes: (1) a universalistic use of 1 Timothy 2:4; (2) the matter of favoritism versus impartiality; and (3) his reference to degenerate Jews. Naturally they all bear on the same basic problem.

The first point, so far as it narrowly concerns 1 Timothy 2:4, may be dismissed by noting that Mayor's interpretation makes it contradict many other New Testament passages. All the more may this Pauline verse be omitted because a similar idea comes in 2 Peter 3:9, and this verse will be discussed in full at the proper place.

Second, choice or love is certainly favoritism, at least if we exclude the pejorative connotations introduced for effect. The term impartiality does not translate *no respecter of persons*. To respect the person of X means to favor X above Y because of X's agreeable qualities. But God did not choose the Israelites because of their merit, person, or station. He clearly favored them, however, above the surrounding nations, and hence was not impartial.

Third, Mayor cannot validly support his universalistic denial of grace by a contemptuous reference to degenerate Jews; for Peter himself, not a forger, but Peter himself in his first epistle, calls the elect a peculiar people (2:9). Commentators who so fully reject the Christian view just naturally misconstrue verses that bear on election, limited atonement, and irresistible grace.

Quite the reverse of Mayor, the New Testament teaches that though God's justice might be the cause of people being condemned for their sins, their faith is due to his mercy. For these reasons the New English Bible translation should be rejected.

1:1c by the righteousness of our God and Savior, Jesus Christ;

What now about righteousness? Does the verse say that believers have been allotted faith by God's righteousness? Or have they been allotted a faith in God's righteousness? One must note that the order of words in the Greek text conjoins faith in righteousness, and does not separate these words as is done in English translations.

The righteousness mentioned is God's, not ours. For this textual reason, as well as for all New Testament theology, Peter does not mean that we earn faith by our works or righteousness. But how is God's righteousness to be fitted into the context? The answer is so easy that the New English Bible appears to have taken quite some trouble to misunderstand it. True, the Greek preposition *en* sometimes means *by;* but more frequently it just means *in*. Thus those to whom faith was given received a faith in God's righteousness. That is, righteousness is the object of belief. The Christian believes in God's justice.

There is no grammatical difficulty here. In the New Testament the object of faith is frequently enough indicated by the preposition *in* with the dative. For example, in John 3:15 the object of faith (in some manuscripts) is *him:* "everyone who believes in *him.*" Paul, also, in Galatians 3:26 speaks of faith in Jesus Christ (*in* with the dative). Other usages are more numerous than *in* with the dative; but this is a grammatically correct possibility for the verse in question: Peter and others have been assigned a faith in God's righteousness. Thus faith as in Paul would be the means of connecting a man with Christ's righteousness.

One needs to note that it is Christ's righteousness. The verse is completed by the words, "faith in the righteousness of our God and savior Jesus Christ." God's righteousness is Christ's righteousness because Christ is God. To avoid this, the American Revised Version inserts an article for which there is no manuscript evidence and makes it read, "of our God and the savior Jesus Christ." This obscures the ascription of deity to Jesus. The text itself is unmistakable. It says quite plainly "faith in righteousness of our God and savior Jesus Christ." For once the Revised Standard Version is better. Admittedly the American Revised Version puts the correct translation in a footnote; and the Revised Standard Version puts the incorrect translation in a footnote. But there was no manuscript reason in either case to include an incorrect form. As Charles Bigg says, "it is hardly open for anyone to translate in I Peter 1:3 *ho theos kai Pater* by 'the God and Father,' and yet here to decline to translate *ho theos kai Soter* by 'the God and Savior.'"

One of the liberal arguments used to deny the authenticity of the epistle is based on the assertion that 2 Peter has a lower view of Christ than has 1 Peter. But no higher view than this verse could be imagined. Other references to "our Lord and Savior Jesus Christ" do not diminish the deity asserted here in 1:1.

1:2 Grace to you and peace be multiplied by knowledge of God and Jesus our Lord.

Again, as was customary in ancient epistles, there comes, after the signature and address, a line of greeting. As the objective sense of faith was the better interpretation above, so here the meaning is objective peace. A subjective feeling that God's in his heaven, all's right with the world, may very well be mistaken. Even a well founded realization that God is no longer our enemy is a meaning that weakens Peter's blessing. The peace intended is not a subjective feeling of comfort, but the actual cessation of hostility: God is no longer our enemy, the war is over, and Peter prays that this peace be extended and that God's grace convey many additional blessings.

Yet one may ask, Does not this thought, that peace be multiplied, show that subjective peace was intended? The war is over, no doubt, and peace has been declared; but for this very reason objective peace cannot be multiplied. Our subjective assurance, our feelings, our emotions can be intensified, but the fact of peace cannot itself be increased or diminished.

This line of reasoning, however, is not sound. It is sound enough, of course, in saying that emotions vary in intensity; but it does not follow that the objective conditions of peace cannot be multiplied. After the war ceases, there comes the work of repairing the devastations. This repair may cause happy emotions, but the repair itself is not a mere emotion: the roads are paved, the food supply is ensured, credit is made available. Thus peace is implemented, extended, or multiplied.

Knowledge stands more in need of explanation. How can these blessings be increased in or by knowledge? Since the word is repeated in 1:3, we may suppose that Peter intended at least some emphasis on knowledge. At the present time a large section of popular Christianity, including both the Arminian fundamentalists and the dialectical liberals, disparages knowledge. They raise a hue and cry against intellectualism and rationalism. No such disparagement is found in Peter. On the contrary, Peter lays stress on knowledge. The more we read the Bible, the more we study theology, "God-ology," the more learned we become—the more of these, the more grace and peace we obtain.

The last words of the salutation are, "of the God and of Jesus the Lord of us." Comparing these words with the previous mention of Jesus Christ, we see here that there is indeed an extra article. The order of words does not necessarily separate *God* from *Jesus the Lord of us;* but neither does it so closely identify them as in the previous line. Peter says it both ways. But it is not good exegesis to minimize, even mistranslate the first form just because he alters it a little a few words later.

This ends the introduction proper: the signature, address, and blessing or salutations. To sum up: the apostle Peter desires an increase in divine knowledge for those to whom God has sovereignly allotted faith in the righteousness of Christ, himself God, that they may receive many additional blessings of grace and peace.

Summary, 1:3–11. Since God who called us has granted us, by means of knowledge, everything that pertains to godliness, we must put forth effort to grow in virtue. Thus we make our election sure and gain entrance into Christ's eternal kingdom.

1:3 in proportion as his divine power has granted us, by the knowledge of him who called us by his own glory and virtue, all things that tend to life and piety . . .

Chapter 1:3 begins a new section, the main body of the letter. But there is no break. Not only does the idea of knowledge continue, but grammatically verses one to four are one sentence, with *hōs* introducing a dependent clause. At least one commentator outlines the epistle so as to make verses two to four *Salutation*. However, the epistolary and conventional address and salutation are logically completed with verse two, for which reason translators often punctuate with a period at this point.

Since the sentence structure is a little complicated, it may be well to show first how 1:3 continues 1:2. "Grace and peace be multiplied to you by knowledge of God and Jesus our Lord, in proportion as his divine power has granted us, by the knowledge of him who called us by his own glory and virtue, all things that tend to life and piety. . . ." With a concluding purpose to make the sentence more cumbersome, no wonder translators split it in two and begin a new sentence with 1:3.

The main part of the letter, then, begins with an emphasis on knowledge. It is by means of knowledge—of course not by knowledge of arithmetic or botany, but by knowledge of the electing or calling God, i.e., a knowledge of theology—that his divine power gives us all things that contribute to life and piety. Note the "all things." No edification, no growth in grace, no advance in piety is possible except by knowledge. Those who wish to preserve and propagate Biblical religion should put more stress on learning. Some zealous groups who claim to be evangelistic offer an emotional experience with little or no evangel. They may read a few verses of the Bible for heart throbs, but certainly not for theology. They should read, and try to understand, 2 Peter 1:2 and 3. As John Trapp wrote in his *Commentary on the New Testament,* "There is not a new notion or a further enlargement of saving knowledge, but it brings some grace and peace with it. All the grace that a man hath, it passeth through the understanding; and the difference of stature in Christianity grows from different degrees of knowledge."

R. H. Strachan *(The Expositor's Greek Testament),* on the word *knowledge,* contrasts *gnōsis* with *epignōsis,* the latter being the word in our text. The former, says Strachan, without the prefixed preposition, designates the imperfect knowledge of the heathen, as in Romans 1:21; while the latter is "the Christian or perfect knowledge of God. . . . *Compare* I Cor 13:12, Col. 1:9, *epignōsis,* involving the complete appropriation of all truth and the unreserved acquiescence in God's will. . . . *Epignōsis* implies a more intimate and personal relationship than *gnōsis.*" Strachan continues by noting that *gnōsis* was associated with Gnosticism, for which reason our text (which he believes Peter did not write) uses *epignōsis.*

There may be a grain of truth in this—the prefix ought etymologically to make some change in the connotation—but Kittel's great *Wörterbuch* hardly emphasizes it. Mayor (pp. 171–174) gives many lexicographical details and comes hesitatingly to a doubtful conclusion. But etymology does not determine the usage of a given author. Rather it is the context and usage that determine the shade of meaning of either of these two words for knowledge. Possibly the prepositional prefix many originally have had some intensive force, but both in Classical Greek and in Koine, it is a common word for ordinary knowledge. Note that in this very chapter the *epignōsis* of 1:2 is designated as *gnōsis* in 1:5, 6. Compare the verbal forms of *epignōsis* in 2:20–21, where the second and third instances hardly designate complete knowledge and unreserved acquiescence in God's will. Finally, the last verse of the epistle uses *gnōsis* in the phrase, "Grow in the knowledge of our Lord and Savior Jesus Christ." A knowledge of Greek is indispensable for an exact understanding of God's Word, but some people quote Greek and then let their imaginations run wild. This is particularly the case with those who cry "Gnosticism!" at every mention of knowledge and repeat, "Not knowledge, but faith."

It is true that Gnosticism in all its heresy or paganism advocated salvation by knowledge. But the knowledge they meant was a cosmological fantasy. The fact that this knowledge does not save is far from implying that some other knowledge cannot. One might as well say that since a knowledge of arithmetic does not cure measles, medical knowledge is of no use.

The next idea in 1:3 comes in the words "his divine power . . . having given . . . by his own glory and virtue." One should note that the *his* in "his divine power" refers to our Lord Jesus. There is no reference to God the Father. Not that Peter is ignorant of the distinction, for it is plain enough in 1:17. But here in the opening verses Peter has fixed his attention on Christ. The grammar supporting this is the singular *his,* and the later word *idia.* Presumably the singular could refer to "God and our Lord Jesus," as these two are mentioned in verse two; but why place an unnecessary strain on a simple and normal construction? It is Christ's divine power that has granted us these things. This is mentioned to add shame to those who would try to remove the deity of Christ from verse one. It is also mentioned to make clear that election and allotting faith is not the work of the Father alone, as if excluding Christ. No doubt the Father gives faith (Matthew 11:25), as he also creates (Acts 17:24); but these are equally and simultaneously actions of the Son as well.

The verb *give, grant,* or *endow* (not the common word for *give,* but one with more stress on the idea of *free gift, gratis, without payment*), especially in a context following *lachousin* of verse one, signifies the liberality and good will of a great monarch who allots his gifts to those whom he selects. Yet the verse does not seem to mean that this sovereign makes these grants *by his knowledge.* The knowledge of verse two identifies the knowledge of verse three as our knowledge. God grants us the means to life and piety by increasing *our* knowledge. For that matter, even without returning to verse two, the phrase, "knowledge of him that called us," would be a most awkward way of referring to God's knowledge of himself. Rather, Christ grants us his gifts *by his own glory and might*. The word *aretē* means *strength* or *excellence*. With this understanding the phrase "him that called us" fits in smoothly. Christ's election and call is an exercise of omnipotent sovereignty. First Peter contains many references to the doctrine of election. The word *election* does not occur in this verse, but the idea of calling reflects the same idea of sovereign choice. For that matter, in verse ten election is associated with calling.

The King James Version can hardly be right when it says that Christ called us to glory and virtue. The manuscript evidence is conclusive in support of *his own;* and it makes no sense to say that Christ called us to *his own* glory and virtue. Even the poorer reading that changes the word *his own (idia)* to *through (dia)* does not mean *to*. It weakens the idea that this glory is Christ's—whose else could it be?—but preserves the thought that God calls us by means of glory and might. This ties in with a supernatural call.

Charles Bigg admits that "All commentators appear to couple *idia doxē kai aretē* with *tou kalesantos,* yet this construction seems extremely difficult. The moving cause of the call is not glory, but mercy." The grammatical construction, however, is entirely normal; and Bigg admits that all commentators are against him. The grammar troubles Bigg because it makes Peter teach a theology Bigg does not like. He writes, "The moving cause of the call is not glory, but mercy." Now, it is true that divine election is an act of mercy. Life and faith and godliness are allotted gratuitously. Salvation is a free gift. Has not Peter already said so? But this does not prevent God from always acting for his own glory. Here Peter sees more clearly than Bigg. Power and might are indispensable for a call that effectively raises a dead sinner to newness of life. Mercy without might is powerless.

1:4 Through which [the which is plural, and most easily refers to *glory* and *might*] **the noble and greatest promises have been granted to us, in order that through these** [either the promises, or even the glory and might] **you might become partakers of a divine nature, by having fled from the corruption that is in the world by reason of lust.**

The New English Bible has a poor translation, and one that contradicts everything in the Bible, when it says, "come to share in the very being of God." The New English Bible has inserted two words that are not in the Greek text: *the* and *God*. A more accurate translation is: "that you may become partakers of a god-like nature." It is amazing enough that a sinful man in some sense can become god-like; but that a created being, even if not defiled by sin, could share in the very being of God the creator, is a metaphysical impossibility. Salvation is not deification—that would be Gnosticism indeed. For Christianity man always remains a temporal being. He is never eternal. Since man has already been created, has already had a first moment, it is too late for him to become eternal. Salvation is a moral rejuvenation.

The idea of sharing in the divine nature can sound like Stoic pantheism or the queer religion of Gnosticism. By so interpreting the verse a liberal commentator can conclude that Peter was not the author and that the letter was written about A.D. 150 because of conditions then obtaining. But this epistle is neither Stoic nor Gnostic. These verses all teach that we become partakers of the divine nature through grace, through the promises, through a sovereign grant to those called. In Stoicism every man by nature has a spark of divinity. It is not a matter of special calling, but of natural law. In fact, an author of A.D. 150 who wanted to appear apostolic and orthodox would probably have avoided such a phrase because of conditions then obtaining. Now, the author of this epistle uses several words current among educated men; these words were familiar in the first century; the author shows less acquaintance with Hellenistic thought than Paul and Luke do; he is not a philosopher; he does not refer to Gnosticism; and as will be shown later, the destruction of the world by fire as described in chapter three is completely non-Stoic. There is nothing here that the apostle Peter could not have written.

Peter in his next phrase makes perfectly clear what he means. We *thus,* not in some other way, but through God's glory and promises, obtain a divine nature, to wit, "by having fled from the corruption that is in the world by reason of lust." Peter's addressees have made good progress in sanctification. The next few verses urge them to further progress. This sanctification anticipates our final complete freedom from sin in heaven. Thus, and not in some other way, we become partakers of a divine nature; we become god-like, or, godly.

1:5, 6, 7 For this very reason and by exercising all zeal furnish excellence by your faith, and knowledge by your excellence,

and self-control by your knowledge, and patience by your self-control, and piety by your patience, and brotherly-love by your piety, and love by your brotherly-love.

"For this very reason," that is, in order to become godly, follow the several instructions in verses five, six, and seven. Grammatically *this very reason* could be *because you have fled corruption.* Peter would then be saying, Strive for patience and self-control *because* you have fled corruption. But this does not make very good sense. It is clearer to say, Having done so well in fleeing from what is evil, now do these further things in order to become positively godly.

Christians should introduce (the verb sometimes means *smuggle in*) into their lives all zeal or earnestness, and supply, even supply lavishly, something with something. These somethings need a little explanation.

The King James Version takes the easy way out. Translating the verb *supply* as *add,* it reduces the following verses to a mere list of items that should be added one after another in order to increase in godliness. There is indeed a sort of list. In this sense 1:5 expands the thought of 1:3. Chapter 1:3 simply spoke of "all things" that increase life and piety. Verse two had specified grace, peace, and knowledge. Now verses four to seven add promises, self-control, patience, and love. The enumeration need not be taken as complete.

However, there are difficulties. For one thing self-control and patience seem to be synonyms; and if so, one wonders why both are mentioned. Similarly brotherly kindness and love do not appear to be very different. For another thing, piety *(eusebeian)* is so all inclusive that either it should be omitted or placed at one end. All this makes it difficult to explain the order in which the items are mentioned.

But first, what about the King James idea of simple addition? Does it do justice to the language and the thought? One point is that the verb *supply* with the preposition *in* or *by* is not exactly identical with *add to.* Ordinarily it means supply something (in the accusative) to something (in the dative without a preposition). Thus 2 Corinthians 9:10 says, "He who furnishes seed to the sower." The verse continues, "and supplies bread (accusative) *toward, for the purpose of,* eating" (also accusative). Here there is no preposition *in* or *by*. Galatians 3:5 speaks of him "who supplies the Spirit to you" (dative without a preposition). But Peter with the preposition seems to say, "Furnish your virtue (excellence) by means of faith and your knowledge by means of your excellence," etc.

But if this interpretation takes us beyond the idea of mere addition to a teleological sense of supply, it still must face the other difficulties previously listed. If one supplies virtue or excellence to faith and then knowledge to virtue, as one supplies seed to the sower for a purpose, the process of edification would begin with faith, proceed to virtue, and then to knowledge. But 1:3 said that God supplies everything else by means of knowledge, so that knowledge should be first in the list.

There is also another difficulty. The text does not make it clear how one of these items is the means to the next. That faith produces virtue may not be too hard to understand; but how is virtue the means to knowledge? There is a traditional phrase, "truth is in order to goodness"; but this verse seems to say goodness is in order to truth. Or, again, although it surprises no one to read that knowledge produces self-control, how can self-control cause patience when patience seems necessary to self-control? The relation between piety and brotherly love also is unclear, and the separate enumeration of brotherly love and love (even if the first is *philia* and the second *agapē*) is puzzling.

Yet there seems to be some sort of progression because faith comes first and love last. That is, faith is the foundation of, or issues in, seven virtues. Perhaps Peter did not intend to assert that the relation of each higher virtue to its preceding virtue is always the same relation. If the motivation is unclear, one can only note that other lists given in the New Testament are equally unclear in the principle of their progression. No wonder then that the King James simply said, "Add."

1:8 for if you have these virtues and they abound, they will not make you lazy and unfruitful with respect to the knowledge of our Lord Jesus Christ.

The conclusion in 1:8, however, is perfectly clear: "for if you have these virtues and they abound, they will not make you lazy and unfruitful with respect to the knowledge of our Lord Jesus Christ." Here again the term *knowledge* may puzzle us. Some commentators have professed to see a difficulty in that this verse suggests that knowledge is the end (for the preposition *eis* often denotes *end* or *purpose*), whereas verse three makes knowledge the beginning. After our difficulties with the list of seven virtues it is a relief to realize that there is little trouble here. The preposition *eis* also means "with reference to"; as is the case in the baptismal formula—into or with reference to the name of the Father, etc. Accordingly verse eight simply means that in this process of edification the foundational knowledge will not fail to produce fruit.

1:9 For the man without these [virtues] is blind, near-sighted [myopic], having forgotten the cleansing of his past sins.

If 1:8 states the result of having these virtues, 1:9 describes the man who lacks them: "For the man without these [virtues] is blind, near-sighted [myopic], having forgotten the cleansing of his past sins."

Modern readers, expecting a climax, are surprised to see *near-sighted* following *blind.* A climax would require blind to follow near-sighted. If, however, the translation had used the English cognate of the Greek term, so that we would read, "the man . . . is blind, myopic..," one would easily suppose that a climax was not intended, but a more accurate description: the person may see what is near at hand, today or yesterday, but he cannot see far into the past when God cleansed him. Presumably this refers to moribund Christians whose state of mind is neither praiseworthy nor enjoyable because in failing to make moral progress they have even forgotten that God once cleansed them. Some commentators, perhaps entertaining sacramentarian notions of baptism, insist that this cleansing must be baptism. Bigg and Mayor both say that the word *past* (the cleansing of his past sins) necessitates the idea of baptism. Lange more reasonably refers it to justification and cites Psalms 51:4; Exodus 29:36–37; Hebrews 1:3, 9:22–23; and 1 John 1:7. The New Testament verses are particularly convincing against the sacramentarian interpretation.

1:10 Therefore rather than this myopic forgetfulness, be zealous [Peter uses the verb three times, 1:10, 15, and 3:14; he has already used the noun in 1:5] **to make your calling and election certain.**

Here there is no difficulty in grammar or translation, but interpretation and theology could raise a difficulty.

A so-called Gospel tract described election as God's voting for you, the devil's voting against you, and if you break the tie by voting for yourself, you are elected. Thus we are supposed to make our election sure. First Peter and all the New Testament show how anti-Christian this is.

But it is no less contrary to the Gospel, if, merely dropping the analogy of ballots, one retains the idea that a man makes certain an eternal divine election that was in itself uncertain. How can anything God has done be made certain by a man? This tract on ballots and its emendation as well point out the fact, the very strange fact, that some people who regard themselves not only as Christians but as superior evangelistic Christians do not really believe in God at all. At all? Well, they doubtless believe in some superhuman person of considerable power, whom they call God. But with some unimportant differences their God is not much more divine than Zeus or Shiva. A little more power, some Christian morality no one would expect in Zeus or Shiva, but no omnipotence and sovereignty. Really no omniscience either. For if God cannot control a man's actions, how could God know whether or not the man would decide to make the uncertain divine decree certain?

The form of the Greek verb provides what evidence it can against the above irresponsible interpretation and also bears on certain further emendations about to be considered. To *make* a thing certain in the above sense, i.e., to do something, would ordinarily require a verb in the active voice. It would be a construction parallel to making a ship, making a house, or manufacturing arrows and swords. But in this verse the verb *make* is not active. The voice is the Greek middle and bears a subjective meaning that does not quite fit in with the preceding view and pretty much rules out the following.

Some Arminians have said that God elects or chooses, not individual persons, but churches or nations, in which conditions favorable to conversion obtain. If the people in these churches or nations make good use of their advantages, they will make the general election certain for themselves.

The idea of considering a general election, already certain in itself as general, and making it certain for oneself is doubtless within the possibilities of the Greek middle voice. Only, one does not make *it* certain. What is made certain is not divine election, for on this view divine election is general. What is made certain is one's own salvation. By doing something or other—Peter's text speaks of patience, self-control, love—a man saves himself. In theological language this is autosoterism and negates grace.

Of course it is true that the Jewish nation was chosen and to it many privileges were given. Jewish children were more likely to hear about the Lord than Egyptian or Babylonian children. But God had chosen Babylon too. He had chosen Assyria and Babylon for the purpose of punishing the Jewish nation; and he chose Rome to wipe them out as a nation. But none of these choices, including the bare choice of the Jews as the matrix from which Messiah was to arise, is what the Bible refers to as election. Biblical election is not a matter of a nation or church in which the Gospel can be heard. Biblical election is election to salvation. Jesus was named Jesus because he would save his people from their sins. The Father gave him a definite people, and of these people he would lose none. He and his Father hold them in their hands and no one can snatch them away. In the future, looking back on his finished ministry, Jesus will see his seed, he will see of the travail of his soul, and shall be satisfied.

The text itself, 1:10, makes no reference to the Jewish nation or any other general group. Peter is speaking to individuals to whom Christ has sovereignly allotted faith. They are the individuals whom Peter exhorts to self-control and godliness, to whom the promises have been made. Such a calling and election is radically individual. And this is the election Peter exhorts us to make certain for ourselves.

To make my divinely decreed election certain to or for myself is simply a matter of assurance. Simply, not because the doctrine of assurance is guaranteed to be devoid of problems; but because it does not face the impossible problem of making God's decree more certain than God could make it. The text deals with assurance. Kierkegaard, who should never be trusted, has a good point, though even in this case he exaggerates, when he says we must in humility always be certain of others' salvation and always doubtful of our own. The idea of becoming assured of one's own salvation is perfectly Scriptural, and part of the method is self-examination. Therefore one commentator's view that we cannot make our own election sure, on the ground that only God can grant assurance, is without foundation; for though it is God who gives us certainty, he does this through several means. The same commentator's suggestion that Peter refers here to our making our election certain to others by our good works is altogether implausible. The idea of assuring others cannot be found in the text. The middle voice means oneself. The second half of 1:10 clearly indicates the individualism of the argument. Furthermore, since God alone can see and judge the heart, another person, an observer, can never be made certain by my good works. These are observable because external; my internal motives, an indispensable element in my moral standing, the observer cannot see.

The Lord may indeed grant me assurance of my election by means of my good works. Nor does this infringe on God's sovereignty or grace. Paul also admonishes us to work out our salvation in fear and trembling, for it is God who works in us not only to cause us to do good works, but even earlier to cause us to will to do them; and it is all of God's sovereign pleasure.

1:10 By so doing you shall never come to grief.

A moment ago the second half of 1:10, to which 1:11 should be added, was mentioned as evidence that Peter was not asking us to assure others. The reference is entirely to one's own salvation. It continues, "By so doing [making your election sure] you shall never come to grief." The usual translation *shall never stumble* gives the impression that one who has received assurance never sins again. All commentators disavow this interpretation. It is not a promise of sinlessness in this life: the next verse shows that it means assured glorification in the life to come.

1:11 For in this way [the way, not only of 1:10, but of 1:5–10] **entrance into the eternal kingdom of our Lord and Savior Jesus Christ is richly provided for you.**

Thus entrance into the kingdom of heaven is the final idea of this section, as the summary, some pages ago, indicated.

This section has now told us that Christ has granted us all things that pertain to life and piety so that we might be godly people. We should therefore zealously practice all the virtues and so assure ourselves that God has elected us into Christ's eternal kingdom.

Summary of 1:12–21: Facing imminent death Peter insists that the Gospel is not a myth but a direct revelation from God.

1:12 Therefore I shall always remind you about these things.

The King James Version depends on a poorly attested reading when it says, "I will not be negligent." Several commentators have trouble with the Greek text because it is an unusual construction. In fact the style of 2 Peter (and its relation to Jude, later to be noted) is so different from 1 Peter that the liberals make a point of it in their rejection of its authenticity.

The matter of style is worth a parenthetical paragraph, for a similar argument is used to discredit the second half of Isaiah. The style of John's Gospel differs considerably from the style of Revelation. But then the style of *Les Misérables* differs considerably from that of *Dieu* and *La Fin de Satan;* yet Victor Hugo wrote them all. If a critic replies that the latter two are poetry and *Les Misérables* is prose, a Christian can note that Revelation is apocalyptic and the Gospel is simple narrative. The subject matter of the two halves of Isaiah also differs. And finally, consider *Thus Spoke Zarathustra* and *Beyond Good and Evil* or some other works of Nietzsche. The styles are strikingly different; but no one dares to assume two authors.

Neither is the wording of 1:12 inconsistent with Peter's authorship. *Mello* with an infinitive, future or present, even in classical Greek, had the meaning of a simple future (compare Goodwin's *Greek Grammar,* 1254, and his *Moods and Tenses,* 73). Classical Greek used the present *mello;* but somebody, obviously, used the future *mellēso* and this somebody could have been Peter as easily as a later impostor. Nor is there any reason why first century Koine could not use the future *mellēso* with a present infinitive. Nietzsche was happy pointing out the bad grammar in the New Testament; but Nietzsche did not know as much Greek as he thought he knew.

There are other peculiarities in the style of 2 Peter; and its differences from 1 Peter are used against its apostolic authorship. But this is nothing new. The ancient church fathers knew about differences in style. Jerome made an interesting conjecture. Peter could have, not exactly *dictated,* but *explained* the message he wanted to write. His secretary, no doubt a trusted personal friend, wrote out the message in his own style. Peter then read it and put his stamp of approval on it. Conservative theologians cannot prove that this is what happened; but neither can liberals disapprove it. Since it could possibly be so, arguments from style cannot prove 2 Peter spurious.

"These things" in 1:12, which Peter will always remind them of, may be the "these things" of 1:10, viz., the several virtues previously enumerated. But the repetition of the idea three times over in 1:12–15 suggests something more. The "these things" of 1:15, with the explanatory clause of the following verse, is a verbal combination that points forward rather than backward. Naturally this does not exclude the earlier exhortations; but it seems to emphasize the contents from 16–21.

1:12 though you know them and are established in the present truth.

The repetitious emphasis in these verses is considerable. Peter is reminding them of what they not only know already, but of "the present truth in which you are firmly established." On this last phrase King James is better than American Revised Version and those commentators who feel obliged to say, "the truth that is with you." "Present" presumably means present in this epistle. Peter reminds them of the truth here present. No doubt it is also with them: they are established in it. But he will do all he can to prevent them from forgetting it.

1:13, 14, 15 For I think it right, so long as I am in this tabernacle, to stir you up in memory, knowing that I shall quickly put aside my tabernacle, as also our Lord Jesus Christ made it clear to me; and I shall also be eager that after my departure you may always be able to bring these things to remembrance.

Not only is *remembering* repeated three times, but the whole is made more emphatic and solemn by Peter's reference to his approaching death. It is not necessary for a Protestant to submit to tradition or receive *Quo Vadis?* as Scripture. The story is suspiciously dramatic. But no Protestant can deny that the Lord predicted an unwelcome death for Peter, one that would in men's eyes rescue him from the odium of his betrayal. Peter was now old—he was not the youngest of the disciples—and at the least it was obvious that his departure from this tabernacle was nearer than before. It is also possible, even probable, that some immediate circumstances convinced him that he would soon be martyred. In these serious circumstances Peter is zealous to remind them of established doctrine.

If any doctrine warrants such impressive asseveration, it is the inerrancy of Scripture, the truth of revelation, the authority of God's word. Chapter 1:16–21 are extremely important. In them two subjects are combined. First, they bear on the authorship of the epistle and either confirm or contradict the account of the Transfiguration in the Gospels. Then, second, this passage is a major contribution to the doctrine of the inspiration of the Bible. Actually these two topics form a unity because the remarks on the Transfiguration are designed to defend the truth of Peter's message, so that the truthfulness of Scripture is the great concern.

Since the matter of authorship as such, however important it is to us, was not Peter's main intention, and even the Transfiguration itself is subsidiary, it is best to get these things out of the way before discussing the main point.

1:16 For we did not follow sophisticated myths when we informed you of the power and presence of our Lord Jesus Christ; on the contrary , we were eye-witnesses of his majesty.

The first word that turns our attention to matters of authorship and authenticity is *parousia.* This term is frequently used to refer to Christ's second coming. But the word itself means simply a visit or presence. The time and occasion of the visit must be determined by the context, and in this context there is no mention of Christ's future presence. The immediately following phrase speaks of Peter's being an eye-witness of the event, and the remainder describes the transfiguration.

The word *eye-witness,* as R. H. Strachan notes in *The Expositor's Greek Testament,* is "used of those who had attained the highest degree of initiation into the Eleusinian mysteries." If such remarks are intended to suggest that pagan religions contributed some ideas to Christianity, one may reply that the paragraph in Peter has nothing to do with agricultural gods, such as Kore and Demeter. Nor does the passage in Peter even concern the hope of a future life. Even if it did, such a hope in two religions, with their different views on the nature of the future life, is no evidence of influence or dependence.

If it is not the intention to find an Eleusinian source of Peter's theology, the remark might mean that Peter claims to have attained the highest level of Christian living and so is superior to the lower Christians. This is a poor view because, in the first place, even though Peter's apostolic authority made him officially superior to most other Christians, personal pride and immodesty are absent from the epistle. In the second place, at the time of the transfiguration Peter had not attained the highest spiritual level. He blurted out some ineptitudes at its conclusion; and of course he later denied his Lord.

Furthermore, while *epoptai* may have been a technical term in the worship of Demeter, it must have had an ordinary sense before being taken over. After being taken over, it still retained its ordinary sense. Even in later centuries, the word was used for a Roman magistrate, and in the Code of Justinian it designates an inspector. First Peter 2:12 and 3:2 use the verb in the most ordinary of senses: it means simply *to see* or *look at*.

Accordingly the author of the epistles reminds the readers that he personally saw the power and majesty of the Lord's visit.

1:17 For having received from God the Father honor and glory, where there was borne to him such a voice by the majestic glory, This is my beloved Son in whom I am well pleased . . .

On this occasion, or during this visit, Jesus received honor and glory. The participle, *having received (labōn),* clearly refers to Jesus. Its grammatical referent is either *the Lord Jesus* of 1:16, or, less likely, *the son* two lines below. The author claims to be an eyewitness of the stupendous event. He not only quotes the voice, the major part of the experience; but he also includes a small detail, as eye-witnesses regularly do—namely, it occurred on a mountain.

Now, if the epistle were not written by Peter, all this makes it a forgery of such arrogant magnitude that Strachan's excuses, referred to earlier, are to be ignored. It is hard to satisfy the liberals. If clear-cut claims are not made, then an epistle shows no evidence of apostolic authorship; but if explicit claims are in the text, then the writer must have been a devout imitator who wanted to add to the apostle's literary legacy. Anything to avoid authenticity.

1:18 And this voice we heard being borne from heaven while we were with him in the holy mount.

With respect to the present incident liberal commentators try to find inconsistencies between 2 Peter and the Synoptics, all three of which describe the transfiguration. One liberal claim is that the Synoptics depict the glory as emanating from within Jesus, while 2 Peter makes its source external: "All three Synoptics speak as though the glory had its source from within. Such can only be the significance of *metemorphōthē* (Matthew and Mark); and the *egeneto . . . heteron* of Luke is an indication of an inward change."

Such interpretations are entirely imaginary. Luke's phrase, "The aspect of his face became *(egeneto)* other" (9:29), gives no hint whether the source was external or internal. Matthew's *metemorphōthē, was transfigured,* is an ordinary passive voice. If it were a middle voice, it might have meant, "he changed himself," but the actual text gives no such hint. Since therefore the Synoptics do not state the source of the glory on Christ's face, they cannot possibly contradict Peter's account. It takes two statements to make a contradiction.

Peter in fact does not explicitly mention the brightness of Christ's face. The word *greatness, honor, glory,* and *majestic glory* could include the white light of his face and garments; but all that Peter explicitly mentions is the voice. If the shining light is intended to be included, it came "from God the Father" as the voice did. Twice Peter says the voice was borne or brought to Christ from the Father out of heaven. The Synoptics mention no other source. To construct a contradiction out of these materials requires an uninhibited imagination.

The reason for mentioning the transfiguration is to assure the readers of the truthfulness of the Gospel message. The former is confirmatory and subsidiary; the latter is the main thought of the paragraph. This main thought starts the section: "It is not, not (I say) sophisticated myths that we have followed when we made known to you the power and presence of our Lord Jesus Christ."

This declaration should always come to mind when the dialectical theologians of today try to reduce the Scripture to mythology. Peter's express statement shows how anti-Christian Bultmann *et al.* are.

That the main point of the paragraph is the truth of Scripture can hardly be missed even by a careless reader; but there is a less noticeable literary device used to build up to a climax. It is the four-fold repetition of the verb *borne*. Chapter 1:17 says that a voice was borne to him. Chapter 1:18 says that this voice was borne out of heaven. Chapter 1:21, no longer referring to the Transfiguration, but to the Old Testament, says that no prophecy was ever borne by the will of man; and then adds that the prophets were borne by the Holy Spirit. This fourfold repetition seems to be intentional. It makes Scripture, particularly the Old Testament, at least as authoritative as the words from heaven.

1:19 And we have the more certain prophetic word, to which you do well to pay attention, as to a lamp shining in a dark place, until the day dawn and the day-star rise in your hearts.

The progress of thought, however, particularly in 1:19, requires more careful attention. A definitive translation must await some decisions on exegesis, but a tentative translation is given above.

There are two difficulties here. In the literal, first half of the verse the meaning of *bebaioteron,* which the King James, American Revised Version, and Revised Standard Version translate as "more sure" or more certain, needs to be determined. The second half of the verse is figurative language, and this is always very difficult to understand. Remember that Christ spoke in parables, not to make his meaning clear, but to prevent the people from understanding what he meant. That Peter's figures are hard to understand is proved by the variety of interpretations commentators give. These will be considered first, and *bebaioteron* afterward.

Mayor believes that the language indicates a development of spiritual life in three stages: the lamp is the Old Testament, the Gospel is the dawn, and the day star in our hearts is the inner light of the Spirit. "The lower degree of faith," he says, "in the written word will be followed by divine insight." This interpretation stretches figurative language to or even beyond its limit. Peter does not tell us what he means by the dawn and the day star; but Mayor's mysticism and his belittling of the written word do not agree with what we know of Peter. Chapter 1:20 and 21 do not put the written word on a level inferior to an inner light, but rather assert the authority of Scripture in the strongest terms. Besides, Mayor's interpretation takes no account of the words spoken at the transfiguration, though they are an integral part of the paragraph.

Another view takes the *eōs* clause, "until . . . ," presumably including both the dawn and the day star, as a reference to the second advent. There is no hint of this in the text, at least if it be acknowledged that *parousia* refers to the transfiguration. The only hint in the text rules out the second advent, for the dawn and day star are something that occurs "in your hearts." This seems to rule out a public descent with angels and trumpets. Peter is urging his readers to continue studying the prophetic word until its meaning dawns in their minds. So exegeted the verse confirms the emphasis on knowledge in the earlier part of the chapter.

A third commentator translates 1:19 as, "Thus we have still further confirmation of the words of the prophets, a fact to which you would do well to give heed." In the second half of this translation the phrase "a fact to which" obscures the obvious Greek sense that it is the word itself to which we must give heed. The New English Bible avoids this obscurity and so expresses the same idea better: "All this only confirms for us the message of the prophets, to which you will do well to attend."

But does Peter mean that the voice from heaven at the transfiguration confirms the Old Testament? The transfiguration, although it does not seem to have been predicted, may yet confirm the Old Testament, insofar as the life of Christ, taken as a whole, confirms the predictions of a Messiah. But something more definite than this is needed, if we are to interpret 1:19 in this sense.

The Greek text does not easily lend itself to the idea of confirmation. True it is that the verb *bebaioō* can means *confirm;* but the comparative degree of the adjective is very awkward so understood. Yet perhaps grammar allows one to say, We have a more confirmed prophetic word. But grammar does not require one to say that the transfiguration confirms the Old Testament. It is even possible to suppose that the divine voice is better confirmed or more certain than the prophecies. One must ask and answer the question, What is the more certain or better confirmed prophetic word? What is more sure than what? If there is a simpler and clearer meaning than these, it ought to be preferred.

If the more certain prophetic word is the voice at the Transfiguration, the sense would be: Thus we, Peter, James, and John, have something more certain than the Old Testament, and therefore you who read this epistle should pay attention to what I say. But while this is grammatically possible for 1:19, the sense does not fit in easily with 1:20 and 21. These refer to the Old Testament. Then too, *kai* is much better taken as *and* or *also* than as *thus*.

If on the other hand the prophetic word is not that spoken at the transfiguration, but is the Old Testament, is Peter saying that Isaiah's and Moses' prophecies are more sure than God's direct voice from heaven? In this case grammar would allow the free translation: We, i.e., you readers and I Peter, have the more sure or better confirmed prophetic word, namely, the Old Testament. To it, you should pay attention since you do not have and therefore cannot pay attention to the voice of Transfiguration.

Admittedly this interpretation seems peculiar at first glance; but is it any more peculiar than saying that the voice from heaven is more certain than the Old Testament? At first glance one might suppose that the direct voice of God on the holy mount is indeed more certain than the words of Moses or Isaiah. Yet the culmination of the paragraph is the divine authority of the words of the prophets. Chapter 1:21 simply does not fit into an argument that makes the direct voice of God more certain than the Old Testament.

If, however, the words from heaven and the words of Moses are equally the words of God, neither is more sure, certain, or authoritative than the other. Then why does the text have an adjective in the comparative degree? One must credit Weymouth with the best solution to these difficulties. He translates, "And in the written word of prophecy we have something more permanent." Obviously the Old Testament, written, is more permanent than the brief duration of God's declaration at the Transfiguration. Those who do not know Greek must take the word of Liddell and Scott that *bebaioteron* means more firm, steady, steadfast, durable. Durable or permanent is therefore a permissible meaning and it makes perfect sense.

Now that 1:19 fits into the argument, some further explanation is needed for 1:20 and 21. The King James and American Revised Version have poor, unintelligible translations: "No prophecy of Scripture is of private interpretation." Perhaps this would make sense to a pope, but Protestants can hardly like it. What does it mean? Let us introduce the explanation with a different translation.

1:20, 21 Knowing this first [of all], that no prophecy of Scripture comes into being by *idias epiluseōs,* for no prophecy was ever brought by the will of man, but men who were borne [along] by the Holy Ghost spoke from God.

The difficulty that makes the King James translation unintelligible centers in the word *epiluseōs*. This word translated *interpretation* in the King James, American Revised Version, Revised Standard Version, and, in a sense, the New English Bible, can stand closer scrutiny. It seems to be a hapax legomenon. Souter's *Pocket Lexicon* gives simply *solution, explanation, interpretation*—no more. Liddell and Scott have also *release* and *discharge*. The verb has two main sets of meanings: (1) loose, untie, set free, release; and (2) solve, explain, confute.

Strachan makes the remarkable translation, "No prophecy is of such a nature as to be capable of a particular interpretation." This means either that no prophecy has any particular meaning and is therefore meaningless, or that a general rule, such as "Thou shalt not steal," cannot be applied to any particular case of theft. This too makes the Old Testament meaningless.

If, however, something less stupid can be extracted from Strachan's words, it will founder on the fact that 1:21 is not a proper reason for the assertion. Whatever 1:20 means, it must be such that 1:21 explains it. No translator can defend his translation without showing that 1:21 is a logical reason for 1:20. Verse 21 must be a premise from which 1:20 follows.

The New English Bible gives and makes more explicit the traditional rendering: "No one can interpret any prophecy of Scripture by himself." Presumably the reason is that the interpretation of one commentator must be checked by another until the consensus of the church is obtained. But however wise it may be for commentators to consider the arguments of other commentators, such a view of 1:20 makes very poor sense. The passage does not deal with the ability of Christians to interpret the Scripture. Its main idea is the Scripture's divine authority. The following verse, given as an explanation of the assertion, makes this absolutely clear. The reason there is no *idias epiluseōs* of prophecy is that prophecy did not come by the will of man, ever. Isaiah did not get out of bed one morning and say, I have decided to write some prophecies today. Revelations are not the results of human volition. On the contrary, God picked Isaiah up and carried him along; and, so supported, Isaiah spoke words from God.

Therefore 1:20 should be translated, "No written prophecy ever came into being by any individual's setting it free [or, more literally] by private release. Because . . .," etc. Peter is asserting the complete absence of human initiative in revelation. Revelation is initiated by God. Therefore since God revealed the message to Moses or Isaiah, it must be true and therefore authoritative.

Facing imminent death Peter wants his readers never to forget it.

Chapter Two

2:1–22 Summary: Beware of false prophets. Their evil is clear in many ways, and God will surely punish them.

This chapter, in addition to the ordinary items of exegesis, presents the problem of being a close parallel to Jude 4–16. Simply by comparing the two passages some critics conclude that Jude was written first, and the mythical writer of the second century copied and arranged the former's material. Since external evidence in no way conflicts with the authenticity of the epistle, anyone able to understand the two passages is competent to arrive at a judgment on authorship. This commentary aims to help the understanding.

First, to introduce the subject, some similarities will be noted, then certain differences, and then possible inferences will be examined.

The two sections both begin with an Old Testament reference to false teachers who even deny the Master. Both authors condemn these men for their lasciviousness *(aselgeia)*. Reasons for believing that their punishment is sure are then given. First the condemnation of the fallen angels is mentioned, each author stating that they are reserved to judgment. Both authors use Sodom and Gomorrah as an example of divine punishment. Soon follows the peculiar reference to the humility of the unfallen angels in not railing at evil. The false prophets rail; they are like Balaam; clouds without water; for whom the blackness of darkness has been reserved *(hois ho zophos tou skotous—eis aiōna—tetērētai)*. A concluding description of these false teachers, in both books, contains the phrase "arrogant things" *(huperogka)*. Second Peter says, "uttering great swelling words of vanity," and Jude says, "their mouth speaketh great swelling words." The verbal similarity is the one word *huperogka*. If this list is not minutely complete, these are at least the main similarities. There are many more differences than similarities. Some of these should also be listed.

The most important difference among those directly connected with the verbal similarities is the chronology of the Old Testament references. Peter orders his material in the familiar historical sequence: angels, Noah, Sodom, and Balaam. The motive or principle behind Jude's order is hard to guess: without mentioning Noah he begins with the exodus, then angels, Sodom, angels again, and finally Balaam. Can this comparison be brought to bear on the question of authorship or the question of dependence? Did a methodical impostor of the second century correct the scatter-brained Jude? Or is some other explanation just barely possible?

In connection with God's judgment upon the fallen angels, the wording of the two authors is completely different, except for the word *angels*, the word *judgment*, and the word *darkness*. Though the idea of these two verses is identical, yet the verbal differences prevent the conclusion that a pseudo-Peter made a loose and longer copy to insert into his short letter. The similarity in thought is much more simply explained: both Peter and Jude knew the Old Testament very well. Indeed, the arguments of some critics almost presuppose that the Old Testament never existed. Then too it is just possible that Peter and Jude had met after some years of separation and, finding that their congregations faced an identical problem, discussed this very matter. Their discussion would impress on their minds for later use the best arguments and even some of the wording.

That the situation among Peter's converts and Jude's was pretty much the same is clear from the main thrust of the two passages. There is, however, a slight difference. Jude describes a situation in which the false teachers (as the Old Testament prophesied) are already active. Peter says that there *were* false prophets in the Old Testament and that there *will* be false teachers among his readers. The difference, however, is not utterly sharp, for in 2:12–15, 17–20, and 3:5 Peter speaks of the false teachers as presently active. Critics who claim that the impostor began to describe a first century situation when the false teachers were still future, and then forgetting his stance described the conditions of his own times, ignore what must have actually happened.

In the early days of any local group, even after the apostle-evangelist had left the city, there would be a period of internal peace and purity. False teachers, false doctrine, and false conduct would take time to develop. The beginning date and the rate of development would vary from congregation to congregation. What then is impossible or even suspicious in supposing that some of Peter's churches had no false teachers yet and that others had not deteriorated very far, while Jude's were more advanced in their corruption? Given these conditions, which must have occurred nearly everywhere, the similarities between 2 Peter and Jude are fully appropriate.

Parenthetically one may note that Paul in 2 Timothy, speaking of false teaching and false living, fixes the present and future tenses. The present occurs in 1:15, 2:18, and possibly 2:25. References to the future occur in 2:16, 17, 3:13, 4:3, 4. The paragraph 3:1–5 has both.*

There are many incidental differences, as there must be when Jude's section is 38 lines long (in one edition) and Peter's is 54. For example, the difference between Peter's accusation that they "even deny the Master" and Jude's that they "even deny our only Master and Lord, Jesus Christ," is interesting. It is of little importance for determining literary dependence one way or another; but it bears on a different point to be discussed a little below.

Jude's mention of Enoch in connection with the Lord's return is not found in 2 Peter; nor does Peter mention the Lord's return in chapter two. This fact may compel a comparison between 3:1–14 and Jude 17–23. But the comparison will not weaken the independence of 2 Peter.

This brief comparison of the texts of 2 Peter and Jude shows not only how precarious it is to deny Petrine authorship, but that the evidence is altogether non-existent. That is to say, the allegations go no distance at all in branding 2 Peter a forgery. To be sure, the above paragraphs are brief. More details will be considered as the commentary proceeds verse by verse.

---

*Second Timothy 3:1–5 may be punctuated as one sentence. Chapter 3:2–5 must be. Chapter 3:1 has the future *enstēsontai*. Chapter 3:2 has *esontai*. Then after the long list of condemnatory predicates, 3:5 has the present participle *echontes* and the perfect middle *ērnēmenoi*, which itself bears a present sense.

2:1 There were also false prophets among the people, as also among you there will be false teachers.

Without forgetting the critical question of authorship, we may now turn to the message itself. It begins by stating that in addition to the holy men who were borne along by the Holy Ghost, there were also false prophets among the Old Testament people. The reference must be to the Old Testament, not only because of the mention of the prophets in 1:20–21, but also because of the word *also* in 2:1, and the past tense of the verb. Further, there is the contrast between "the people" and "you," among whom there will arise false teachers in the near future. Does one need to be reminded of the impiety before the time of Christ? Idolatry itself was not eradicated before the Babylonian captivity. The depravity of the northern kingdom is described in 1 Kings 22. Jeremiah 2, 17, 23 *et passim* castigate the sins of the southern kingdom. And Christ lamented, O Jerusalem-rulers, how often would I have gathered your common citizens, but you rulers opposed!

Accordingly Peter warns his converts that false teachers will infiltrate their churches too. The change in wording from *pseudo prophētai* to *pseudo didaskaloi* may indicate that prophets and apostles are on a level, but that teachers are on a lower level. At any rate the Christian community of the second century, as well as the first, made a sharp distinction. Some evidence for this is found in the procedure of the Gnostics. Had forgery been uniformly regarded as pious, or had it been regularly undetected through the stupidity of the early ignorant Christians, the Gnostics could have relied on writing extra Gospels and epistles. They actually appealed to unwritten, secretly communicated, allegedly apostolic teaching. In this they are witnesses to the Christian public's view of apostolic authority in sharp distinction from other writers.

Better evidence that the early Christians regarded apostolic messages as the word of God comes from Clement of Rome (A.D. 90). In chapter 42 he says, "The apostles received the Gospel for us from the Lord Jesus Christ; Jesus Christ was sent from God. The Christ therefore is from God and then apostles from the Christ." And, to make the present point clear, we, i.e., Clement and others, rank below the apostles. This conclusion is supported by the reference to Apollos in chapter 47. There is "blessed Paul, the apostle"; he had written to you "concerning himself and Cephas, and Apollos, because even then you had made yourselves partisans. But that partisanship entailed less guilt on you; for you were partisans of apostles of high reputation and of a man approved by them." Clearly Apollos' position depended on the approval of the apostles. Ignatius (A.D. 100) *To the Romans*, chapter 4, says, "I do not order *(diatassomai, command)* as did Peter and Paul: they were apostles." Similarly in *Trallians*, chapter 3, he repeats, "I do not think myself competent, being a convict, to command you like an apostle."

Archbishop Wand* (and how strange for an Anglican with delusions of apostolic succession), ignoring the evidence, writes: "The distinction between prophet and teacher, if ever it was very sharp in the early Christian community, seems already to be wearing thin." Quite the contrary: if there was any change at all, it was toward a greater sharpness. The *Epistle of Barnabas*, chapter 13, makes sense only on the supposition that Paul's epistles are equal in authority to the Old Testament. Nor are these the only evidences.

2:1b These [false teachers] **will introduce heresies of destruction** [into the church].

The first question is, What is heresy? Is it partisanship, schism, and nothing else? Is it immoral conduct? Or is it theological and intellectual in nature? The anti-intellectualists, of course, who favor either the first or second meaning, wish to deny that heresy is a matter of doctrine, for they hold that doctrine is unimportant in Christianity.

Strachan in *The Expositor's Greek Testament* defends the moral definition of heresy and comments, "The cardinal distinction between the true and false prophet lay in the moral character of their teaching (Jeremiah 23:21, 22)." In reply to Strachan one may say that this was not really true of the false prophets in the Old Testament, and Jeremiah does not say it was. Jeremiah complains that the false prophets had not stood in God's council (American Revised Version; *counsel*, King James); that is, the false prophets do not agree with God's judgment and thought. The message they proclaim is not God's message. If they had given the people God's words, the people would have turned from

---

*J.W.C. Wand, Archbishop of Brisbane, *The General Epistles of St. Peter and St. Jude* (London, 1934).

their evil ways. Obviously the people engaged in evil conduct; maybe the false prophets did too, but the text does not say so. Jeremiah's complaint against the false prophets is that they did not preach God's words. This is the cardinal distinction between the true and false prophet. As in Jeremiah, so also in Peter. The cardinal distinction is not their conduct. Of course, their conduct was iniquitous, and Peter condemns it severely, as we shall see. But basically the trouble is the intellectual content of their message. Chapter one has already indicated Peter's great interest in knowledge. Chapter three will show this interest again. We must not minimize this emphasis in chapter two.

Furthermore, a short survey of the word *heresy* in the New Testament will show that it is essentially intellectual. In Acts 5:17 the Sadducees are called a "sect." The word is *hairesis*. It has no particular reference to immoral conduct, as if the Sadducees were worse than the Pharisees. It is simply a designation of a school of thought. Acts 15:5 speaks of the sect or heresy of the Pharisees who believed. In Acts 24:5 Paul is a pestilent fellow and a mover of insurrection. But this is not the chief charge against the sect or heresy of the Nazarenes. Though it is not mentioned in Acts 24:2–9, the charge was that Paul taught against the people and the law and this place, the temple (Acts 21:28). Further Paul wanted to bring the Gentiles (Acts 22:21) into the kingdom of God. Ordinary civil disturbances would not have inflamed Paul's enemies so highly. They were wrought up because of his message.

It is not necessary to trace the word *heresy* all the way through the New Testament, for the present passage itself mentions the doctrinal aberration. So serious is it that it goes to the incredible length of "even denying the Master" himself. The text is too brief to determine in precise detail what the doctrinal aberration was. It is not even certain that *Master* means Christ. But whatever they denied, it was a matter of theological belief rather than observable immoral conduct. Chapter 3 also indicates doctrinal divergence with respect to the second advent. Heresy therefore is basically theological.

The text hints, or seems to hint, at a denial of redemption: the false teachers "deny the Master who bought them." This is often thought to mean that Christ bought them with his blood and they deny it. But a second reading will show that there is no mention of Christ's blood, his death, or resurrection, as is most common in the New Testament passages that speak of Christ's buying us or redeeming us. It is necessary therefore in the first place to determine whether *Master* means Christ.

Liberal theologians, desiring to minimize the Scriptural evidence of Christ's deity, might be tempted to deny that *Master (despotēn)* refers to Christ. J. B. Mayor argues that *despotēs* always refers to the Father.* He points out that with one exception every instance of *despotēs* in the New Testament rather clearly means the Father. The one instance, unfortunately, is Jude 4; and this bears on the meaning in 2 Peter 2:1. But if every other instance refers to the Father, how could Jude call Christ the *only* Master (*ton monon despotēn*)? Mayor then acknowledges that the grammar favors the translation, "our only Master and Lord, Jesus Christ." A reference here to the Father, says Mayor, "seems to contradict the general rule that, where two nouns denoting attributes, are joined by *kai,* if the article is prefixed to the first noun only, the second noun will then be an attribute of the same subject." (This is the rule used above in the exegesis of 1:1.) Mayor, however, wishes to make exceptions for the nouns *God* and *Lord,* and he gives a half page of examples. The evaluation of the evidential examples is tedious. But granting them reasonable credit, it still does not follow that one must so understand Jude 4. After all, the regular and simple rule makes it, "our only Master and Lord, Jesus." If there are some exceptions to the rule, why must this be one?

Jude, therefore, must be understood to call Christ our only Master and Lord. If this weakens the explanation of 2:1, about to be given, one must suffer along and base the argument on all the other instances of *despotēs.*

Liberal presuppositions often effect liberal exegesis. In this case, however, John Gill, a rigid Puritan, who would have been scandalized beyond measure at a suspicion of diminishing support of Christ's deity, used Mayor's arguments almost two hundred years earlier. He says that Christ and redemption by his blood are completely absent from 2:1. To forestall the charge of minimizing Christ's deity, he argues that while *Kurios* is a proper title for Christ, *despotēs,* indicating power and ownership but without connotations of redemption, more properly belongs to the Father.

---

*I do not assert that his argument was motivated by liberal desire. Read on.

The complications continue. If the verse in Jude refers to the Father, then 2 Peter 2:1 would be the only instance where *despotēs* means Christ—if indeed it does so here. This would be peculiar, so peculiar that it would almost force us to Mayor's and Gill's view. On the other hand, if Jude refers to Christ, as simple grammar would prefer, it would not conclusively prove that Peter does, no matter how much conversation they enjoyed together. Yet must not Peter refer to Christ by reason of the participle *bought?* He speaks of denying the Master who bought them. Is this not redemption by Christ's blood?

Now, if liberal presuppositions are sometimes active in liberal exegesis, no doubt Reformed presuppositions are active in Reformed exegesis. John Gill was an enthusiastic Calvinist. He believed that Christ died for and actually saved the elect—no one else. Therefore, either Christ had bought these heretics and had saved them (this could be true either on the basis of universalism or on the assumption that they later repented) or Christ had not bought them (in which case the text is troublesome). John Gill, thoroughly opposed to universalism, and finding no evidence that these heretics later repented, but rather the reverse, decided to look more closely at the wording. He relied heavily on the position that *despotēs* refers to the Father and that therefore there is no reference whatever to Christ's redemption. But if anyone complains that this is a Calvinistic prejudice, he can hardly direct the complaint against J. B. Mayor.

Gill, of course, must explain what the participle *bought* means. Regularly throughout the New Testament wherever reference is made to Christ's purchase of his people, some circumstance, some description of the price or method, usually determines the sense. For example, "redeemed . . . with precious blood" (1 Peter 1:19); "purchased with his own blood" (Acts 20:28); "redemption through his blood" (Ephesians 1:7). Here no phrase is added. Furthermore, not only does the first half of the verse center on the Old Testament, the remainder of the chapter does too. Even 3:4–5 refers to creation and the flood. This may seem strange in Christian ears today. But consider: First Peter is explicitly addressed to Jews. Since the author was the apostle to the Jews, it is very probable that 2 Peter was also addressed to the Jews. To them purchase and redemption had for centuries been connected with their salvation from Egypt. Therefore the line of thought would not have seemed at all unfamiliar to them. Peter was saying: God rescued you from Egypt; do you therefore repay him with heresy and immorality?

Twentieth-century Christians are likely to misjudge the conditions of a church largely Jewish rapidly becoming Gentile. The great contrast between the sacrifices of the Mosaic ritual and their abolition with Christ's fulfillment is familiar to us but dim. The pressing necessity of the Jerusalem Council is poorly appreciated. How many congregations were disturbed, and from the opposite direction, how the Gnostics attacked the Old Testament, remain poorly understood. Therefore Gill's exegesis seems farfetched to us. But it is not farfetched, when one pictures the historical conditions of the year A.D. 60. The meaning of 2:1 is, then, that the false teachers even deny the God who delivered the Israelites from Egypt. They were on a par with the false prophets whom Jeremiah condemned.*

One gives a sigh of relief to see that the last four words of the verse, "bringing upon themselves sudden destruction," occasion no difficulty whatever. The word *swift, tachinēn,* is of some help in understanding 1:14. Peter's death is *tachinē;* the destruction of the false teachers is *tachinēn.* It seems to make little difference whether we translate it as suddenly or swiftly. The root meaning is swift. Either meaning makes perfectly good sense in each of the two verses; and neither meaning strengthens the case for forgery.

2:2 Many shall follow their lewd conduct, through whom the way of truth shall be blasphemed.

For some unimportant verbal parallels see Romans 2:24, Psalm 119:30, and Acts 16:17, 19:9, 23. Heresy is basically intellectual; but it results in evil conduct just as orthodox belief produces sanctification. The reason deserves emphasis wherever people propose a non-doctrinal Christianity. What a man does is controlled by what he thinks. Lewd conduct is always the result of wrong ideas. Similarly orthodox theology inevitably produces good works. When the Jews attacked Paul's doctrine of justification by faith alone, he replied that justification

*This repudiation of Old Testament teaching does not prove that Peter's false teachers were Gnostics—who also repudiated the God of the Old Testament. Jeremiah's false prophets were not Gnostics.

necessarily produces sanctification. There is no such thing as dead orthodoxy. Right thinking is followed perforce by right living.

It is not enough, however, to condemn false doctrine. The evil conduct of heretics is usually more noticeable than their doctrinal divergences because uneducated Christians are often deceived by poor reasoning. Furthermore, immorality is an immediately pressing problem, and Peter in his situation must deal with it energetically. The verse says that the false teachers will make many disciples and the disciples will bring the Christian community into disrepute. So they did.

2:3 In covetousness they will exploit you—make gain of you—by contrived arguments. Their ancient condemnation is not without force and their destruction is not dormant.

It would be difficult to estimate what financial gain these false teachers were able to make. An impostor could no doubt "sponge on" a simple Christian's hospitality. No doubt he could also collect some offerings. The false teachers had to get their living somehow. But covetousness is not always for money, nor is "making gain of you" necessarily financial. There is also prestige. Men covet honor. Teachers want their teaching recognized. Less honorably lascivious teachers covet their neighbor's wives. The passage should not be narrowly restricted to money.

Against these heretics a judgment had been pronounced centuries before. This sentence of condemnation is not without force, nor does the righteous judge sleep. It may seem so, both to the false teachers themselves and to the distressed faithful. Against this misconception Peter directs a heavy argument.

2:4 If God did not spare angels who sinned, but committed them to *sirais* of darkness . . .

The main thought of the argument from 2:4–10, namely, that God will punish the false teachers, is too clear to need explanation. That they shall be punished was asserted in 2:1. From 2:4 on, Peter gives evidence that the sentence shall in fact be executed. But though some general idea is sufficiently clear, there is a troublesome subsidiary point right at the start.

There are two words in Greek, *siros* or *seiros,* meaning a pit or excavation for the storage of grain, and *sira* or *seira,* a chain or fetter.

The former reading occurs in the best uncial manuscripts, א , *A, B, C*. The latter is supported by a mediocre papyrus, *K, P,* ψ, and a large number of cursives. The Aland-Black-Metzger-Wikgren edition favors *sirais, chains* or *fetters*. But the combination of א , *A,* and *B* ought to stand up against nearly anything. So far as the sense is concerned, it seems to make little difference whether the angels were reserved for judgment in fetters or in a dark pit. At first *chains* seems slightly better, but the participle *having cast them down into hell* (all one word) favors a dark pit. If Isaiah 24:22 includes angels *(high ones),* and if Peter had that verse in mind, it would support *pit.* The plural *pits,* however, is a trifle awkward, if one thinks of hell as a single pit; whereas *chains* is naturally plural. The parallel verse in Jude definitely has chains; but it is a different word, not *sirais,* but *demois.* Because Mayor is sure that an impostor copied Jude, he prefers *chains (sirais)* in 2 Peter. This and other details of his argument are too hypothetical. A decision based on א *A B* can claim more objectivity, but everyone agrees that there is little assurance on either side.

Well, then, the false teachers must not be emboldened nor the faithful discouraged by the prevalence of heresy, "for," to resume, "if God did not spare angels who sinned, but committed them to pits of darkness, cast them into hell, and reserves them for judgment. . . ."

Here one might expect the conclusion: neither will God spare these false teachers and their disciples. But Peter thinks of another evidence of divine punishment, an event which he intends to make use of in chapter 3, and this leads his thought on, as we shall now see.

2:5 and if he did not spare the ancient world, but preserved the eighth, Noe, a preacher of righteousness, when he brought a cataclysm on the world of impiety . . .

After the mention of angels there begins here a list of examples of divine punishment on evil men. The first item contrasts, at least by implication, the great number who perished in the flood with the few who were saved. Yet, as some critics delight to notice, for it seems to them an evidence that the impostor copied from and corrected Jude, whereas Jude speaks only of punishment, "the more merciful" forger includes this act of salvation. It is amazing that writers of scholarly pretensions can be impressed by the flimsiest of arguments. Nor is the above the flimsiest. Archbishop Wand (previously mentioned), in his attempt to make Jude the source from which 2 Peter copied, also writes (p. 133), "II Peter seems occasionally to be acting on a hint from Jude. Thus Enoch is called by Jude 'the seventh from Adam.' II Peter does not mention this but the number occurs in 2:5, where he describes the company saved by the flood as 'Noah with seven others.'"

That Peter "seems occasionally to be acting on a hint from Jude" is a very mild statement of a very possible fact. This is not to say that an impostor rewrote Jude. It is quite possible that Jude and the real Peter met, and it is altogether probable that similar conditions prevailed in their churches. With this probability the certainty that they were both familiar with the Old Testament undermines all such attacks on the authenticity of 2 Peter.

But Archbishop Wand proceeds to the flimsiest extreme by his reference to the number seven. He had written, "Enoch is called by Jude 'the seventh from Adam.' II Peter does not mention this, but the number occurs in 2:5, where he describes . . . 'Noah with seven others.'" Unfortunately for the cleric there is no number seven in 2 Peter. The number is eight. Hence the argument must be: Jude says that Enoch is seventh. Second Peter says Noah was eighth. Therefore an impostor copied from Jude!

Furthermore, in his commentary Wand correctly translates it "the eighth." But his critical introduction where he attacks the authenticity of the epistle makes no use of the correct translation. It contains only the erroneous "with seven others." Possibly Wand may have been depending here, not on the Greek text he correctly translates, but on his memory of the incorrect translation in the American Revised Version (or the English Revised Version).

The text reads, "preserved the eighth, Noe." What is meant by *eighth?* Does it mean "with seven others"? Does it mean the "eighth from Adam"? Or does it mean "the eighth preacher of righteousness"?

That God preserved Noah with seven others is a perfectly good interpretation, however wrong a translation it is. First Peter 3:20 says, "in which a few, that is, eight souls were saved by [not from] water." Yet this faces one objection. If eight *(okto)* souls were saved, why is Noah called *eighth (ogdoon)?* True enough, Peter's aim of impressing the reality of God's judgments against sin is well served by contrasting the few saved with the many lost; whereas the phrase *eighth from*

Adam or *eighth preacher of righteousness* does not do so. But this is of little help in explaining the ordinal in place of the cardinal.

No good reason can be given for supposing that Peter meant the eighth in a list of preachers of righteousness. There is no such list. It is even more difficult, in fact impossible, to believe that Peter meant to call Noah the eighth from Adam. Peter knew the Old Testament. Genesis 5:21ff. says that Enoch (whom both Jude and Genesis number the seventh) begat Methuselah, who begat Lamech, whose son was Noah. This makes Noah the tenth from Adam. It also leaves no reason to suppose that the present verse was somehow distilled from Jude.

Perhaps then Noah was the eighth to be saved because he went into the ark last and God shut the door. But Genesis hints that Noah went in first. All things considered, however, the American Revised Version's mistranslation, not without some small difficulty, appears to be the best interpretation.

Noah is called a preacher of righteousness. This causes no difficulty here, but it bears on the exegesis of 1 Peter 3:19.

2:6 and the cities of Sodom and Gomorrah he condemned in a catastrophe, having turned them into [or, covered them with] ashes, setting an example for those who should live ungodly lives, . . .*

This is the third example of divine judgment. In the last phrase a variant reading makes better sense. "Setting an example for," or "to," should be followed by a dative noun. The best attested text has a genitive participle followed by the normal infinitive. Insert one letter in the infinitive and it becomes the proper dative. The translation would then be, "setting an example to the ungodly of what will happen" to them. The dative occurs in a few manuscripts, including one papyrus of the third century.

2:7 and he rescued righteous Lot, who was ill-treated by the conduct of the lawless in indecency.

The verb *kataponoumenon (ill-treated)* occurs in Acts 7:24, where it is applied to the Israelite whom an Egyptian was maltreating.

---

*Some modern Greek editions omit *catastrophe*. It may be redundant; but 2 Peter is often redundant, and the textual evidence favors it.

Moses murdered the Egyptian. The verb therefore has a definitely rough sense. Lot made a poor choice when he went to live in Sodom. Financially it seemed to be an excellent choice. But in addition to preliminary troubles, he finally lost his wife and barely escaped with his daughters. Even at the end he wanted to delay his escape. Peter says he was righteous, justified by faith. However strange this may seem, there are many Christians today who are in no position to criticize. They should listen to the rumblings of the volcano beneath them.

2:8 for by seeing and hearing, this just man, since he lived among them, from day to day tortured his righteous soul by their lawless deeds.

This verse puts Lot in a better light. Though he may have been foolishly and even sinfully attracted for financial gain, his righteous soul was daily vexed by the pervasive immorality.

The verse gives a reason for something: either for God's rescuing Lot, or for Lot's being ill-treated and distressed by Sodom's evils. The latter seems preferable. Mayor translates it, "Righteous in look and in hearing he tortured himself at their lawless deeds while he lived among them." In order to make *dikaios (righteous* or *just)* modify *sight* and *hearing,* Mayor has to omit the article. The article occurs in nearly all the manuscripts. The gain in sense, on which Mayor depends for his translation, seems illusory. There is no difficulty with the American Revised Version and similar versions.

2:9 The Lord knows . . .

The last few paragraphs must have seemed tedious to the reader, and unless he has carefully followed in his Bible, he is probably lost by now. Peter's sentence is indeed cumbersome. Chapter 2:9 is the apodosis of a long and involved conditional sentence beginning in 2:4 and continuing through 2:10. The main idea is: If God did not spare the angels and the Sodomites, he will not spare present day workers of iniquity. This is precisely the argument in Jude. But the "more merciful" Peter has complicated the grammar by introducing examples of salvation also. The immediately preceding verse, 2:8, is one of them. Therefore Peter's rather more complicated sentence is: If God punished Sodom, but rescued Lot, "the Lord knows how to rescue the pious from trial and to reserve the unjust for punishment until the day of judgment." One commentator asserts that here the day of judgment is identified with the second coming of Christ. No such thing, True it is that the Father has handed all judging over to the Son, and he himself judges no man (John 5:22, Acts 17:31). True also that Jude 14–15 explicitly connects the judgment with the return of Christ. Accuracy of interpretation, however, must distinguish between what is undoubtedly true and what a particular verse says. The verse in 2 Peter, taken alone, says merely that the wicked are now being reserved for judgment, and that such a day will come. It does not mention the second advent. The American Revised Version, "Keep the unrighteous *under punishment* unto the day of judgment," does not seem so clear as "reserve the unjust *for punishment* until the day of judgment," when the punishment will come as at Sodom.

Having now given his argument against those who doubt that God will punish, Peter, concerned with the spiritual growth of his converts and disturbed by the dangers they face, continues his description and condemnation of the wicked. Of course the two ideas are easily connected.

2:10 [God will punish] especially those that follow after the flesh in the desire of defilement, scorning lordship.

The word *especially* could mean that the punishment of this group of evildoers, is especially certain. This ties in with the general argument of the section that punishment is certain. It could also mean that God will punish these people with especial severity. Since the punishment in both cases is equally certain, the difference might be the severity. The text does not decide between these two meanings.

As for the remainder of the verse, surely Alford is wrong in paraphrasing as "lust hankering after . . . polluting use of the flesh." Alford's idea is not at all bad, but "desire of defilement" is only a Hebraism that means "defiled desire." This is similar to "heresies of destruction" (2:1), which meant "destructive heresies." That the wicked hankered after defilement is certainly true; but this is not the literal meaning of the words.

Peter adds one further phrase: these heretics "scorn lordship." Contemporary English might prefer "despise authority." Does this mean apostolic authority, the authority of angels, or the lordship of

Christ? On the assumption that the same idea is repeated in the next few lines, we shall conclude the paragraph right here in the middle of 2:10.

Chapter 2:4 to the middle of 2:10 is one sentence. Here a new paragraph begins. The first half of 2:10 not only concluded the long conditional sentence, it also introduces a further description of the heretics' wickedness.

2:10b Headstrong, arrogant, they do not tremble [hesitate] to abuse [blaspheme] dignities . . .

Following upon the unexplained idea of scorning authority, Peter describes the evildoers as "shameless, arrogant." The second word can be construed as an adjective modifying "shameless men." But adjectives can also be construed as substantives. These men "blaspheming glories do not tremble." Presumably *glories* and *lordship* refer to the same thing.

2:11 whereas angels who are greater in strength and power do not bring an abusive [blasphemous] judgment against them before the Lord.

Here Peter contrasts these wicked men with the angels. The comparative *greater* can only mean that the angels are greater than the false teachers. Though this may be so obvious as not to need mention, one can justify it on the ground (1) that it heightens the contrast between good angels and evil men; and that (2) if these evil men were Gnostics, as one commentator suggests, they may have scorned angels on the ground that angels created the material and therefore the evil universe. The text, however, does not favor the view that these false teachers were Gnostics. They seem more like down to earth, earthy, antinomians. Perhaps materialistically minded. In this case they may have despised angels either because they did not believe such existed or because, if existing, were too unsubstantially spiritual. In any case, if lordship and glories refer to angels, the text says they despise them. But there is considerable room for hesitating between detailed possibilities.

Jude is more definite in some particulars. An example of the humility of angels is Michael's refusal to blaspheme Satan; but the heretics blaspheme everything they do not understand. Without mentioning Michael, Peter contrasts the angels' refusal to blaspheme the *heretics* (for so much the word *them* be understood) with the heretics' willingness to blaspheme angels. Some exegetes try to refer *them* *(autōn)* to the *glories* of 2:10. This would make some angels blaspheme against other angels—an idea not supported in the rest of the text. Still, there is no record of angels showing their humility by refraining from condemning evil men.

Just what an abusive or blasphemous judgment is may be hard to say. One ordinarily thinks that blasphemy can be directed only against God. It seems meaningless to speak of blaspheming Satan or heretics. Apparently the word here must refer to immoderate, exaggerated, irrational, and therefore untrue accusations. It certainly does not mean that angels, or even men, are forbidden to judge between good and evil; for Michael, though he did not blaspheme against the devil, nonetheless said, "The Lord rebuke thee."

2:12 These, like dumb beasts, born natural objects for capture and destruction, blaspheming on matters of which they are ignorant, shall be destroyed in their destruction.

The slight difference in thought between this verse and Jude 10 causes no difficulty to those who believe both epistles to be apostolic. The two men had a similar thought and developed it as each saw fit. The word *their* must be reflexive. It makes no sense to refer it to animals slaughtered for food; therefore, it must be the false teachers who shall be destroyed in their own destruction. One might possibly read into the verse an allusion to their destroying others by their false teaching and evil example. Then a paraphrase would be: the same conduct by which they destroy others will destroy them themselves. But it is probably better to take the phrase as a sort of emphatic Hebraism. "Hearing they shall hear" and "seeing they shall see" are simply emphatic statements that they hear and they see. In this case, they shall be destroyed by or in their own destruction.

2:13 suffering wrong *(adikoumenoi)* as the hire of wrongdoing [American Revised Version] **"shall receive *(komioumenoi)* the reward of unrighteousness** [King James]. . .

The American Revised Version depends on the original reading of א , *B, P,* and *p* 72. The King James follows a corrected reading of

א and *A, C,* and *K* plus a long list of cursives. This is too even a division of the evidence to choose either with confidence; but the American Revised Version is slightly better with the help of the papyrus.

The King James, which is the easier reading, receives some help from Colossians 3:25, "for the unjust person shall receive the wrong he has committed." Yet the future participle *komioumenoi* is a strange member of a list of seven present participles.

A contention that one commentator directs against both readings, and therefore against the author, namely, the contention that they identify the hire of wrong-doing as the final destruction of the sinner, whereas in 2:15 it applies to the quite material reward promised to Balaam, is completely without merit. One might better complain that this verse gives the false teachers their pay, whereas Balaam never got his. But this new objection applies only to the King James reading. The other reading (since this verse is still the same sentence with 2:12) can be taken as: being unjustly defrauded of the wages of injustice (in this case, popularity and money, as Balaam was) by being destroyed in their own destruction. This construction has two advantages. First, it attaches the participle *being cheated* to the preceding verb. A semicolon can then be put at the end of the phrase, before continuing with verse 13. Second, it makes a better parallel with Balaam. Balaam and the false teachers both lose the reward they wanted.

2:13b considering pleasure [to be] luxury in the daytime. . .

This translation was deliberately made unintelligible in order to emphasize the difficulty of interpretation. Three words can each be taken in either a good or bad sense: *pleasure,* though often evil, can be good; *day* or *daytime* changes its connotation with the other two; *luxury (truphēn)* can also be good or bad. For example, the only other instance of the noun *truphē* in the New Testament is Luke 7:25, where the fine clothes and luxury of a king's palace are contrasted with the haircloth and locusts of John the Baptist. But the verse does not imply any moral condemnation of high officials. If Luke thus uses *luxury* in a neutral sense, the LXX sometimes uses it in a positively good sense. Proverbs 4:9, Psalm 36:8, and several references to the garden of Eden use *truphē* for *heavenly joys.* Taking everything in the best possible sense, Bigg translates it, "counting our sober daylight joy mere vulgar pleasure." This is well nigh impossible, since there is nothing in the context to suggest that the luxury or joy is "ours." All the activities mentioned are those of the heretics.

James 5:5 uses the verb *truphaō* in a bad sense: "You have lived luxuriously . . . you have killed the righteous one." Taking the words thus in an evil sense, the translation becomes, as in the American Revised Version, "count it pleasure to revel in the day-time." However, to say that the ungodly consider day-time debauchery a pleasure is hardly a profound statement. Debauchery is pleasure no matter what time of day or night. Some sense, nonetheless, may be found by attaching to it the meaning that it is not enough to get drunk at night—these people must continue their lascivious doings all day. And this is about the best that can be done with this enigmatic phrase.

2:13c Spots and blemishes, luxuriating in their deceptions, while they feast with you.

This is the final phrase, a phrase that supports the idea that pleasure and luxury belong to the evildoers and do not refer to our sober daylight joy.

The phrase "spots and blemishes" no doubt has as its background the kinds of animals that the Jews were forbidden to sacrifice to the Lord. "Luxuriating" is a compound of the previous verb *truphaō*.

"Deceptions" *(apatais)* is by far the better reading. *Agapais,* love feasts, the Agape, by which Bigg tries to support his interpretation of our heavenly joys, is very poorly attested. The fact that Jude 12 uses *agapais,* along with "spots" and "feasting together," is no reason for altering the manuscripts of 2 Peter. Nor can one justifiably conclude that "II Peter has deliberately altered Jude either in order to correct him or to make a grim pun on his phraseology" (Wand). This commentator himself gives a very interesting excursus on the *Agape* (pp. 221–231). He shows both how much variation there was in the early churches and how much we today do not know about them. Under these conditions it does not stretch the imagination to suppose that Jude's churches and Peter's, though facing essentially the same dangers from similar false teachers, differed enough in custom to require or at least permit variations in the apostles' phraseology.

It is no doubt true that "feasting together with you" refers to love feasts. This does not undermine the interpretation here selected. It rather indicates a situation similar to that at Corinth, where a certain number regularly got drunk. The emphasis is on the evil, not on sober joys.

2:14 Having eyes tainted with an adulteress and never ceasing from sin, enticing unstable souls, having a heart exercised in covetousness, children of cursing.

The last phrase is another Hebraism. Compare the similar Hebraism of opposite meaning in 1 Peter 1:14, "children of obedience." It is unlikely that a post-apostolic writer would use such literary forms. The farther the date is pushed into the second century, the less likelihood there is. But to date an alleged forger early is to bring him within the observation of many who knew Peter personally. They would have protested against the imposture.

There is no difficulty in translation or understanding this verse. What twentieth-century Christians might well notice is the sharp difference between the respect paid to false teachers today and the treatment they received from the apostles.

2:15 Leaving the straight [and narrow] path, they wandered away, having followed the way of Balaam, [son] of Bosor, who loved the wages of unrighteousness.

The previous phrase, children of cursing, can be considered as a transition to the mention of Balaam whom Balak wanted to curse Israel. The first words of the verse, another participial clause, still refer back to the false prophets of 2:1, or in strict grammar depend on *these, (houtoi)* of 2:12.

The only difficulty is the name of Balaam's father. The Old Testament says Beor. The Greek manuscripts are heavily in favor of Bosor. One scholar supposes that the Hebrew gutteral in Beor was mispronounced and softened in the slovenly speech of Galilean Aramaic and then became an S in Greek. It is an ingenious supposition.

The final phrase contains a small item that must prove embarrassing to the "agapeic" theologians. These men distinguish between *agapaō* and *phileō*. They say that the latter is an earthly love while the former is some superior, spiritual emotion that can do wonders. The licentious theory of situation ethics insists that anything, even murder and adultery, motivated by *agapē* is right and good. If so, it was right and good for Balaam to try to please Balak because he loved *(ēgapēsen,* aorist of *agapaō)* the wages of unrighteousness. And the Pharisees also would be justified, Luke 11:43, in loving *(agapatē)* the chief seats in the synagogues.

There is a second point in these few words. Note that Peter is castigating the false teachers because they share the vice of Balaam. Dr. Calvin Seerveld* has an interesting exegesis of Numbers 22–24, the passage describing the historic encounter. The point now to be made, and Seerveld's point also, is not just the exegesis of the Numbers passage, but rather a critique of three methods of understanding Scripture.

The first method is that of evangelical fundamentalists. Seerveld has collected phrases from Alexander Maclaren, W. B. Riley, Clarence Edward Macartney, and others who note that (1) Balaam had a strong passion for earthly honor; (2) he wanted the best of two incompatible worlds; (3) he beat his ass unmercifully. Now we should not put earthly honor first among our choices; we should seek righteousness first of all; and we should not be cruel to dumb animals. Seerveld continues his list with a number of such applications and moral lessons.

The second method is that of the liberal destructive critics. They carve up the three chapters in Numbers into various hypothetical documents, *et cetera*. The present argument does not concern this method.

The third method Seerveld assigns to the "remnants of staunch orthodox churches; and he cites Hengstenberg and Calvin. This method notes that Numbers 23:19 is a clear statement of God's immutability. This divine dependability extends to the covenant with Abraham, which therefore applies to the Israelites whom Balak wanted Balaam to curse. In the account the fulfillment of the covenant is prophesied in the words, "There shall come forth a star out of Jacob." And there is considerably more in the passage.

Seerveld disapproves of each of these methods of understanding the Scriptures. He proposes another method. "Simply telling the story" is his first recommendation. "Noticing closely the literary contours" is his second. The third is, "Detecting the history-making context of the piece." "Listening and hearing the kerygmatic message" is the last.

On the whole Seerveld's sixteen pages of recommendations are

---

*De Graaff and Seerveld, *Understanding the Scriptures* (Toronto, 1968).

not particularly objectionable. Most of the material is very good. The question, however, is, how do these recommendations differ from the evangelical-fundamentalistic and the orthodox Calvinistic methods?

The trouble with the method of the Reformers, so he says, is that they always sought "truths that can be theoretically formulated and held to be universally valid, consistent Bible teaching against all attack." But is this a bad method of Biblical interpretation? Is it not rather entirely commendable? To be sure, a Calvinistic exegete (like the present writer) may make mistakes, he may overemphasize some lesser points, he may, like Hengstenberg, who is rather an exception, let his imagination soar at inappropriate intervals; but if this means that the method is poor, how could any method be good? Seerveld himself, in my opinion, makes mistakes, overemphasizes, and lets his imagination soar.

The trouble with the evangelical fundamentalist method is said to be that it "is interested in the practical lessons we can learn from it." As a matter of fact, so was Calvinism. The Westminster Larger Cathechism and innumerable Puritan sermons show this practical interest. Nor, conversely, are the fundamentalists so uninterested in doctrine as Seerveld seems to think. In fact they are usually disparaged because they stress doctrine too much (at least a few doctrines) and have poor standards of morality. A more sober appraisal of these methods as such, apart from this or that writer's idiosyncracies, would identify them. They are not incompatible or mutually exclusive. In fact, Seerveld's method, excluding his idiosyncracies, cannot be distinguished from the other two.

Or, if it can be distinguished, it is because of his negations and denials, rather than because of his positive recommendations. What vitiates Seerveld's application of his method is that it flatly contradicts Scripture itself. And this returns the discussion to Balaam and 2 Peter.

Seerveld writes (p. 68), "Quite wrong about the method . . . is this: Numbers 22–24 is not about Balaam, Balak, and their doing, except incidentally. . . . To make Balaam a warning model for the reader is to distort the nature of biblical narrative and ignore the historical solidity of God's disclosure. Scripture never gives biographic snatches to serve as ethical models."

In this quotation there are several serious flaws. But the worst and most obvious is his implied accusation that the apostle Peter "distort[ed] the nature of biblical narrative and ignore[ed] the historical solidity of God's disclosure," when he used "biographic snatches" of Balaam's conduct "to serve as ethical models," for this is precisely what Peter is doing.

If one must choose between Professor Seerveld's method of using the Bible and an apostle's, which should one prefer?

2:16 But he got a rebuke for his particular disobedience: a beast of burden without speech opened his mouth in human speech and prevented the madness of the prophet.

It does not seem to make too much sense to translate the first phrase as, "he was rebuked for his own disobedience." Some commentators want to expand the sense into, "he was rebuked for his own disobedience by the disobedience of the beast." The text itself does not mention the beast's refusal to obey his master's command; but if anyone wish the verse to allude to such, it can be done as well, and with a more delicate touch, by taking his *particular* sin as a contrast with the animal's disobedience.

2:17 These people are wells without water and mists propelled by a squall, for whom the blackness of darkness is reserved.

Thus Peter in picturesque language continues his denunciation of the false teachers. Noting that Jude speaks of "clouds without water carried along by winds," Mayor suggests that pseudo-Peter thought "he was adding clearness and point to the parallel in Jude." But he did not quite succeed because *squall* "seems an unnecessarily strong expression here." Mayor does indeed refer to the squall on the Lake of Galilee in Mark 4:37 (though he does not see that this could be a reminiscence of Peter himself), and speculatively attaches the word *mist* to the garden of Eden. Mayor further criticizes, as inappropriate to wells and winds, *the blackness of darkness;* though in Jude it is "appropriately used of the meteors, which flame out for a moment and then disappear into the blackness of darkness for ever."

Most probably the greatest fault of every commentator, and certainly of every ordinary reader of the Bible, is to see too little in the text. As God's word, the verses carry implications that all of us miss. Jesus condemned the Pharisees, and we condemn them too; but how many of us, like Christ in Matthew 22:32, could have deduced the doctrine of the resurrection from the Old Testament phrase, "the God of Abraham"? Though such inability to reason out inferences is doubtless our greatest shortcoming, some commentators occasionally see too much. I cannot believe that Peter had the mists of Eden in mind when the Sea of Galilee was so prominent in his memory. Nor can one validly infer that Jude was talking about meteors burning out into darkness. The words *asteres planētai* refer to planets. For this meaning Liddell and Scott cite Xenophon and Aristotle. There is no mention of comets, much less of shooting stars. The idea behind the expression is that planets wander. The so-called fixed stars move in a regular path; there are other lights in the sky, like Venus and Mars, that go backward and forward in a way that much interested the ancients. They called them *wanderers (planētai).* This designation is quite suitable to false prophets, who have wandered from the regular path of righteousness and are headed towards the blackness of darkness that has nothing to do with meteors. Furthermore, if anyone wants to push the matter, meteors do not visibly wander, and they extinguish themselves too quickly to resemble the false teachers' longer career.

Nor need one be disturbed by the fact that the darkness follows wells and mists. The literary metaphor must have an end as well as a beginning. Once the metaphor is ended, the main idea rules again: namely, "these [false teachers] for whom" destruction is determined, as in the last phrase of 2:1.

2:18 Uttering vain and arrogant [words] they entice with lewd fleshly lusts those who are just escaping those living in error.

This is a difficult verse. It is a reason why the false teachers are destined to hell, but the precise significance of several phrases is not very clear. First there is repetition: *uttering (pheggomenoi).* This causes no difficulty. It is repetition because it is what Balaam's ass did. Only the ass did not speak vain and arrogant words.

Repetition also occurs in *entice (deleazousin),* used in 2:14, "enticing unstable souls." But it is translation and interpretation, not repetition, that cause trouble here. The sentence is complicated, and in two instances the connection of the words is in doubt.

"They entice," of course, means that the false teachers "entice . . . those who are just now fleeing. . . ." *Oligōs* means *slightly* or *just:* those who are now fleeing and have got only slightly away. *Oligōs* is probably the correct reading; but *ontōs* has more than meagre attestation. The sense would then be: those who have *really* or completely escaped. But it is more likely that those who have *recently* fled and got *slightly* away could be enticed than those who had completely escaped. Let us therefore choose *recently* or *just now*.

The next difficulty is the participle *fleeing (apopheugontas)*. This is a present participle, and the meaning would be, "those who are just now fleeing." But there is also an aorist reading, *apophugontas,* not very well attested. This aorist occurs also in 2:20, where it means "after having fled" and in 1:4, "having escaped." These two verses, in fact chapter one as a whole and the last five verses of chapter 3, give the impression that Peter is addressing stable Christians who have pretty much, or even really *(ontōs)* escaped the enticements of evil. But though so advanced, they still need an exhortation against the heretics. This makes good enough sense; and if it does not positively require *ontōs,* it surely seems to exclude *oligōs*. On the other hand, the present participle, with which *oligōs* so well fits, would seem to envisage a minority in the church who, having been converted so recently, have not made much progress. Such a situation is not only possible, but highly probable. Its difficulty lies in the apparent shift in address from the main body to a smaller group. All through the epistle, the main body of stable Christians is in view, and now a smaller unstable group comes on the scene without proper textual introduction. But if *oligōs* is the better reading, it must be accepted. Furthermore, the alleged shift is more imaginary than real. Peter is in process of enumerating the sins of the heretics. One of these sins, he tells the main body and church as a whole, is that they entice the new converts.

The next difficulty is the phrase that follows "those who are just escaping." The phrase is, "those who are reared in error" or, equally well, "those who are returning in [to?] error"; or, best, "those who live in error." *Anastrepho* can have any of these meanings. But are these people the false teachers from whom the converts have just escaped? This accusative would then be identical with the nominative that is the subject of the main verb *entice*. The verse would then mean, The false teachers are enticing the new converts who are just escaping the false teachers. If this is barely possible, it is at least extremely awkward.

Now, if these people in the accusative case are not the false teachers, they may be the heathen in general from whom the converts have just fled. This is not a bad meaning, for it is more likely that recent converts have fled the heathen community than that they have just fled the heretics in the church. They have not yet had time to follow and then to flee the heretics. This is the view of Keil, Alford, and Bigg.

There is a third possibility. The phrase in question can be taken as appositive: "those who are fleeing, namely, those who live [were living] in error." Jerome holds that these people have fled but were now reverting to error. Thus the Vulgate. This view has a hard time with the present participles: *just now fleeing* and *presently living* in error. Furthermore, if the second participle is in apposition to the first, there is nothing stated that the converts flee *from*. The simplest understanding of these words is: those just fleeing the people who live in error.

The final difficulty in this very difficult verse lies in the words so far omitted: *en epithumiais sarkos aselgeiais*. In literal crabbedness: in desires of flesh lewdnesses. If only the latter noun were an adjective! Alford says, "they entice in lusts by licentiousnesses of the flesh." But "lusts of the flesh" is the more normal phrase. Either of the two dative nouns can be instrumental. *En epithumiais* can mean *by means of desires*. Of course it can also mean *in desires*, but this makes little sense with the verb *entice*. Similarly *aselgeiais* without a preposition can be a simple dative of means or manner. This makes possible the expanded translation: they entice the recent converts in the sphere of, or, through fleshly desires by means of lewdnesses.

Putting the whole complicated sentence together now, we get: "Mouthing arrogant vanities, they seduce, through fleshly desires by means of lewdnesses, those who are just escaping from those living in error."

2:19 promising them liberty while they themselves are bound by corruption; for by whatever a man is defeated, to that he is enslaved.

Or the last phrase can equally well be, "for by whom a man is defeated, to him he is enslaved." Although the noun corruption more or less suggests *what* rather than *whom* (the fact that the relative is not feminine does not bear on the matter), the practice in warfare makes the *whom* more appropriate. Besides, there is Christ's similar phraseology in John 8:34, "Everyone who commits sin is the slave of sin."

The truth of this verse is particularly applicable to conditions here in America in the seventies. Situational ethics wants freedom or liberty from moral rules. The law of God is repulsive and restrictive to those who lust. But in freeing themselves from the commandments, they become enslaved to sin. Romans 1:18–32 describe their plight. With this warning of Peter they are without excuse.

2:20 For if, having fled the *miasmata* [this is an English word as well as Greek, meaning defilements] **of the world by the knowledge of our Lord and Savior Jesus Christ, they are again entangled and defeated by them, the final affairs are worse than the first.**

The description of the evil actions of the false teachers virtually ended with 2:19. The concluding three verses of the chapter contain a solemn condemnation, phrased as a reason for saying in 2:19 that they are slaves.

Several things are to be noted. First, the escape from the defilements of the world was accomplished by means of knowledge. This echoes the thought of 1:2ff.

Second, again going back to the previous chapter, 1:1 said, "our God and Savior Jesus Christ." Some liberals wanted to translate it, "our God and the Savior Jesus Christ" (who is not quite God). But here in 2:20 we have the identical construction, "our Lord and Savior Jesus Christ." No one dares translate it "our Lord and [the different person] our Savior Jesus Christ."

Then a third difficulty concerns the referent of the participle *having fled*. Several commentators think it refers to the recent converts who had just fled heathen customs in 2:18.

A superficial reading makes this interpretation very plausible. Who else has fled the heathen customs besides the converts? Yet another interpretation, somewhat implausible at first sight, seems to be the correct one. It is that the false teachers themselves had fled heathen customs. One reason for this identification is that the item is only one in a long list describing the sins of the heretics, nearly all of which are introduced by participles. The more compelling reason is the sense of the final three verses, the conclusion of the paragraph as a whole, to which 2:20 is a fitting transition. But this engages us in a fourth difficulty.

The fourth difficulty is not grammatical, but theological. A quick reading has given the Arminians and Romanists the idea that people who have been previously regenerated can later be lost. Since this idea contradicts a dozen verses elsewhere in the New Testament, or two dozen, either the Bible is self-contradictory or a less superficial reading of the verse is required.

Now, it must be admitted that these persons mentioned here finally and totally fell away into perdition. One need not gratuitously suppose that they later became Christian. The text says they were entangled and overcome by the pollutions of the world. And surely the Arminians do not want to soften this judgment, for they would then undermine their own position.

Agreeing that these false teachers are lost—and their condemnation is found not only in 2:20, but in all the description that precedes—the Calvinist must argue that they had never been regenerated in the first place. The question then becomes, What does the chapter imply as to the earlier spiritual status of these false teachers? One may also ask, What does the whole Bible say about similar cases?

Matthew 7:22–23 say, "Lord, Lord, have we not prophesied in thy name . . . and in thy name done many wonderful works? And then will I profess unto them, I never knew you." Note that the Lord does not say, "I once knew you, but I no longer know you." He says, "I *never* knew you." The passage shows the possibility of persons being active in Christian endeavors and therefore giving the appearance of being Christians, while all the time they are not Christian at all.

Acts 19:13 speaks of certain vagabond or itinerant Jewish exorcists who made use of the name of Jesus. Judas, too, although he was a devil (John 6:70), and the son of perdition (John 17:12), was outwardly so much a genuine disciple that the others never suspected he stole their money and would betray Christ.

What is said of the false teachers in 2 Peter, namely, that they had fled the corruptions of the world through their knowledge of Christ, could also be said of Judas and the persons Christ condemned in the Sermon on the Mount. By what they had learned they were able to avoid the most obvious iniquities of the pagan world. The Holy Spirit had for a time restrained their proclivity to sin in a greater degree than he restrains those who have no knowledge of Christ.

Note parenthetically that *knowledge* here is *epignōsis*. Clearly those commentators are wrong who, in their interpretations of 1:2, 3, try to distinguish *epignōsis* as a higher form of spiritual knowledge as opposed to the lower and probably unspiritual knowledge called *gnōsis*. The two cognate words are synonymous. What they mean in particular must be determined by the context; and the context of 1:2, 3 is manifestly different from that of 2:20, 21.

It would seem that there are sufficient passages in the New Testament to show that some people have a form of godliness though they repudiate its power. Even Herod heard John the Baptist gladly (Mark 6:20). First Corinthians 13:3 intimates that some insincere professors can make a number of astonishing sacrifices in the name of Christ—sacrifices more remarkable than anything here ascribed to these false teachers.

But knowledge, profession, and association with Christ or Christians increases one's responsibility and makes these false teachers all the more culpable.

2:21–22 It was better for them not to have known the way of righteousness than once having known it to withdraw from the holy commandment delivered to them. The true proverb applies to them, The dog turned to his own vomit, and, The washed pig to wallowing in the mud.

This final verse, part of which comes from Proverbs 26:11, concluding the denunciation of the false teachers, rather clearly indicates that they had never been regenerated. When it speaks of a dog's returning to his own vomit and a sow to the mire, the implication is that these acts are natural to dogs and pigs. They have never been anything else than dogs and pigs, even though for a time they might have been cleaned up externally. Hence the false teachers had never been Christians and the verse does not teach that a regenerated person can become unregenerated.

Recapitulation: False teachers are a real and present danger. Their sins are numerous and serious. God will surely destroy them, for their knowledge of Christianity makes them all the more culpable.

Chapter Three

Summary: The prophets and the Lord himself foretold the age of mockers and false teachers who deny the return of Christ. Their uniformitarian view of history is falsified by the flood, and their sense of time is not God's. God has a reason for the delay, but he will suddenly destroy the world with fire. For this reason you must live a holy life and look for the day of God. Our beloved brother Paul, through his God-given wisdom, has written you the same things.

3:1 This is now the second epistle, my friends, that I write to you; in both of which I awaken your pure intellect.

"This second epistle" raises again the question of authorship and forgery. M. R. James, *The Second Epistle General of Peter* (Cambridge, 1912), following the liberal line, writes (p. xxxii), "Is not the writer of 2 Peter guilty of forgery . . .? [No.] If there were an element of conscious deceit connected with the writing it must have lain principally in the manner in which the Epistle was introduced to the Church."

Let us do a little arithmetic. Civil War (1861–1865) veterans had not all died by 1925. Suppose Abraham Lincoln had never issued the Emancipation Proclamation. Now in 1925 a devout forger, wishing to enhance Lincoln's reputation, writes and publishes the document, including some references to the first inaugural address and one of Lincoln's early Springfield experiences. Would not several veterans easily see and indignantly expose the forgery? Therefore it is unlikely that a devout Christian in A.D. 125 could have forged a letter in Peter's name without instant exposure. Nor would a devout Christian have thought it necessary to enhance Peter's reputation, any more than people in 1925 thought Lincoln needed such help. Nor, finally, would a devout Christian have so ignored the commandment, Thou shalt not bear false witness. One should conclude therefore that the words "This second epistle" came from Peter himself.

The word *pure* can mean *unbiased* or *unconfused;* Plato in *Phaedo* 66A uses the phrase to designate a mind unconfused by sensation; but the word can also mean *morally pure*. The material in the previous chapter makes the latter sense quite plausible. Nevertheless since false doctrine was also mentioned in the previous chapter, and since Peter considers their minds to have escaped these heresies, the intellectual meaning of unbiased cannot be ruled out, even though Plato's meaning of being unbiased by sensation is not mentioned in the context at all.

The other New Testament instances of the word *pure* or *purity* are these: Philippians 1:10, where either intellectual or moral purity makes good sense; 1 Corinthians 5:8 where intellectual or doctrinal purity is indicated in the verse itself, though the preceding verses are moral; 2 Corinthians 1:12 is predominantly intellectual; and 2 Corinthians 2:17 relates to knowledge and the word.

One of the critical objections to the authenticity of this epistle is that it is too intellectual and does not fit the general devout-emotional-non-intellectual tone of the New Testament. Fundamentalists also, as well as liberals, minimize intellect. This verse and the quoted instances of the term *pure* show that such people have missed an important New Testament emphasis.

3:1 I awaken your pure intellect to remembrance . . .

3:2 to remember . . .

This repetition is not good English style, but it passes in Greek and causes no surprise in Hebrew.

3:2 to remember the words previously spoken by the holy prophets and the commandment of the Lord and Savior [recorded] by your apostles.

In spite of the fact that M. R. James thinks that *your apostles* "is one of the phrases which suggests that the Epistle belongs to the subapostolic age," the reverse seems more reasonable. The situation was as follows: Both Peter and Paul preached in Rome and Rome claimed these two as peculiarly their apostles. It is likely that Peter and Jude at some time ministered to the same congregations. Certainly the lesser known apostles did some preaching and founded some churches. These churches would think of them as particularly *their* apostles. Since Peter, the real Peter, knew all this, he naturally writes "your apostles."

3:3 Knowing this first, that in the last days mockers will come in mockery, advancing according to their own desires . . .

"The last days," which so many people think refers to what is still future at the end of this age, clearly means the time of Peter himself. First John 2:18 says it is, in his day, *the last hour.* Acts 2:17 quotes Joel as predicting the last days as the lifetime of Peter. There are also verses that refer to the end of this age and some where the exact reference is unclear. Compare John 6:39, 40, 44, 54; 2 Timothy 3:1; James 5:3, and some other places. Peter obviously means his own time.

"Advancing according to their own desires" can be made more colloquial by the paraphrase "going their own way" or "following their own ideas." The point is that they reject revelation. If they were Gnostics, they accepted "sophisticated myths;" or if they were some other sort of third rate philosophers, they trusted their own religious experience and allegedly new inspiration of the Spirit. But the written word, they rejected.

3:4 And saying, where is the promise of his presence?

The translation *coming* instead of the correct meaning *presence* or *visit* gives rise to some confusion. Views on the second advent go astray when several events are compressed into a single moment. *Parousia* often refers to a king's visit to or progress through a country. It does not indicate that when certain events are to take place "at his coming," they are to be interpreted as occurring simultaneously. Since the phrase *the day of the Lord* is very common, it is interesting to note that Luke 17:26 speaks of the *days* of the Son of Man in comparison with the days, indeed the years of Noah. In this extent of time prophesied events can take place at intervals.

It is clear from these verses that the apostles had instructed their converts concerning Christ's return. Peter urges his churches to remember this teaching. But the mockers question the divine promise,

3:4 From the day the fathers fell asleep, all things continue in the same fashion from the beginning of creation.

At first sight there seems to be an awkwardness or exaggeration in the mockers' argument. They refer to all time since the creation of the world. Yet, so far as the return of Christ is concerned, only the years after Christ's first advent should have been mentioned. The promise made in Acts 1:11, for example, cannot be doubted on the length of centuries before the Incarnation. The doubt must be based on the length of time since the ascension.

Some thirty years had elapsed between the resurrection and the writing of Peter. In comparison with the four thousand years of Old Testament history, this seems a ridiculously short time on which to base a doubt about Christ's return. Nevertheless, in these thirty years many of the early Christians had died. From Acts 1:6–7 it is incontestable that these people had expected Christ to return in their lifetimes. Now the mockers ask, Where is the promise of his return, for—and here is where their reference to the time since the creation is seen not to be so greatly out of place—history is not eschatologically, teleologically, and supernaturally controlled. The positivistic laws of history are uniform, and irruptions *ab extra* have been shown to be impossible, if not yet by David Hume, at least by Aristotle and Epicureans.

That is where you are wrong, replies Peter. Not to mention miracles, which are eschatological only in an attenuated sense, the great supernatural irruption and judgment on sin that ruins the secular theory is the flood. For . . .

3:5 For they willfully ignore the fact that heavens were of old and an earth was formed of water and by means of water by the Word of God . . .

This is a crabbed, literal rendering that shows the need of interpretation to put it into intelligible English. Could Peter have meant, "heavens were ancient, perhaps eternal, but on the other hand an earth was more recently formed of water"?

Aside from other details, Peter surely could not have meant that the heavens were eternal, while the earth was constructed. True, the word *constructed (sunestōsa)* is feminine singular, referring to *earth (gē);* but this is not an insurmountable difficulty, for agreement is often attracted to the number and gender of the nearest noun. Since too the concluding phrase *by the word of God* presumably belongs with *heavens* as well as with *an earth,* the intervening words also would seem to attach to both heavens and earth. Then we should read, "Of old the heavens and the earth were constructed out of water by the word of God."

The compound phrase *out of water and by means of water* is obscure. It can hardly be for the purpose of emphasis or contrast. A single mention of water in this verse with the additional mention in the next verse is quite sufficient to make the contrast with the coming destruction of the world by fire. Some commentators try to argue that the pseudo-Peter relies on imaginative Jewish traditions that complicate the account of creation. Such imaginations occur today also between the first two verses of Genesis. But sober interpretation stays with what is written.

To avoid the awkwardness of this redundancy, Keil separates *heavens* from *an earth:* heavens are of old, but an earth was made of water. However, as stated above, this attaches *by the word of God* to the earth alone, and in contradiction to Genesis makes the heavens eternal. Even a pseudo-Peter, if he had the slightest notion of the Old Testament would not have said this.

Though it is difficult if not impossible to picture the processes referred to, the dependence on the Old Testament is clear. Genesis 1:2, 6, and 7 read, "The earth was waste and void; and darkness was upon the face of the deep: and the Spirit of God moved upon the face of the waters. . . . And God said, Let there be an expanse in the midst of the waters, and let it divide the waters from the waters. And God made the expanse and divided the waters which were above the expanse." Does this mean that our present continents rose out of the oceans? Who can say? The detailed processes are not specified.

3:6 through which the cosmos of that day, having suffered a cataclysm of water, was destroyed.

The *which* in "through which" is genitive plural. The only plural noun in the preceding verse is *heavens.* It is somewhat remote for an antecedent. Therefore Mayor conjecturally emends the relative pronoun to the masculine singular, making it refer to the word of God. Although this makes good sense—the word of God through which the world was destroyed—the textual evidence is almost unanimously against the singular. Emending to the singular also violates the common rule that the more difficult reading is preferable; and *hon*, the plural, is surely difficult. Another attempt makes the repetitive phrase *of water and through water* the antecedent. But while it makes sense to say that the world was destroyed by water, the grammar is extremely awkward.

It is less awkward to take the remote word *heavens* as the antecedent, possibly in conjunction with *earth*. Then the text would say, "The heavens were of old composed of water and they destroyed the cosmos in a cataclysm of water." This presupposes the idea that it was the rains from heaven that caused the flood. The fountains of the deep were also broken up. Some allusion to this source of the waters of the flood may be found in the phrase "an earth composed of water and by water." But the connection is not so smooth as one could wish.

To repeat: "Through which the cosmos of that day, having suffered a cataclysm of water, was destroyed."

Mayor objects: "By *cosmos* is meant the material world made up of heaven and earth. . . . The Mosaic account gives no support to this story of the absolute destruction of the earth, far less of the heaven by the deluge." But *cosmos* does not mean an aggregate of matter, which could meet absolute destruction only by complete annihilation. *Cosmos* means a particular orderly arrangement. The flood destroyed this arrangement. Whether or not this destruction requires "flood geology," the text does not say. But quite clearly some arrangements were destroyed. Therefore there is no justification for complaining that pseudo-Peter took "an exaggerated view of the deluge."

3:7 But the present heavens and the earth have been kept for fire, reserved to the day of judgment and destruction of impious people.

Liberal commentators who wish to divorce the New Testament from its Old Testament background and find the source of its ideas in Greek philosophy and religion seize upon this verse as a clear indication of Stoic thinking, for the Stoics taught that the world was to be destroyed by fire. The idea of a final conflagration is not very Jewish. The Sibylline Oracles (*c.* 140 B.C.) mention it several times; there are a few earlier references; and it occurs sparsely in the rabbinical literature. Since, on the other hand, it is a prominent idea in Stoicism, having been adopted from Heraclitus, the liberals are willing to see Stoic influence on their pseudo-Peter.

On this point Mayor is one of the less dogmatic liberals. He says only, "A similar belief prevailed among the Greeks, see Heraclitus . . . Plato, *Timaeus* 22 b-c. . . . The chief upholders of this doctrine at the time of the Christian era were the Stoics. . . . Origen answer[ed] the charge of Celsus that the Christian belief . . . was derived from the Greeks. . . . As we have evidence in this epistle of familiarity with Stoic phraseology, such as *theia, phusis,* and *aretē,* it is probable that the writer's conception of the end of the world may have been influenced by Stoic teachers" (pp. 154–155). But the text of the epistle, even though Mayor is so modest and undogmatic in his statement, makes it improbable rather than probable.

There are two main reasons for rejecting the idea of Stoic influence. The first has to do with physics and the second is very strictly religious. In Stoicism the final conflagration is a gradual, natural process inherent in the constitution of matter. (See von Arnim, *Stoicorum Veterum Fragmenta,* Vol. II, 596–632.) The process is cyclical and continuous. All bodies have arisen from the primitive fire as the universe cooled; then they grow hotter until they resume the form of undifferentiated fire; after which world history repeats itself *ad infinitum.* Peter, on the other hand, announces a sudden, non-cyclical, virtually instantaneous cataclysm. This ends world history. There is no repeat. Augustine later used this contrast to convict the Stoics of pessimism. Their world process is like the labors of Sisyphus. Furthermore, Stoic physics, which is the matrix of their conflagration theory, is totally absent from the New Testament.

The second reason why Stoicism cannot be the source of the apostle's ideas is strictly religious. Whereas the Stoic conflagration is purely natural, Peter's is a divine judgment and punishment of a sinful human race. This idea is as absent from Stoicism as theirs is from Peter.

Dies irae, dies illa
solvet saeclum in favilla . . .

Or, let us ask, how recently has your congregation sung,

That day of wrath, that dreadful day
When heav'n and earth shall pass away!
What pow'r shall be the sinner's stay?
How shall he meet that dreadful day?
When, shrivelling like a parched scroll,
The flaming heav'ns together roll;
When louder yet, and yet more dread,
Swells high the trump that wakes the dead;
O on that day, that wrathful day
When man to judgment wakes from clay,
Be thou the trembling sinner's stay,
Though heav'n and earth shall pass away.

3:8 And don't forget this one thing, beloved, that with the Lord one day is as a thousand years and a thousand years as one day.

This echo from Psalm 90:4 is appropriate not only to the false teachers but also to the most devout. The false teachers assume that unless God fulfills his predictions in less than fifty years, there will be no fulfillment. Liberals today adopt and adapt their predecessors' complaint. Sometimes they assert that the apostles expected Christ to return during their own lifetimes, and that their disappointment shows the fallibility of their writings. Peter, however, was not of this opinion. Christ had prophesied his death. No doubt Paul too had read Psalm 90. Their sense of time and their view of world history was not what the liberals believe it to have been.

True Christians, while they realize that the Gospel had to be preached to every nation and tribe before Christ should return, are also, not deceived, but sometimes cast down and sorrowful that Christ seems to delay his coming. This is a natural state of mind for the longing heart. But however much we wish that Christ would come today, we understand what Peter said in the next verse:

3:9 The Lord does not delay his promise, as some calculate delay . . .

The remainder of this verse is separated here because it presents a problem quite different from that of the second coming.

3:9b but is long-suffering to you [or, on our account], not willing that some [plural] **should perish, but that all should withdraw** [from the world?] **into repentance.**

"Long suffering toward you" is surely the correct text. I think only two manuscripts read "on account." Mayor prefers the poorer reading because it makes better sense. But since Peter is writing to Christians, it makes a minimal difference whether he includes himself and other churches or more pointedly singles out his readers.

If it had been fully realized that Peter was addressing Christians, a great deal of theological confusion would have been avoided. Arminians have used the verse in defense of their theory of universal atonement. They believe that God willed to save every human being without exception and that something beyond his control happened so as to defeat his eternal purpose.

The doctrine of universal redemption is not only refuted by Scripture generally, but the passage in question makes nonsense on such a view.

Since God has made and appointed the wicked for the day of evil, as 2:3, 4 have already said, as 2:9 virtually implies, and as is distinctly stated in Romans 9:17–22, 2 Thessalonians 2:11–12, or as Proverbs 16:4 says, "The Lord has made everything for its own end, yea even the wicked for the day of evil," it follows that God does not will the salvation of every member of the human race. It is not his will that every man without exception should repent. Repentance is a gift of God, and if God willed to, he would give everyone repentance. But obviously he does not. So much for the Scripture in general.

The verse 3:9 would make no sense otherwise. Peter is telling us that Christ's return awaits the repentance of certain people. Now, if Christ's return awaited the repentance of every individual without exception, Christ would never return. Already many have died unrepentant, and their number grows larger every day. The only time when every individual had come to repentance was when Adam and Eve repented and were clothed with skins. The Arminians, unwittingly to be sure, imply that Christ should have returned them—his second advent antedating his first.

This is no new interpretation. The *Similitudes* viii, xi, 1 in the *Shepherd of Hermas* (*c.* A.D. 130–150), which because of the date serves as evidence for the epistle's authenticity, says "But the Lord, being long-suffering, wishes *[thelei]* those who were called *[tēn klēsin ten gēnomenēn]* through his Son to be saved." This quotation shows how the verse was understood in the second century. It is the called or elect whom God wills to save.

Peter therefore is saying simply that Christ will not return until every one of the elect has come to repentance. Or, as the hymn writer said,

Ten thousand times ten thousand
In sparkling raiment bright,
The armies of the ransomed saints
Throng up the steeps of light.
Bring near thy great salvation,
Thou Lamb for sinners slain;
Fill up the roll of thine elect,
Then take thy power and reign.

3:10 [Though the delay seems long] Yet the day of the Lord will come [unexpectedly] like a thief . . .

As Matthew 24:42–44 say, and 1 Thessalonians 5:2, "in which [day] the heavens will disappear with a thundering crash, and the elements will be destroyed in a feverish heat." *Elements, stoicheia,* is the regular word for the material elements, which the Greeks identified, not as hydrogen, copper, and uranium, but as earth, air, fire, and water. Since the earth is mentioned next in the verse, some commentators try to refer *stoicheia* to angels. They find what support they can in Isaiah 34:4, "All the host of heaven shall be dissolved and the heavens shall be rolled together as a scroll; and all their host shall fade away as the leaf fadeth from off the vine. . . ." Maybe the first instance of the word *host* (LXX, *dunameis*) refers to angels, but the second instance is *astra, stars.* In any case Isaiah is far from suggesting a sudden destruction by fire: he speaks of the stars as fading away and withering like a leaf.

3:10b the earth also and its works shall be discovered.

The verb here, *heurethēsetai,* is difficult to understand. But it is the best attested reading. Both these considerations indicate its correctness. A more poorly attested reading is *katakaēsetai,* "will be burned up." This makes easy sense. But since a conflagration has already been mentioned, so necessity forces a repetition. Critics and commentators have tried emendations. One inserts an *ouch,* not: the earth will not be found—it will have disappeared. This is completely conjectural. Another changes a few letters in the verb reading *kruēsetai* or even *diaruēsetai* (which does not occur in Liddell and Scott) and translating "the earth and its works will be redeemed." This expedient combines poor textual criticism with worse sense.

It is best therefore to take the best reading and figure out what Peter meant by saying that the earth and its works will be discovered. Nor is this impossibly difficult. Remember first that God is a consuming fire. Silver is tried in the fire. If any man builds gold, silver, hay, or stubble on the foundation of Christ, each man's work shall be made manifest because it will be revealed by fire, and the fire will test what sort of work each man has done. . . . If any man's work is burned up, he [or, it] shall be punished; but he himself shall be saved, as if he had gone through the fire. When therefore Peter says that the world and its works will be discovered, he means that the fire of destruction will reveal their worthlessness.

3:11 Accordingly,* since all these things are being destroyed, what sort of people ought you to be in holy conduct and piety, . . .

Although "being destroyed" is present tense, it is best taken as a vivid anticipation of the future. In the next verse *tēketai* is present, "are melting," but the sense is future. Verse 13 also has the present *katoikei, dwells* or *inhabits;* though here the sense could possibly be present.

The thought of the verse is perfectly simple and clear. As agents in eschatological history we must adjust our conduct to the end in view. Thus the next verse continues . . .

3:12 waiting and hastening the presence of the day of God, by which the heavens in flame shall be destroyed and the elements burning are melting.

---

*This is one of many instances where Aland, Black, Metzger, and Wikgren print the poorer reading.

In view of the coming judgment the Christian is obligated to live a life of piety. Assenting to God's plan he waits the day. Just how any creature of God can hasten that day is not so obvious. "Earnestly desiring" makes easier sense, but is not a good translation. "Seeking eagerly" would be possible. Since it is not possible to alter God's timetable, since nothing can be made to happen before its fulness of time has come, one must ask how we can hasten the day of God. The best explanation is found in Acts 3:19–21. In these verses it is clear that the time is fixed. Christ must remain in heaven until the time of restoration as the holy prophets have said; but men must repent *so that* times of refreshing may come and that he may send Christ who has been appointed for you. In this sense, by our repentance, our pious life, and holy conduct, we bring or hasten God's day of judgment.

The remainder of the verse repeats for the sake of emphasis what had just been said: the heavens and the elements (stars?) shall be destroyed by fire. Destruction, however, is not the last word . . .

3:13 But according to his promise, we await new heavens and a new earth in which righteousness dwells.

Why should anyone have explained this passage as due to Stoic influence? Peter's conflagration results in a heavenly and earthly home of righteousness. This is not Stoic. It comes from Isaiah, whose prophecies were perfectly well known to all the apostles. Isaiah 32 begins, "Behold, a King shall reign in righteousness," and pictures conditions never obtaining on earth to date. Isaiah 65:17 says, "For behold, I create new heavens and a new earth. . . . I will rejoice in Jerusalem . . . there shall be heard in her no more the voice of weeping. . . . And they shall build houses. . . . They shall not labor in vain. . . . The wolf and the lamb shall feed together. . . . They shall not hurt nor destroy in all my holy mountain, saith the Lord."

In the following chapter and final verses of the prophecy, Isaiah concludes, "As the new heavens and new earth that I will make shall remain before me, . . . so shall your seed and your name remain. . . . And [you] shall look upon the carcasses of the men that have transgressed against me: for their worm shall not die, neither shall their fire be quenched."

This is not pagan Stoicism but the divine message of prophets who spoke from God, being borne along by the Holy Spirit.

3:14 Therefore, beloved, as you await these events, undefiled and unblemished in his sight, be eager to be found at peace.

The word *beloved* here, as in 3:8, as well as the contents of the last three verses, leaves no doubt that Peter is addressing Christians. This word therefore reinforces the fact that God is not willing for any Christian to perish.

To prepare for the home of righteousness that will be ushered in by fire and judgment, the Christians must persevere in the process of sanctification and strive to live an unblemished life.

3:15 And believe that the long-suffering of our Lord is salvation, as also our beloved brother Paul wrote to you according to the wisdom given to him.

The false teachers had believed God's long-suffering to be delay, and, even worse, to be an evidence that the prophecies were empty deceptions. Peter now repeats the idea that God "delays" judgment until all the elect have been brought into the church. Some of these elect, like the apostle Paul, had lived very rebellious lives. But the long-suffering of God leads them to repentance. Therefore Peter, quite naturally, refers to Paul and his epistles.

The implications of this reference to Paul have been variously understood, and the decision depends largely on the antecedent of the phrase "as Paul wrote to you." The preceding thought, that the long-suffering of the Lord contributes to salvation, has a *prima facie* claim because of its immediacy. It is plausible also because Romans 2:4, "Do you despise . . . [God's] long-suffering, unaware that the goodness of God is leading you toward repentance?" is what Paul wrote. But in conjunction with Peter's word "to you" *(humin),* this would imply that Peter's epistle was addressed to the church at Rome. This is not inconsistent with Peter's addressing Jews, for there were many Jews in Rome. Yet, if this epistle had been sent to Rome, the early Christian church should have had much less difficulty and taken far less time to decide that the epistle was apostolic. Of course, there may have been circumstances that could explain this peculiarity, such as an aloofness or even antagonism between the Jewish and Gentile Christians in Rome. But all such attempts at explanation, so far as they relate to the destination of 2 Peter and its canonicity, are completely conjectural.

There are two other possible antecedents for the phrase "as Paul wrote." Instead of limiting the idea to the long-suffering of God, one can include the ideas of "undefiled and unblemished." These are not very remote. Or, in the third place, one could include all the eschatology of 3:8–13. Certainly it is hard to rule out these two possibilities because verses 14, 15, and 16 are all one sentence. On this understanding, Peter does not limit himself to certain verses in Romans. Any remark on sanctification, in Ephesians for example, would be satisfactory. If eschatology is also included, then 1 Corinthians and both Thessalonians qualify. Nor is it necessary to suppose that Paul and Peter addressed a letter to the same church. The dative *humin* can mean, not *to you,* but *for you.* Thus Paul, though he sent a letter to the Romans and another to the Galatians, wrote these letters for all Christians, and consequently for the Christians whom Peter addresses. The following verse supports either the second or third interpretation as against the first.

3:16 as also in all epistles speaking about these things . . .

The reference therefore is not to Romans alone, nor to one thing alone. The epistles and the antecedents are both plural.

3:16b in which some things are hard to understand, which the uneducated and flighty warp, as they do also the other Scriptures, to their own destruction.

This is a most interesting verse, not so hard to understand, but which nevertheless the liberals warp to their own destruction. Minor interest attaches to the things hard to understand. Peter certainly did not mean predestination and limited atonement. He himself here as in his first epistle teaches these doctrines. More likely the difficulties belong to meat offered to idols and other problems of conduct connected with blemishes and defilement. Eschatology would also be one of the difficult subjects, if we accept the third antecedent discussed above.

The more important point in this verse is Peter's classification of the Pauline epistles with the Old Testament Scriptures. Mayor, for all his liberalism, not only admits that *graphas* refers to the Old Testament Scriptures, but also furnishes abundant evidence of the fact. It occurs many times in the Synoptics, a dozen times in John, at least a half dozen times in Acts, and so on. Indeed, Mayor seems to agree that this verse puts the Pauline epistles on a level with the Old Testament. But he escapes the real force of the words by dating the epistle in the second century and by remarking that the canonical New Testament had not been assembled during the real Peter's lifetime.

M. R. James gives the following negative argument. "If the phrase had occurred in a later document, we should not hesitate to render it 'the rest of the Scriptures' and to take it as including both Old Testament and New Testament Scriptures. But the fact that we have here a writing under the name of an Apostle, and of early date, causes a difficulty. We shall be overstating the case if we say that the writer here places Paul's Epistles exactly on the level with the Old Testament and implies the existence of a body of Christian Scriptures that were so regarded: but it is fair to say that he knows of the Pauline Epistles as writings read to Christian congregations and on the way to be put upon the level of Canonical Scripture."

This type of phraseology is sufficiently ambiguous to be literally true while conveying an impression that contradicts the sense of the epistle. Let us analyze the wording. It is true that if Peter's statement concerning the other Scriptures "had occurred in a later document, we should . . . take it as including both Old Testament and New Testament Scriptures." While true, this is irrelevant, for all a conservative theologian need maintain is that the "other Scriptures" are the Old Testament. Because Provost James includes the New Testament he can refer to "the existence of a body of Christian Scriptures that were so regarded." But if one takes Peter's word as referring to the Old Testament, no difficulty arises from the true but irrelevant fact that the canon was not fixed during the first century. What Peter definitely says is that the Pauline epistles are on a par with the Old Testament books. Rather than suggesting otherwise, critics would be more forthright if they should admit this exegesis, even though they might add that neither Old Testament nor New Testament is divinely inspired. But that Peter asserts the equal inspiration of both should never be doubted.

3:17–18 You, accordingly, beloved, since you know this already, take care lest, being carried away with the error of the

lawless, you fall from your own support. But grow in grace and knowledge of our Lord and Savior Jesus Christ. To him the glory both now and to day of age. Amen.*

This concluding exhortation presents neither critical nor exegetical difficulty. It ends on a theme with which the epistle opened, namely knowledge. The word here is *gnosis,* a word some commentators try to connect with Gnosticism and contrast with some other type of knowledge called *epignosis.* Peter clearly uses the two words interchangeably.

Peter's emphasis on knowledge is not unique in the New Testament. Ephesians 1:17–18 stress the idea by using it five times (the word itself twice) in two lines: *sophias (wisdom), apokalupseos (revelation), epignōsei, (knowledge),* and *pephatismenous (enlightened),* and *eidenai (to know).*

Contemporary popular Christianity, both the semi-modernists and the "New-evangelicals," has seriously ignored Peter's exhortation. They have fallen off their foundation and are carried away with various wicked errors. Anti-intellectualism is the root of their other disobediences. Serious study is decried as cold, dead orthodoxy. Spirituality is identified with fuzzy thinking and the empty platitudes that pass for piety. Will this perverse generation heed the apostle and studiously grow in grace and knowledge of our Lord? To whom be the glory, now and forever, Amen.

---

*Here again Aland, Black, and Wikgren consider the *Amen* doubtful, though only one manuscript of any importance omits it.

Scripture Index

INDEX

The Crisis of Our Time

Historians have christened the thirteenth century the Age of Faith and termed the eighteenth century the Age of Reason. The twentieth century has been called many things: the Atomic Age, the Age of Inflation, the Age of the Tyrant, the Age of Aquarius. But it deserves one name more than the others: the Age of Irrationalism. Contemporary secular intellectuals are anti-intellectual. Contemporary philosophers are anti-philosophy. Contemporary theologians are anti-theology.

In past centuries secular philosophers have generally believed that knowledge is possible to man. Consequently they expended a great deal of thought and effort trying to justify knowledge. In the twentieth century, however, the optimism of the secular philosophers has all but disappeared. They despair of knowledge.

Like their secular counterparts, the great theologians and doctors of the church taught that knowledge is possible to man. Yet the theologians of the twentieth century have repudiated that belief. They also despair of knowledge. This radical skepticism has filtered down from the philosophers and theologians and penetrated our entire culture, from television to music to literature. *The Christian in the twentieth century is confronted with an overwhelming cultural consensus—sometimes stated explicitly, but most often implicitly: Man does not and cannot know anything truly.*

What does this have to do with Christianity? Simply this: If man can know nothing truly, man can truly know nothing. We cannot know that the Bible is the Word of God, that Christ died for the sins of his people, or that Christ is alive today at the right hand of the Father.

Unless knowledge is possible, Christianity is nonsensical, for it claims to be knowledge. what is at stake in the twentieth century is not simply a single doctrine, such as the virgin birth, or the existence of hell, as important as those doctrines may be, but the whole of Christianity itself. If knowledge is not possible to man, it is worse than silly to argue points of doctrine—it is insane.

The irrationalism of the present age is so thorough-going and pervasive that even the Remnant—the segment of the professing church that remains faithful—has accepted much of it, frequently without even being aware of what it was accepting. In some circles this irrationalism has become synonymous with piety and humility, and those who oppose it are denounced as rationalists—as though to be logical were a sin. Our contemporary anti-theologians make a contradiction and call it a Mystery. The faithful ask for truth and are given Paradox. If any balk at swallowing the absurdities of the anti-theologians, they are frequently marked as heretics or schismatics who seek to act independently of God.

There is no greater threat facing the true church of Christ at this moment than the irrationalism that now controls our entire culture. Totalitarianism, guilty of tens of millions of murders, including those of millions of Christians, is to be feared, but not nearly so much as the idea that we do not and cannot know the truth. Hedonism, the popular philosophy of America, is not to be feared so much as the belief that logic—that "mere human logic," to use the religious irrationalists' own phrase—is futile. The attacks on truth, on revelation, on the intellect, and on logic are renewed daily. But note well: The misologists—the haters of logic—use logic to demonstrate the futility of using logic. The anti-intellectuals construct intricate intellectual arguments to prove the insufficiency of the intellect. The anti-theologians use the revealed Word of God to show that there can be no revealed Word of God—or that if there could, it would remain impenetrable darkness and Mystery to our finite minds.

Nonsense Has Come

Is it any wonder that the world is grasping at straws—the straws of experientialism, mysticism, and drugs? After all, if people are told that the Bible contains insoluble mysteries, then is not a flight into mysticism to be expected? On what grounds can it be condemned? Certainly not on logical grounds or Biblical grounds, if logic is futile and the Bible unintelligible. Moreover, if it cannot be condemned on logical or Biblical grounds, it cannot be condemned at all. If people are going to have a religion of the mysterious, they will not adopt Christianity: They will have a genuine mystery religion. "Those who call for Nonsense," C.S. Lewis once wrote, "will find that it comes." And that is precisely what has happened. The popularity of Eastern mysticism, of drugs, and of religious experience is the logical consequence of the irrationalism of the twentieth century. There can and will be no Christian revival—and no reconstruction of society—unless and until the irrationalism of the age is totally repudiated by Christians.

The Church Defenseless

Yet how shall they do it? The spokesmen for Christianity have been fatally infected with irrationalism. The seminaries, which annually train thousands of men to teach millions of Christians, are the finishing schools of irrationalism, completing the job begun by the government schools and colleges. Some of the pulpits of the most conservative churches (we are not speaking of the apostate churches) are occupied by graduates of the anti-theological schools. These products of modern anti-theological education, when asked to give a reason for the hope that is in them, can generally respond with only the intellectual analogue of a shrug—a mumble about Mystery. They have not grasped—and therefore cannot teach those for whom they are responsible—the first truth: "And ye shall know the truth." Many, in fact, explicitly deny it, saying that, at best, we possess only "pointers" to the truth, or something "similar" to the truth, a mere analogy. Is the impotence of the Christian church a puzzle? Is the fascination with pentecostalism and faith healing among members of conservative churches an enigma? Not when one understands the sort of studied nonsense that is purveyed in the name of God in the seminaries.

The Trinity Foundation

The creators of The Trinity Foundation firmly believe that theology is too important to be left to the licensed theologians—the graduates of the schools of theology. They have created The Trinity Foundation for the express purpose of teaching the faithful all that the Scriptures contain—not warmed over, baptized, secular philosophies. Each member of the board of directors of The Trinity Foundation has signed this oath: "I believe that the Bible alone and the Bible in its entirety is the Word of God and, therefore, inerrant in the autographs. I believe that the system of truth presented in the Bible is best summarized in the Westminster Confession of Faith. So help me God."

The ministry of The Trinity Foundation is the presentation of the system of truth taught in Scripture as clearly and as completely as possible. We do not regard obscurity as a virtue, nor confusion as a sign of spirituality. Confusion, like all error, is sin, and teaching that confusion is all that Christians can hope for is doubly sin.

The presentation of the truth of Scripture necessarily involves the rejection of error. The Foundation has exposed and will continue to expose the irrationalism of the twentieth century, whether its current spokesman be an existentialist philosopher or a professed Reformed theologian. We oppose anti-intellectualism, whether it be espoused by a neo-orthodox theologian or a fundamentalist evangelist. We reject misology, whether it be on the lips of a neo-evangelical or those of a Roman Catholic charismatic. To each error we bring the brilliant light of Scripture, proving all things, and holding fast to that which is true.

The Primacy of Theory

The ministry of The Trinity Foundation is not a "practical" ministry. If you are a pastor, we will not enlighten you on how to organize an ecumenical prayer meeting in your community or how to double church attendance in a year. If you are a homemaker, you will have to read elsewhere to find out how to become a total woman. If you are a businessman, we will not tell you how to develop a social conscience. The professing church is drowning in such "practical" advice.

The Trinity Foundation is unapologetically theoretical in its outlook, believing that theory without practice is dead, and that practice without theory is blind. The trouble with the professing church is not primarily in its practice, but in its theory. Christians do not know, and many do not even care to know, the doctrines of Scripture. Doctrine is intellectual, and Christians are generally anti-intellectual. Doctrine is ivory tower philosophy, and they scorn ivory towers. The ivory tower, however, is the control tower of a civilization. It is a fundamental, theoretical mistake of the practical men to think that they can be merely practical, for practice is always the practice of some theory. The relationship between theory and practice is the relationship between cause and effect. If a person believes correct theory, his practice will tend to be correct. The practice of contemporary Christians is immoral because it is the practice of false theories. It is a major theoretical mistake of the practical men to think that they can ignore the ivory towers of the philosophers and theologians as irrelevant to their lives. Every action that the "practical" men take is governed by the thinking that has occurred in some ivory tower—whether that tower be the British Museum, the Academy, a home in Basel, Switzerland, or a tent in Israel.

In Understanding Be Men

It is the first duty of the Christian to understand correct theory—correct doctrine—and thereby implement correct practice. This order—first theory, then practice—is both logical and Biblical. It is, for example, exhibited in Paul's epistle to the Romans, in which he spends the first eleven chapters expounding theory and the last five discussing practice. The contemporary teachers of Christians have not only reversed the order, they have inverted the Pauline emphasis on theory and practice. The virtually complete failure of the teachers of the professing church to instruct the faithful in correct doctrine is the cause of the misconduct and cultural impotence of Christians. The church's lack of power is the result of its lack of truth. The *Gospel* is the power of God, not religious experience or personal relationship. The church has no power because it has abandoned the Gospel, the good news, for a religion of experientialism. Twentieth century American Christians are children carried about by every wind of doctrine, not knowing what they believe, or even if they believe anything for certain.

The chief purpose of The Trinity Foundation is to counteract the irrationalism of the age and to expose the errors of the teachers of the church. Our emphasis—on the Bible as the sole source of truth, on the primacy of the intellect, on the supreme importance of correct doctrine, and on the necessity for systematic and logical thinking—is almost unique in Christendom. To the extent that the church survives—and she will survive and flourish—it will be because of her increasing acceptance of these basic ideas and their logical implications.

We believe that The Trinity Foundation is filling a vacuum in Christendom. We are saying that Christianity is intellectually defensible—that, in fact, it is the only intellectually defensible system of thought. We are saying that God has made the wisdom of this world—whether that wisdom be called science, religion, philosophy, or common sense—foolishness. We are appealing to all Christians who have not conceded defeat in the intellectual battle with the world to join us in our efforts to raise a standard to which all men of sound mind can repair.

The love of truth, of God's Word, has all but disappeared in our time. We are committed to and pray for a great instauration. But though we may not see this reformation of Christendom in our lifetimes, we believe it is our duty to present the whole counsel of God because Christ has commanded it. The results of our teaching are in God's hands, not ours. Whatever those results, his Word is never taught in vain, but always accomplishes the result that he intended it to accomplish. Professor Gordon H. Clark has stated our view well:

> There have been times in the history of God's people, for example, in the days of Jeremiah, when refreshing grace and widespread revival were not to be expected: the time was one of chastisement. If this twentieth century is of a similar nature, individual Christians here and there can find comfort and strength in a study of God's Word. But if God has decreed happier days for us and if we may expect a world-shaking and genuine spiritual awakening, then it is the author's belief that a zeal for souls, however necessary, is not the sufficient condition. Have there not been devout saints in every age, numerous enough to carry on a revival? Twelve such persons are plenty. What distinguishes the arid ages from the period of the Reformation, when nations were moved as they had not been since Paul preached in Ephesus, Corinth, and Rome, is the latter's fullness of knowledge of God's Word. To echo an early Reformation thought, when the ploughman and the garage attendant know the Bible as well a the theologian does, and know it better than some contemporary theologians, then the desired and awakening shall have already occurred.

In addition to publishing books, the Foundation publishes a monthly newsletter, *The Trinity Review.* Subscriptions to *The Review* are free; please write to the address below to become a subscriber. If you would like further information or would like to join us in our work, please let us know.

The Trinity Foundation is a non-profit foundation tax-exempt under section 501(c)(3) of the Internal Revenue Code of 1954. You can help us disseminate the Word of God through your tax-deductible contributions to the Foundation.

And we know that the Son of God has come, and has given us an understanding, that we may know him that is true, and we are in him that is true, in his Son Jesus Christ. This is the true God, and eternal life.

John W. Robbins

INTELLECTUAL AMMUNITION

The Trinity Foundation is committed to the reconstruction of philosophy and theology along Biblical lines. We regard God's command to bring all our thoughts into conformity with Christ very seriously, and the books listed below are designed to accomplish that goal. They are written with two subordinate purposes: (1) to demolish all secular claims to knowledge; and (2) to build a system of truth based upon the Bible alone.

Philosophy

Behaviorism and Christianity, Gordon H. Clark $6.95

Behaviorism *is a critique of both secular and religious behaviorists. It includes chapters on John Watson, Edgar S. Singer Jr., Gilbert Ryle, B.F. Skinner, and Donald MacKay. Clark's refutation of behaviorism and his argument for a Christian doctrine of man are unanswerable.*

A Christian Philosophy of Education, Gordon H. Clark $8.95

The first edition of this book was published in 1946. It sparked the contemporary interest in Christian schools. Dr. Clark has thoroughly revised and updated it, and it is needed now more than ever. Its chapters include: The Need for a World-View, The Christian World-View, The Alternative to Christian Theism, Neutrality, Ethics, The Christian Philosophy of Education, Academic Matters, Kindergarten to University. Three appendices are included as well: The Relationship of Public Education to Christianity, A Protestant World-View, and Art and the Gospel.

A Christian View of Men and Things, Gordon H. Clark $10.95

No other book achieves what A Christian View *does: the presentation of Christianity as it applies to history, politics, ethics, science, religion, and epistemology. Clark's command of both worldly philosophy and Scripture is evident on every page, and the result is a breathtaking and invigorating challenge to the wisdom of this world.*

Clark Speaks From The Grave, Gordon H. Clark $3.95

Dr. Clark chides some of his critics for their failure to defend Christianity competently. Clark Speaks *is a stimulating and illuminating discussion of the errors of contemporary apologists.*

Education, Christianity, and the State $7.95
J. Gresham Machen

Machen was one of the foremost educators, theologians, and defenders of Christianity in the twentieth century. The author of numerous scholarly books, Machen saw clearly that if Christianity is to survive and flourish, a system of Christian grade schools must be established. This collection of essays captures his thoughts on education over nearly three decades.

Essays on Ethics and Politics, Gordon H. Clark $10.95

Clark's essays, written over the course of five decades, are a major statement of Christian ethics.

Gordon H. Clark: Personal Recollections $6.95
John W. Robbins, editor

Friends of Dr. Clark have written their recollections of the man. Contributors include family members, colleagues, students, and friends such as Harold Lindsell, Carl Henry, Ronald Nash, Dwight Zeller, and Mary Crumpacker. The book includes an extensive bibliography of Clark's work.

John Dewey, Gordon H. Clark $2.00

America has produced many philosophers, but John Dewey has been extremely influential. Clark examines his philosophy of Instrumentalism.

Language and Theology, Gordon H. Clark $9.95

There are two main currents in twentieth-century philosophy—language of philosophy and existentialism. Both are hostile to Christianity. Clark disposes of language philosophy in this brilliant critique of Bertrand Russell, Ludwig Wittgenstein, Rudolf Carnof, A.J. Ayer, Langdon Gilhey, and many others.

Logic, Gordon H. Clark $8.95

Written as a textbook for Christian schools, Logic *is another unique book from Clark's pen. His presentation of the laws of thought, which must be followed if Scripture is to be understood correctly, and which are found in Scripture itself, is both clear and thorough.* Logic *is an indispensable book for the thinking Christian.*

Logic Workbook, Elihu Carranza $11.95

Designed to be used in conjunction with Clark's textbook, Logic, *this* Workbook *contains hundreds of exercises and text questions on perforated pages for ease of use by students.*

Logic Workbook Answer Key, Elihu Carranza $4.95

The Key *contains all the answers for the convenience of logic teachers.*

The Philosophy of Science and Belief in God $5.95
Gordon H. Clark

In opposing the contemporary idolatry of science, Clark analyzes three major aspects of science: the problem of motion, Newtonian science, and modern theories of physics. His conclusion is that science, while it may be useful, is always false; and he demonstrates its falsity in numerous ways. Since science is always false, it can offer no objection to the Bible and Christianity.

Religion, Reason and Revelation, Gordon H. Clark $7.95

One of Clark's apologetical masterpieces, Religion, Reason and Revelation *has been praised for the clarity of its thought and language. It includes chapters on Is Christianity a Religion, Faith and Reason, Inspiration and Language, Revelation and Morality, and God and Evil. It is must reading for all serious Christians.*

Thales to Dewey: A History of Philosophy paper $11.95
Gordon H. Clark hardback $16.95

This volume is the best one volume history of philosophy in English.

Three Types of Religious Philosophy, Gordon H. Clark $6.95

In this book on apologetics, Clark examines empiricism, rationalism, dogmatism, and contemporary irrationalism, which does not rise to the level of philosophy. He offers a solution to the question, "How can Christianity be defended before the world?"

Theology

The Atonement, Gordon H. Clark $8.95

This is a major addition to Clark's multi-volume systematic theology. In The Atonement, *Clark discusses the covenants, the virgin birth and incarnation, federal headship and representation, the relationship between God's sovereignty and justice, and much more. He analyzes traditional views of the atonement and criticizes them in the light of Scripture alone.*

The Biblical Doctrine of Man, Gordon H. Clark $6.95

Is man soul and body or soul, spirit, and body? What is the image of God? Is Adam's sin imputed to his children? Is evolution true? Are men totally depraved? What is the heart? These are some of the questions discussed and answered from Scripture in this book.

Cornelius Van Til: The Man and The Myth $2.45
John W. Robbins

The actual teachings of this eminent Philadelphia theologian have been obscured by the myths that surround him. This book pene-

trates those myths and criticizes Van Til's surprisingly unorthodox views of God and the Bible.

Faith and Saving Faith, Gordon H. Clark $6.95

The views of the Roman Catholic church, John Calvin, Thomas Manton, John Owen, Charles Hodge, and B.B. Warfield are discussed in this book. Is the object of faith a person or a proposition? Is faith more than belief? Is belief more than thinking with assent, as Augustine said? In a world chaotic with differing views of faith, Clark clearly explains the Biblical view of faith and saving faith.

God's Hammer: The Bible and Its Critics $6.95
Gordon H. Clark

The starting point of Christianity, the doctrine on which all other doctrines depend, is "The Bible alone is the Word of God written, and therefore inerrant in the autographs." Over the centuries the opponents of Christianity, with Satanic shrewdness, have concentrated their attacks on the truthfulness and completeness of the Bible. In the twentieth century the attack is not so much in the fields of history and archaeology as in philosophy. Clark's brilliant defense of the complete truthfulness of the Bible is captured in this collection of eleven major essays.

Guide to the Westminster Confession and Catechism $13.95
James E. Bordwine

This large book contains the full text of both the Westminster Confession (both original and American versions) and the Larger Catechism. In addition, it offers a chapter-by-chapter summary of the Confession and a unique index to both the Confession and the Catechism.

The Incarnation, Gordon H. Clark $8.95

Who is Christ? The attack on the Incarnation in the nineteenth and twentieth centuries has been vigorous, but the orthodox response has been lame. Clark reconstructs the doctrine of the Incarnation building and improving upon the Chalcedonian definition.

In Defense of Theology, Gordon H. Clark $9.95

There are four groups to whom Clark addresses this book: the average Christians who are uninterested in theology, the atheists and agnostics, the religious experientialists, and the serious Christians. The vindication of the knowledge of God against the objections of three of these groups is the first step in theology.

The Johannine Logos, Gordon H. Clark $5.95

Clark analyzes the relationship between Christ, who is the truth, and the Bible. He explains why John used the same word to refer to both Christ and his teaching. Chapters deal with the Prologue to John's Gospel, Logos and Rheemata, Truth, and Saving Faith.

Pat Robertson: A Warning to America, John W. Robbins $6.95

The Protestant Reformation was based on the Biblical principle that the Bible is the only revelation from God, yet a growing religious movement, led by Pat Robertson, asserts that God speaks to them directly. This book addresses the serious issue of religious fanaticism in America by examining the theological views of Pat Robertson.

Predestination, Gordon H. Clark $8.95

Clark thoroughly discusses one of the most controversial and pervasive doctrines of the Bible: that God is, quite literally, Almighty. Free will, the origin of evil, God's omniscience, creation, and the new birth are all presented within a Scriptural framework. The objections of those who do not believe in the Almighty God are considered and refuted. This edition also contains the text of the booklet, Predestination in the Old Testament.

Sanctification, Gordon H. Clark $8.95

In this book, which is part of Clark's multi-volume systematic theology, he discusses historical theories of sanctification, the sacraments and the Biblical doctrine of sanctification.

Scripture Twisting in the Seminaries. Part 1: Feminism $5.95
John W. Robbins

An analysis of the views of three graduates of Westminster Seminary on the role of women in the church.

Today's Evangelism: Counterfeit or Genuine? $6.95
Gordon H. Clark

Clark compares the methods and messages of today's evangelists with Scripture, and finds that Christianity is on the wane because the Gospel has been distorted or lost. This is an extremely useful and enlightening book.

The Trinity, Gordon H. Clark $8.95

Apart from the doctrine of Scripture, no teaching of the Bible is more important than the doctrine of God. Clark's defense of the orthodox doctrine of the Trinity is a principal portion of a major new work of Systematic Theology now in progress. There are chapters on the deity of Christ, Augustine, the incomprehensibility of God, Bavinck and Van Til, and the Holy Spirit, among others.

What Calvin Says, W. Gary Crampton $7.95

This is both a readable and thorough introduction to the theology of John Calvin.

What Do Presbyterians Believe? Gordon H. Clark $7.95

This classic introduction to Christian doctrine has been republished. It is the best commentary on the Westminster Confession of Faith that has ever been written.

Commentaries on the New Testament

Colossians, Gordon H. Clark $6.95
Ephesians, Gordon H. Clark $8.95
First Corinthians, Gordon H. Clark $10.95
First John, Gordon H. Clark $10.95
New Heavens, New Earth (First and Second Peter) $10.95
Gordon H. Clark
First and Second Thessalonians, Gordon H. Clark $5.95
The Pastoral Epistles (I and II Timothy and Titus) $9.95
Gordon H. Clark

All of Clark's commentaries are expository, not technical, and are written for the Christian layman. His purpose is to explain the text clearly and accurately so that the Word of God will be thoroughly known by every Christian

The Trinity Library

We will send you one copy of each of the 40 books listed above for the low price of $250. You may also order the books you want individually on the order blank on the next page. Because some of the books are in short supply, we must reserve the right to substitute others of equal or greater value in The Trinity Library. This special offer expires June 30, 1995.

ORDER FORM

Name ____

Address ____

____

Please:

- ☐ add my name to the mailing list for *The Trinity Review*. I understand that there is no charge for the *Review*.
- ☐ accept my tax deductible contribution of $______ for the work of the Foundation.
- ☐ send me ______ copies of *New Heavens, New Earth*. I enclose as payment $______.
- ☐ send me the Trinity Library of 40 books. I enclose $250 as full payment for it.
- ☐ send me the following books. I enclose full payment in the amount of $______ for them.

____

____

____

____

____

____

____

Mail to:

The Trinity Foundation
Post Office Box 700
Jefferson, MD 21755

Please add $2.50 for postage on orders less than $10. Thank you.
For quantity discounts, please write to the Foundation.